PRENTICE HALL STUDIES IN INTERNATIONAL RELATIONS

ENDURING QUESTIONS IN CHANGING TIMES

Charles W. Kegley, Jr., *Series Editor*

In the era of globalization in the twenty-first century, people cannot afford to ignore the impact of international relations on their future. From the value of one's investments to the quality of the air one breathes, international relations matter. The instantaneous spread of communications throughout the world is making for the internationalization of all phenomena, while the distinction between the domestic and the foreign, the public and the private, and the national and the international is vanishing. Globalization is an accelerating trend that is transforming how virtually every field of study in the social sciences is being investigated and taught.

Contemporary scholarship has made bold advances in understanding the many facets of international relations. It has also laid a firm foundation for interpreting the major forces and factors that are shaping the global future.

To introduce the latest research findings and theoretical commentary, a new publication series has been launched. *Prentice Hall Studies in International Relations: Enduring Questions in Changing Times* presents books that focus on the issues, controversies, and trends that are defining the central topics dominating discussion about international relations.

 **W9-APH-354**

United Nations Politics

International Organization in a Divided World

Donald J. Puchala

University of South Carolina

Katie Verlin Laatikainen

Adelphi University

Roger A. Coate

University of South Carolina

PEARSON

Prentice
Hall

Upper Saddle River, New Jersey 07458

To the peoples of the world who truly need an effective United Nations in the twenty-first century and especially those involved with the UN—from diplomats to aid workers, from those in the field to those at headquarters—who work tirelessly to make it so.

Library of Congress Cataloging-in-Publication Data

Puchala, Donald James,
   United Nations politics : international organization in a divided world / Donald J.
   Puchala, Katie Verlin Laatikainen, Roger A. Coate.
      p. cm.
   Includes bibliographical references and index.
   ISBN-13: 978-0-13-172765-6 (alk. paper)
   ISBN-10: 0-13-172765-6 (alk. paper)
   1. United Nations.   I. Laatikainen, Katie Verlin,   II. Coate, Roger A.
   III. Title.
JZ4984.5.P83 2007
341.23—dc22

                                      2006023791

Editorial Director: Charlyce Jones Owen
Executive Editor: Dickson Musslewhite
Editorial Assistant: Jennifer Murphy
Senior Marketing Manager: Emily Cleary
Marketing Assistant: Jennifer Lang
Senior Managing Editor: Lisa Iarkowski
Production Liaison: Fran Russello
Manufacturing Buyer: Mary Ann
   Gloriande

Cover Design: Bruce Konselaar
Cover Illustration/Photo: Getty Images, Inc.
Manager, Cover Visual Research &
   Permissions: Karen Sanatar
Composition/Full-Service Project
   Management: GGS Book Services/
   Karpagam Jagadeesan
Printer/Binder: RR Donnelley & Sons
   Company

Credits and acknowledgments borrowed from other sources and reproduced, with permission, in this textbook appear on appropriate page within text.

Pearson Education LTD. London
Pearson Education Singapore, Pte. Ltd
Pearson Education, Canada, Ltd
Pearson Education–Japan
Pearson Education Australia PTY, Limited

Pearson Education North Asia Ltd
Pearson Educación de Mexico, S.A. de C.V.
Pearson Education Malaysia, Pte. Ltd
Pearson Education, Upper Saddle River,
   New Jersey

                                    10 9 8 7 6 5 4 3 2 1
                                    ISBN: 0-13-172765-6

Contents

CHAPTER 4
The United Nations: The Last Bastion of Sovereignty?   64

CHAPTER 5
In Search of Leadership   88

CHAPTER 6
The Politics of Culture   117

Preface

Despite the evolution and institutionalization of complex processes of global governance—including the increased importance of non-state actors and international bureaucracies—many of the challenges to multilateralism today stem from the tension between these broader developments and the political proclivities of national governments to defend sovereign prerogatives. This volume assesses the political challenges facing the United Nations and evaluates the capacities of the organization to face them. Our conclusions, contrary to much of the writing on global governance, emphasize political realism because the politics of competing national interests continue to define this world organization that is after all mainly a club of sovereign states.

The book adopts a political perspective for understanding the challenges that the UN multilateral system faces in responding to a variety of global problems in the 21st century. The fundamental elements of UN politics include Western hegemony and resistance to it, a lack of member governments' commitments to cooperate within the UN despite the organization's considerable capacity for action, persisting sensitivies about protecting sovereignty, and obstacles to finding consensus and exercising leadership in a world deeply divided by relative wealth, unequal power, contending ideologies and poorly communicating cultures. We explore the nature of UN politics in debates over issues of universal values and human rights, peacekeeping, and development and human security. The concluding chapter assesses the capacity of the UN system to respond to 21st century challenges. Our conclusion, perhaps not entirely welcome, is that the United Nations is unlikely to respond very well to foreseeable challenges because the political environment within and without the organization will probably remain inhospitable to enhanced global governance. We end our long essay on UN politics with a practical reconsideration of the UN that acknowledges the fundamental political nature of the United Nations while identifying the prospects for transformation that are absent from current discussions of UN reform.

This study employs a political, intergovernmental focus that is increasingly neglected in the literature on the UN and global governance. Recent scholarship has concentrated upon conceptualizing global governance, on underlining the growth of international civil society and on explaining the development of international norms. There appears as well in the literature the curious notion that the United Nations is an autonomous actor in world affairs that can and does take action independent of the will and wishes of the member governments that constitute the organization. Realistically speaking, what UN does or more often does not do in global affairs results mainly from the interplay of intergovernmental politics. Yet, intergovernmental politics at the UN are seldom highlighted in analyses of the organization and also rarely integrated into criticisms of the organization. While acknowledging and explaining that processes of global governance are complex, this volume focuses primarily on contention among governments and factions within the UN and highlights the perceptions and behavior of national governments in responding via international organization to a turbulent world. *United Nations Politics* gauges the tensions between a world where multilateral cooperation is imperative and a world politics that limits incentives to cooperate.

United Nations Politics is intended to serve as a rich, readable text, appropriate for introductory as well as advanced university courses on the United Nations, International Organizations, and/or International Relations. Unusual in the literature on the United Nations, this lively volume draws on hundreds of interviews with UN diplomats and secretariat officials conducted between 2000 and 2005 and integrates their reflections and perspectives—often in their own words—to vividly capture the political dynamics of the UN.

Donald Puchala
Katie Laatikainen
Roger Coate

CHAPTER 1

The United Nations at the Turn of the Twenty-First Century

The occasion of the fiftieth anniversary of the United Nations (UN) in 1995 was one of celebration and broad support for the world body that in the aftermath of the Cold War was asked to be ever more central in issues of peace and security. In this new post–Cold War world, the UN was also expected to be more active in fostering economic and social development worldwide, and it was to be newly energized in the goal of supporting universal human rights and democracy. Yet, ten years later, UN members found themselves struggling with the consequences of a war in Iraq that was entered into in direct defiance of the Security Council and arguably in contravention of the United Nations Charter. Among other things, the unilateral action by the United States in militarily invading and conquering Iraq set public opinion around the world to wondering what had happened to the authority of the UN. Is not preventing preventable wars the chief mission of the United Nations? As if to add injury to insult, in 2003 when the UN was finally invited into Iraq to assist with postwar humanitarian relief and reconstruction, its headquarters in Baghdad was attacked by terrorists whose massive car bomb caused more than a hundred casualties, including twenty-two deaths, among UN personnel. Emotional shocks, as well as political fallout, from this event were still impacting the UN Secretariat years afterward.

What is more, in this first decade after the UN's fiftieth anniversary, the world organization's commitment to human development was challenged by the failure to meet most of the targets outlined in the Millennium Declaration in 2000.[1] Meanwhile, the Security Council, whose newly found solidarity

---

[1]Kofi Annan, *We the Peoples: The Role of the United Nations in the 21st Century, Millennium Report of the Secretary-General of the United Nations* (New York: United Nations, April 4, 2000).

appeared to be a welcomed consequence of the end of the Cold War, reverted to a divisive politics of narrow national interest. Elsewhere in the UN, rhetorical questions about the universality of human rights continued to be asked, and the potentials for cultural conflict remained undiminished. The UN's abilities to protect human rights and provide humanitarian assistance were bound up in contentious debates over cultural relativism and humanitarian intervention. Suspicions exchanged between the Islamic world and the West intensified after 9/11, and these degenerated in some quarters into manifest hostility after the American attack on Iraq. Rather uncharacteristically, and for the UN most unfortunately, in 2004 the Secretariat itself became publicly suspect in the so-called oil-for-food scandal. Sizable private fortunes were apparently amassed by some high UN officials, as well as by some prominent national delegates, who profited handsomely by managing exchanges of food and medicine for Iraqi oil under the sanctions regime between 1996 and 2003. Already hemorrhaging credibility, one thing that United Nations clearly did not need in 2004 was a fraud, bribery, nepotism, and embezzlement scandal.

THE UNITED NATIONS IN A NEW AGE OF INSECURITY

In many ways, the UN was as unprepared for the first decade of the new century as it was for the last decade of the old one. The institution was designed to provide collective security by protecting states from one another. Ironically, a fair number of states, as reflected in the positions of governments, are seeking today to be protected *from the UN*, or at least from members of the Security Council bent upon "humanitarian intervention," which some read rather cynically as "Western intervention." Otherwise, the end of the Cold War did not eliminate the scores of festering inter-state disputes about borders and resources or struggles over all manner of symbols, icons, institutions, and atavisms about which states and peoples choose to be indignant and intolerant. Although the end of the Cold War eliminated the imminent danger of nuclear war between the superpowers, it may also have increased the longer-run danger of nuclear war between lesser powers. It now appears that many long-standing political-military rivalries are rapidly transforming, via nuclear proliferation, into nuclear rivalries, as, for example between India and Pakistan, India and China, and potentially also between North Korea and Japan and Israel and Iran. The terrorist attacks on New York and Washington on September 11, 2001 crystallized further challenges facing the UN in a new and turbulent world. Before the world had moved much more than a year into the new century, it became apparent that protecting people from transnational terrorists is to be as significant a threat to physical security as protecting states from one another. Despite the glitter and glow of globalization, some apparent progress in democratization, and the gradual uplifting of humanity that some see occurring, what may have actually dawned with the turn of the twenty-first century is a new Age of Increasing Insecurity.

If "chronic" appropriately describes evolving conditions of national insecurity in international relations today, the only way to describe conditions of
human insecurity is to label them "acute." Physical threats of considerable
magnitude presently confront countless people living in various failed states,
where conditions of civil anarchy are engulfing and destroying millions of
lives. Others are falling prey to ethnic cleansing or falling victim to perpetra-
tors of genocide. Mass murder, with accompanying brutality, mutilation, torture, rape, and all other forms of atrocity tend to occur today with shocking
frequency. These horrors are most often deliberately planned and perpetrated as political acts inflicted upon people either by their own governments,
by factions opposed to governments, or by brigands operating where there are
no longer effective governments.[2]

Elsewhere, in places where violations of human rights do not attain to
mass murder, they nevertheless relentlessly and extensively deprive people of
freedom, voice, employment and income, family, solace and safety. Political
prisoners, forced laborers, and asylum seekers today number in the hundreds
of thousands. Smashed printing presses, jailed or murdered editors and
closed radio and television stations, silenced writers and artists, banned political parties and persecuted leaders likewise number in the thousands. Slavery
is not an archaic institution; slave trading today is a profitable business, particularly as regards trafficking in women and children.[3] Armed children, some
younger than ten years old, forcibly inducted into guerrilla armies, are today
killing men, women, and other children in western and central Africa, in
southeast Asia, and elsewhere in the Third World.[4] Peoples in many places are
denied an identity because practicing their cultures, speaking their languages,
worshipping their gods, and publicly recalling their histories are politically
forbidden. There are over seven million refugees in the world today, the
majority of them forced from their homes by fear for their lives.[5]

Poverty remains the greatest contributor to human insecurity today.
Wretchedness is present even in the midst of the material abundance of the
northern societies. It is pervasive in much of Africa, in South Asia, in much of
the Caribbean and Central America, in parts of South America, in China, in
Central Asia, parts of the Balkans, and in Russia. What poverty means for
human insecurity is limited choice, limited control over one's life, poor
health, limited information, exposure to exploitation, almost no meaningful

[2]Robert D. Kaplan, *The Ends of the Earth: From Togo to Turkmenistan, From Iran to Cambodia—A Journey to the Frontiers of Anarchy* (New York: Vintage Books, 1997); Philip Gourevitch, *We Wish to Inform
You that Tomorrow We Will Be Killed with Our Families: Stories from Rwanda* (New York: Farrar, Straus,
and Giroux, 1998).

[3]William Greider, *One World, Ready or Not: The Manic Logic of Global Capitalism* (New York: Simon &
Schuster, 1997), p. 348.

[4]P. W. Singer, *Children at War* (Washington, D.C.: The Brookings Institution, 2004).

[5]United Nations Development Programme, *Human Development Report 1998* (New York: Oxford
University Press, 1998), p. 36.

leisure, high anxiety, and little expectation of change.[6] Despite some amelio-
ration in a few places like China and India, poverty appears to be increasing
rather than decreasing as an aspect of the human condition in the twenty-first
century.[7] In 2005 the 2.8 billion people living on less than $2 a day constituted
44 percent of humanity.

Of all of this, the heightening physical insecurity, the relentless persecu-
tion of minorities, the quashing of freedom, the mass murder and the
wretchedness, the members of the United Nations are well aware. It cannot be
otherwise. Throughout its existence the UN has been monitoring and reporting on the human condition, and in recent years the organization has produced thousands of reports, amounting to millions of words describing the
state of world. But describing the world is one thing while acting to change it
for the better is something quite different. According almost all analyses, from
perspectives of the North, the South, the West, and the Non-West and both
within the UN House (as the Secretariat is called) and without, UN responses
to the insecure world that it faithfully monitors have been less than satisfactory.

This is not because the organization has been allotted limited capacity.
The United Nations Charter remains a remarkable document, wherein its signatories have agreed to allow their organization to function toward establishing
peace and security, toward furthering social and economic development,
toward promoting human rights, toward creating international law and adjudi-
cating under it, and toward ushering peoples to political independence. The
Charter establishes means and mechanisms for making collective decisions. It
also gives the UN the authority to establish all manner of subsidiary organizations that might be deemed necessary to fulfill its missions. Under the Charter,
the UN can provide global governance; it can make international public policy and it can act. Most notably, this historic treaty even grants supranational
prerogative to the Security Council because the principle of non-intervention
enshrined in Article 2, Paragraph 7 is qualified in that same paragraph with
the affirmation that "this principle shall not prejudice the application of
enforcement measures under Chapter VII." In effect, the Security Council is
empowered to decide when it will act under Chapter VII, and when it acts
under Chapter VII it can pretty much do what it wants.

Nor in attempting to explain the shortcomings of the United Nations
can we realistically fall back on the old saws of incompetence and bureaucratic inertia. Our interactions with both the Secretariat staff and the national
delegations over a period of several years revealed that in terms of intellectual
and administrative talent the UN compares very favorably with other public
bureaucracies and indeed with many private-sector bureaucracies as well. Top-
echelon personnel in the Secretariat, for example, consistently work up to
very high standards of performance, even under constantly stressful conditions brought on by insufficient resources, unreasonable demands, and the

---

[6]Amartya Sen, *Development as Freedom* (New York: Anchor Books, 1999).
[7]Http://newsvote.bbc.co.uk/mpappas/pagetools/print/news/bbc.co.

urgent and chaotic outside world. At lower levels the ratio of dedicated international civil servants to underachievers not only very much favors the former but also challenges the myth of incompetence at the UN. As for the diplomatic corps that populates the UN "worlds" of New York, Geneva, Vienna and elsewhere, they are for the most part well trained, remarkably knowledgeable regarding the multitude of issues before them, and savvy regarding the opportunities and constraints that accompany multilateralism. They reliably represent their governments. Most member states continue to post their best people to UN missions because for many the UN is a convenient center for both multilateral and bilateral diplomacy. Although it is probably still true that "a diplomat's life is made up of . . . protocol, Geritol and alcohol," at the United Nations, it tends to be an extremely busy life that is at the same time very frustrating because of the tedious and too often inconsequential nature of UN diplomacy.[8] We have come to understand that one of the reasons that diplomats at the UN are so often frustrated is actually because they are so talented and might in other settings accomplish more for their countries.

Ultimately, in seeking to explain the poor performance of the United Nations, one must reach the conclusion that the organization cannot be a vehicle for international cooperation, and hence a motor for collective action toward ameliorating the ills of the human condition, as long as it remains a crucible of world political conflict. Too many scholarly analyses of the United Nations miss the mark of veracity by assuming that international cooperation is mainly what takes place at the UN. What the United Nations excels at producing, and reproducing, is politics. This volume assesses the political challenges facing the United Nations and evaluates the capacities of the organization to face them. Despite the evolution of complex processes of global governance, including the increased importance of nonstate actors and international bureaucracies, many of the challenges to multilateralism today stem from the tension between these broader developments and the political proclivities of national governments to defend sovereign prerogatives and to competitively promote national and factional interests.

Pondering the UN system evokes competing visions of the perceived and desired roles of international institutions in contemporary world affairs. Some observers, for example, view UN multilateralism as a stepping-stone toward creating more effective, authoritative regimes of global governance, whilst others view the UN as a forum for the pursuit of national interest. Still others view the system of international agencies as a mechanism for promoting a particular hegemonic order that preserves a status quo favoring the powerful and the rich. These differing conceptions have shaped the interpretation of politics within the UN. Analysis in *United Nations Politics* acknowledges these different explanations of strategies adopted by member states and other participants in

---

[8]The remark is attributed to Adlai Stevenson and cited in "Thoughts on the Business of Life," *Forbes,* January 20, 2003, p. 120.

international policy making. Our conclusions, however, emphasize the extent to which multilateral politics within the UN continue to reflect world politics outside the UN. In our view, the UN system does not transcend world politics but rather functions as a distinctive prism through which these broader dynamics are reflected in particular patterns.

TAKING POLITICS SERIOUSLY

In *United Nations Politics* we purposely avoid entering into any of the theoretical debates swirling about in our discipline of international relations. Yet this should not be taken to mean that we are unfamiliar with our colleagues' work or that we find theoretical questions uninteresting. What we offer is a text informed by social science theory but not about it. Our own theoretical standpoint, if it warrants being labeled as such, is Lasswellian: politics is about "who gets what, when, how," and this certainly includes intergovernmental politics at the UN.[9] Regarding approaches to the study of international relations, we observe that the essential dynamics of contemporary UN politics cannot be adequately understood from the perspective of American social science paradigms and theoretical orientations such as idealism, liberalism, institutionalism, or functionalism that are conventionally used to frame examinations of the world organization. In the contemporary discourses of our discipline, all of these frameworks either positively or critically focus analytical attention on phenomena of global governance, which have to do with managing anarchy or interdependence by making and enforcing rules that constrain governments' international behavior.[10] "Global governance" in meek, mild, and faltering forms does happen as a result of deliberative and bureaucratic processes at the UN. But the UN is not mainly about global governance, or, put differently, global governance is not mainly what happens within the political confines of the UN or as a result of UN deliberations. Making the study of the United Nations into a search for global governance therefore misses the point. The organization is mainly a club of governments, and their principal mode of interaction is conflict emanating from differing interests. This intergovernmental conflict does not produce global governance, at least not very much of it, although it does yield a somewhat distorted mirror image of the politically fragmented world of the early twenty-first century.

There appears as well in the literature on international organizations the curious notion that the United Nations is an autonomous actor in world affairs that can and does take action independent of the will and wishes of the

---

[9]Harold Dwight Lasswell, *Politics: Who Gets, What, When, How* (New York: P. Smith, 1936).

[10]See, for example, Stephen D. Krasner, ed., *International Regimes* (Ithaca, N.Y.: Cornell University Press, 1983); Robert O. Keohane, *After Hegemony: Cooperation and Discord in the World Political Economy* (Princeton, N.J.: Princeton University Press, 1984); Oran R. Young, *Governance in World Affairs* (Ithaca, N.Y.: Cornell University Press, 1999).

member governments that constitute the organization. Champions of the organization therefore speak of the UN doing much good in world affairs, sympathetic critics frequently ask why "the UN does not do more," and unsympathetic critics blame the UN for perpetrating messes and causing disasters. But the United Nations is not an autonomous agent, and the last thing that most of its member states would want is that the organization per se should become more autonomous. Realistically speaking, what the UN does or does not do in global affairs results mainly from the preferences of its members or more precisely from the interplay of intergovernmental politics among them. In this way, what the UN does—or more frequently does not do—cannot be separated from the proclivities of its members. Yet intergovernmental politics at the UN are seldom highlighted in analyses of global governance and also rarely integrated into criticisms of the organization by its skeptics. This volume therefore focuses primarily on politics within the UN and highlights the perceptions and behavior of national governments in responding via international organization to a turbulent world.

The particular set of theoretical lenses that we adopted for examining the workings of the United Nations is informed by the work of scholars such as Robert Cox, Craig Murphy, Nicholas Onuf, Susan Strange, Robert Keohane, James Mittelman, Herman Schwartz, and others who center our attention on structural sources of political order and tensions implicit in the imposition of hegemony.[11] It draws in particular on the insights of those who have attempted to build on the worldview of Antonio Gramsci, although we do not consider ourselves "Gramscian" because we do not accept the historical materialism that Gramsci inherited from Marx and that writers like Cox and Murphy borrowed from Gramsci. Otherwise, our perspective is somewhat constructivist, though not doctrinally so, because we believe there are material and constitutional givens that influence the functioning of the UN. Still, we also understand that "the UN is very much what its members make of it," through their visions,

---

[11]Robert Cox, ed., *The New Realism: Perspectives on Multilateralism and World Order* (London: Macmillan for UNU Press, 2000); Cox, *Production, Power and World Order: Social Forces in the Making of History* (New York: Columbia University Press, 1978); Robert Keohane, *Power and Governance in a Partially Globalized World* (London: Routledge, 2002); James Mittelman, *Globalization: Critical Reflections* (Boulder: Lynne Rienner Publishers, 1996); Mittelman, *The Globalization Syndrome* (Princeton, N.J.: Princeton University Press, 2000); Mittelman, *Whither Globalization? The Vortex of Knowledge and Ideology* (London: Routledge, 2004); Craig Murphy, *International Organization and Industrial Change* (Oxford: Oxford University Press, 1994); Nicholas Onuf, *World of Our Making: Rules and Rule in Social Theory and International Relations* (Columbia: University of South Carolina Press, 1989); Herman Schwartz, *States Versus Markets: History, Geography, and the Development of the International Political Economy* (New York: St. Martin's Press, 1994); Susan Strange, *Mad Money* (Manchester: Manchester University Press, 1998); Strange, *Casino Capitalism* (Oxford: Blackwell Publishers, 1986); and Strange, "The 'Fall' of the United States: Peace, Stability, and Legitimacy," in Geir Lundestad, ed., *The Fall of Great Powers: Peace, Stability, and Legitimacy* (Oxford: Oxford University Press, 1994), pp. 197–211.

aspirations, and expectations.[12] Some would define our approach as "realist," inasmuch as we do focus on governments and their essentially self-interested pursuits. However, we are certainly not structural realists because we do not accept that power and its distribution determines all. Nor can we accept that interests are somehow exogenous to systems of political interaction, especially within the UN context. If our approach must be theoretically pigeonholed, we would prefer to be labeled "realistic" rather than "realist" because we believe we have captured, and we reliably describe, the central dynamics driving the UN today.

Our perspective was shaped by interactions with a number of scholar-practitioners and career diplomats to whom we are greatly indebted. While they would hardly recognize the ways in which they contributed to our thinking and should in no way be associated with particular conclusions we have reached, Jacques Fomerand, Thomas Weiss, Ramesh Thakur, John Ruggie, Edward Luck, David Malone, Pierre Schori, Kishore Mahbubani, Gelson Fonseca, Brian Urquhart, and John Washburn shared insights born of experience and enlightened us concerning nuances and complexities in ways that only insiders can. The analysis presented in *United Nations Politics* also draws on hundreds of interviews with UN diplomats and Secretariat officials conducted between 2000 and 2005 and integrates their reflections and perspectives—often in their own words—to capture the political dynamics of the UN. As agreed with the subjects of our interviews in order to solicit frank and unrestrained responses, no individual is cited by name unless formal approval was given. To the extent that this diminishes the scientific rigor of our analysis from the perspective of some readers, it is unfortunate. Yet our task, similarly to how we defined it in our previous studies, was to solicit, report, and interpret the most forthright and frank perceptions possible. Our respondents offered these, and our work was enriched as a result. This methodology has served us well in the past. We believe it continues to do so here.

THE CONTOURS OF UN POLITICS

The perceptions of so many of the insiders that we encountered and quote in subsequent chapters highlight the fractious and divided politics of the UN. For example, former Canadian ambassador David Malone observed that "the intergovernmental process at the UN, especially stuck in the dynamics of the immediate post-Colonial period, is probably the greatest challenge facing the organization, poisoning most substantive debates and reducing virtually all issues to questions of process and tactical advantage." Making similar observations, another Canadian diplomat, Michel Duval, concluded that "the agendas of most Member States being played out in the politics surrounding

---

[12]To paraphrase Alexander Wendt, "Anarchy Is What States Make of It: The Social Construction of State Politics," *International Organization*, 46 (1192): 33–70.

peacekeeping reform are largely obstructionist." A Latin American diplomat who was deeply frustrated by the cultural politics being played out at the General Assembly described the atmosphere as "not cooperation, rather confrontational" and said "not anymore" to the proposition that consensus building was occurring between the Non-West and the West. Similarly frustrated over political obstructionism, was the East European ambassador who observed that governments were hiding behind sovereignty to blind the outside world to their abuses of human rights, and as concerns the UN, these governments "are most interested in establishing procedures that would effectively make . . . interventions impossible." The world's "only remaining superpower" was also perceived by insiders as working through its own agenda of national self-interest, or as a Secretariat official told us, the UN "has to become the organization of its members, not the tool of one of its members." This was seconded by the Latin American diplomat who observed that "the U.S. is using the organization for its own purposes and interests which are not necessarily those of the international community."

For many developing states, the perceived purpose of their participation and the basis of their political positions at the United Nations are to enhance national security by protecting autonomy. Felt insecurity is not military only, but also political, economic, and cultural, and it tends to be founded on suspicions of the First World, that is, the United States, Europe, and the several other countries that in political-economic issue-areas constitute the North and in political-cultural affairs constitute the West. Third World governments are wary of being dominated and exploited by those who command inordinate power. Specters haunt Third World discourse: "neo-imperialism," "neo-colonialism," "hegemonism," "westernization," "globalization," and other such symbols that imply domineering motives or external control.[13] Governments in Asia, Africa, and Latin America are sensitive about the enormous disparities in power between the Third World and the First, and they are anxious that the First World's power will be applied self-interestedly. They anticipate that for them this would mean political autonomy constrained, economic destiny distorted, resources exploited, and national culture overwhelmed. They suspect not only the motivations of First World governments, the United States government in particular, but also the intentions and behavior of international institutions controlled by these governments. Among these Northern- or Western-controlled institutions, most would list the UN Security Council, the International Monetary Fund, the World Bank, the World Trade Organization, the Human Rights Commission, and even the United Nations Development Programme. Since the war in Kosovo, NATO has joined the ranks of perceived instruments of Northern control. In many places, "economic adjustment" as prescribed by Northern-controlled international institutions is interpreted to mean de-nationalizing Third World economies. "Peacekeeping" is observed

[13]Claude Ake, "The New World Order: A View from Africa," in *Whose Order?* Hans Henrick Holm and Georg Sorensen, eds. (Boulder, Colo.: Westview Press, 1995), pp. 26 ff.

to mean military intervention mandated by Americans or Europeans to contain or displace bothersome Third World governments. Nowadays, UN peacekeeping is also coming to be looked upon rather cynically as sending Third World soldiers to pacify Third World trouble makers and thereby to keep the messiness from spilling out from the Third World. In the context of world politics in our dawning age of insecurity, it matters little whether such Third World perceptions of First World malevolence are accurate or inaccurate, or whether they are genuine perceptions or images politically contrived for domestic or other self-serving purposes. The discourse itself tends to drive much of Third World behavior within the United Nations and to sour relations between the developing and developed world.

For their part, member states from the First World perceive themselves to be under siege at the United Nations, because they collectively represent a world geopolitical and geoeconomic status quo that largely favors them. They wish to preserve this status quo, and they correctly perceive that a majority of others do not. First World peoples also share cultural norms that they had come to accept as both good and universal and that were not perceptibly threatened, at least from the Third World, until recently. The Europeans especially are using the fora of the UN to defend Western culture, symbolically, that is, to protect the eighteenth-century Enlightenment from twenty-first century revisionists. The intensity of the West–Non-West cultural confrontation should not be underestimated. Representatives of the United States, whom we sometimes think would probably not like to be at the UN at all, share European concerns about the Third World assault on Western cultural norms. But Washington is also fixed on using the UN to buttress the security of the United States. This is to be accomplished by promoting liberal economic policies and practices both between and within countries, and by promoting transitions to democracy in countries deemed nondemocratic. In Washington's conception, a world safe for the United States is a world of liberal democracies and open market economies, and if the world needs to be changed to match this image, the UN ought to be used as an instrument to bring change about. If the United Nations proves to be a blunt instrument for advancing American interests, Washington has other instruments at its disposal and, much to the annoyance of even the Europeans, does not hesitate to use them. Neither the European member states nor the United States would like to see the United Nations become in any way stronger or more autonomous, and this is one interest they incidentally share with the Third World. The First World, furthermore, would certainly not wish to see its institutional power within the UN, and specifically within the Security Council, diluted. Together, Europeans and Americans at the UN perceive their interests jeopardized by turmoil in the Third World and they favor using UN instrumentalities, although not necessarily European and American military forces, either to quell the turmoil or at least to keep the chaos at arm's length. Humanitarian intervention is a good thing, as long as Third World countries are the objects.

A CHANGED LANDSCAPE FOR UN POLITICS

Without wishing to reopen the old debate about whether the United Nations mirrors the broader world of international relations, let us simply assert that it does not. The UN is a world of international relations unto itself. As regards many things like the relative importance of different issues, the relative influence of different actors and agencies, and the relative disproportion in outputs of words and deeds, the UN fails to mirror the broader structure, functioning, and substance of contemporary international relations. Still, the inside world of the UN is crucially affected by the outside world of contemporary international relations, and there are also important reciprocal effects. Among the aspects of the outside world presently impinging upon the UN, the following resurfaced frequently during the course of our interviews in New York. First, the end-of-the-Cold War euphoria is clearly over. The idealism of newfound peace combined with expectations about harmony among powers and aspirations about a "collective management" of world order faded from world affairs not long after the Gulf War. The euphoria dissipated at the UN about the same time. Politics among major powers, without the UN as well as within, reverted to bargaining aimed at furthering national interests. Among regional rivals, neither the post–Cold War euphoria nor its disappearance changed very much.

But the ending of the Cold War also ended bipolarity and left the world with a single superpower, the United States of America. American power is a fact of early twenty-first century international life, and the United States affects the world partly because it is overwhelmingly present and cannot be ignored and partly because it wants to affect the course of twenty-first century history. The world's "only remaining superpower" defines its security as military superiority, economic openness, and ideological hegemony, and as the United States pursues its security, it pleases some but threatens many others. The United States looms as large, powerful, and willful within the UN as without, and while some believe that it may have lost its credibility, perhaps even its respectability, in the organization because of its inclination to heap abuse, no one suggests the United States has lost its influence.

The ending of the Cold War surely changed the bases of intergroup conflict in the world, although commonplace descriptions of what has happened are somewhat misleading. It is not the case, as some suppose, that with the ending of the superpower rivalry the mode of international conflict shifted from interstate to intrastate. Even during the Cold War most intergroup conflict in the world in fact took place within countries. What is different today is that such conflicts are much less likely to be ideologically based and much more likely to be ethnically based. And what is also different nowadays is that it is much more likely that the UN will become involved in such intrastate conflicts than was the case during the Cold War. At the United Nations, this situation is referred too as a "heightened demand for peacekeeping." In some quarters there is considerable consternation about both the UN's capabilities and its obligations to meet the demand by supplying peacekeepers.

The "Third World" has probably disappeared, at least as an economic stratum or a cluster of political-economically like-minded countries. The end of the Cold War had very little to do with this. Regrettably neither did the UN with its sloganized panaceas and its "decades of development." Successful, market oriented, yet state guided, economic development first in Asia and then in Latin America and elsewhere catapulted a score or more countries out of LDC status and effectively undermined the solidarity of the Group of 77. Other factors like differential affinities for privatization, marketization, and structural adjustment also contributed to ruining Third World cohesion. Practically speaking, the end of the Cold War did in the nonaligned movement because it is not especially meaningful to be "nonaligned" in a unipolar world. Yet, rather remarkably, while the Third World has probably disappeared, or at least dissipated, outside the UN, its presence is still being felt inside the organization. The G-77 and the NAM remain parts of the UN's political structure, and movement is afoot to resuscitate them by rebuilding their economic solidarity around a critique of globalization and their political solidarity around the appeals of "non-Westernism." The sides have been lining up for quite some time for an ideological confrontation that pits western liberalism against antiliberalism arrayed in a variety of cultural, religious, nationalistic, or ethnic garbs. This confrontation is already being joined in various parts of the world, but its center stage is probably going to be the UN. North–South relations are much more prominent within the UN than they are in the world of international relations outside the organization. But then, they always were.

The so-called Fourth World has not disappeared. Many countries and hundreds of millions of people remain mired in poverty. The gap in relative well-being between the very rich and the abysmally poor in the world is astronomical—and widening! Myriad forces and factors, including demographic explosion, environmental degeneration, the indifference of markets, and the rather dramatic dropping off of official development assistance in recent years, are driving the poor into deepening desperation. A hugely disproportionate number of impoverished countries and desperate people are located in Africa, where human deprivation is having harsh social and political repercussions. Africa in our time has become a region of continuing crisis. The Fourth World is marginal in contemporary international relations. But it is central at the United Nations, at least on the development side of the organization. Much the same is the case regarding Africa, which captures relatively little attention in the world but considerable attention at the UN. "Human security" is much of what the UN is about these days, and the poorest countries are much of what of human security is about.

Globalization is certainly not a phenomenon of the last ten years, but in many ways the widespread awareness of globalization is a rather recent occurrence. The awareness of economic and financial interdependence is rather recent, and the full implications of these conditions are not yet understood. Nor is there yet even a modest understanding of the implications of instantaneous worldwide communication. The awareness of an emergent transnational civil society is also relatively recent, and the political, economic, and social implications of such a crazy quilt of associations and organizations functioning in a world that has become indifferent to traditional political borders are not yet fully discernable. That a globalized culture is homogenizing elites appears to be true. Whether this English-speaking, cell-phone-toting, pop music listening, five-star-living transnational community will overwhelm traditional cultural diversity is doubtful. Globalization appears to be affecting the UN much as it is affecting the world more generally. It is causing confusion because its implications are not understood, and it is provoking defensive opposition because it appears threatening to established institutions and practices. Because national sovereignty or even nation-states as such could become possible victims of globalization, no small amount of defensive concern is being voiced by national governments within the UN.

OUTLINE OF THE STUDY

This study represents an updating of two monographs on "the state of the United Nations" written by Puchala and Coate for the Academic Council on the United Nations System (ACUNS) more than a decade ago. *The State of the United Nations* was published in 1988, and *The Challenge of Relevance: The United Nations in a Changing World Environment* appeared a year later.[14] At the time, we described the UN as an organization struggling to deal with profound challenges to its relevance in a rapidly changing global political climate. The Cold War had just come to an end, and political space seemed to be opening for multilateral action. Our first study, however, pictured a teetering, tottering, battered, and smarting organization that was suffering greatly from its marginalization during the Cold War, from the wounds inflicted during the political battles over the New International Economic Order, and from abuse heaped on it by its wealthiest member state. The second report, issued a year later, reflected a slightly improved political climate at the UN and a growing realization that many of the most important problems confronting peoples everywhere could not be dealt with through unilateral or strictly governmental means. This realization seemed to provide impetus for collective action and for reaching beyond the traditional confines of sovereignty-based diplomacy. The challenge to sovereignty appears to have grown significantly during the last decade, but so have governments' tenacious commitments to preserving and protecting their sovereign prerogatives. *United Nations Politics* gauges the tensions between a world where multilateral cooperation is imperative and a world politics that limits capacities to cooperate.

[14]Donald J. Puchala and Roger A. Coate, *The State of the United Nations, 1988*, Reports and Papers, No. 2, Academic Council on the United Nations System, 1988; and *The Challenge of Relevance: The United Nations in a Changing World Environment*, Reports and Papers, Academic Council on the United Nations System, 1989.

United Nations Politics might be looked upon as a sequel to our earlier inquiries concerning the state of the United Nations. However, the essays that compose the chapters in this volume delve considerably deeper than was the case with the earlier studies into the causes of the conditions that characterize the UN today. The picture of the United Nations that we ultimately paint will be seen by some as unflattering: the state of the UN today is problematic and the relevance of the organization in world affairs is questionable. However, we seek here to do more than simply paint this picture because the objective of our analyses is to explain as best we can why the state of the UN today is as it is. The explanation we offer is multifaceted, although the central theme of competitive politics reappears often. Successive chapters of this book were originally written as discrete essays, and they may be read as such in any order that suits readers' inclinations. Even the last chapter is less a summary and conclusion than it is another attempt to explain the current condition of the United Nations. It possibly invites another study of the state of the UN that might be conducted five or ten years hence.

Chapters 2, 3, 4, and 5 of our book establish the context for understanding the challenges that the UN multilateral system faces in responding to a variety of global problems in the twenty-first century: Western hegemony and the resistance to it, the unfulfilled institutional capacity inherent in the United Nations Charter, the persistence of state sovereignty, and obstacles to finding consensus and exercising leadership in a world deeply divided by relative wealth, unequal power, contending ideologies, and poorly communicating cultures. Our analysis begins with an interpretation of the historical, structural, and holistic context of the UN system. From birth, the UN was part vision, part ideology, part war weariness and frustration with the evolving deadliness and costliness of war. It was in large measure a product of a realistic assessment of and response to the state of world affairs and the structure of international relations at the time. The resultant UN system represented the firm conviction that a new world order—based in the political, moral, and economic foundations of liberalism—the ideology—was essential for promoting, building, and maintaining world peace and stability. The foundation of this new order was plagued from the beginning by the tensions and forces inherent in two often contentious, if not contradictory, globalizing paradigms: the European interstate diplomatic legal order, which privileged the separateness and autonomy of states, and a universalistic liberal ideological order, which at the very least imagined a global marketplace and a moral unity of humankind. As a system of intergovernmental organizations with the national state as the primary unit of membership and action, the UN system was just that, a diplomatic-legal institutional forum of representatives of states playing out their diverse and often conflicting foreign policies and intrigues. It was first and foremost a Westphalian sovereignty-based institution with rules, procedures, norms, and principles based accordingly. On the other hand, it was also an institutional form founded and structured around liberal ideological tenets, assumptions, and goals. The invisible hand of markets, not state directives and intervention, was viewed by the UN's main architects as the way and means of promoting, building, and maintaining world peace and stability. This would be buttressed by universally endorsed codes of appropriate international behavior that would emerge from shared values and continuing dialogue among reasonable people.

These ideas and principles are constitutive of the "Western hegemonic" order that has grown to encapsulate the postwar global order, including the United Nations. However, as was the case in the beginning, these ideas and values have not prevailed without contention. Ideas, values, interests, and perceptions are shaped by history and events, and tensions rise and fall and grow and wane accordingly. The substantive focus of politics has evolved in the post–Cold War environment to include new issues such as the legitimacy of humanitarian intervention, the implications of the Bush Doctrine of preventive war, the meaning of "good governance," the role of civil society and the private sector in global governance, and the threat of transnational terrorism. But the tension between Westphalian state-centrism and liberal ideological conceptualizations and aspirations continue to shape UN politics.

Chapter 3 provides an assessment of the remarkable but as yet unrealized capacity for collective action inherent in the United Nations Charter. This expansive capacity assumes member state commitment for its realization, and in subsequent chapters we detail how politics has undermined that commitment. Capacity for collective action is most detailed and expansive in the area of peace and security, and the Charter provides for ever more expansive application of collective action subject to consensus in the Security Council. But this is not the only area in which the Charter provides the means for the collective will to be exercised efficiently. In the area of economic and social cooperation, the UN Charter provides for a central coordinative role for the UN. On human rights the Charter itself provides for very little capacity, but the Charter does open the door for the development of human rights machinery and the consideration of human rights issues by the General Assembly and the Security Council. Member states have over the past several decades availed themselves of this possibility by creating new bodies and commissions, although the politics of the UN reform effort in 2005–2006 shows how tenuous developing institutional capacity remains. One area in which the UN capacity for action was successfully realized was in the area of self-determination and Third World decolonization. The chapter presents self-determination as a case study of how the international community can realize the promise of the Charter and further develop capacity to realize collective action. However, the bulk of Charter-derived capacity remains unrealized. The chapter concludes with an assessment of the unbalanced institutional development of the General Assembly, the Economic and Social Council, and the Security Council, which reflects the political proclivities of member states rather than any deficiencies stemming from the Charter itself.

Chapter 4 presents the challenge and persistence of sovereignty in a globalizing world by examining the debates over humanitarian intervention and the role of nongovernmental organizations (NGOs) within the UN. The argument is simple. There has been much ink spilled by scholars of international relations on the question of whether sovereignty is being eroded. In the broadest sense, state sovereignty is assailed by forces of globalization and the growth of interdependence. The nature of contemporary global challenges—from the warming of the earth's atmosphere to the menace of international terrorism—confounds notions of interstate politics as well. Arguments about the erosion of sovereignty have emerged in the analyses of the UN system itself, where supranational authority is seen to be emerging from above and NGO participation in global governance undermines national sovereignty from below. These questions about the endurance of sovereignty cut to the heart of the tensions of Westphalian and liberal perspectives on UN multilateralism. In support of human rights, for example, UN secretary-general Kofi Annan has challenged the concept of absolute state sovereignty while ever greater access to the political process within the UN by nongovernmental organizations represents another apparent assault on sovereignty. Such advocacies and openings have been criticized and resented by member states that continue to be preoccupied with protecting national sovereignty, national interests, and keeping the United Nations a strictly intergovernmental system. This chapter elaborates the tensions between member-state preoccupation with sovereignty and some of the forces eroding it. The chapter also examines ways in which questions of sovereignty affect the UN's capacities in dealing with a number of pressing political issues.

Leadership, the focus of Chapter 5, is critical in global political processes, and the early twenty-first century appears to be an era of constrained leadership at the UN. Nothing much happens at the United Nations, unless governments or coalitions exercise leadership. Yet leadership is complicated in the context of the UN, which is comprised of member states that are "sovereign equals" according to international law but vary rather dramatically in the international distribution of power and their capacity to act. These structural factors condition the exercise of leadership even though structural distributions of power are not determinative of leadership by states or individuals. Further, leadership does not necessarily guarantee successful international outcomes or policies. Using concepts of structural leadership, entrepreneurial leadership, and intellectual leadership, this chapter assesses the impact of U.S. unilateralism and Washington's ambivalence about multilateralism. It evaluates the leadership record and potential of an emergent European Union committed to multilateralism but steeped in Westernism nevertheless. The most likely contenders for structural leadership, the United States and the European Union, have divergent worldviews regarding the organization. The former is content with a marginal role for the UN in world affairs while the latter presses for a much more central one, and such tensions within the West are notably impacting the organization. Our analysis in Chapter 5 also ponders the absence of leadership *within* the Group of 77 and the nonaligned movement that restricts these groups from providing leadership within the UN more generally. Entrepreneurial leadership in discrete issue-areas by ad hoc coalitions of middle powers and NGOs, and intellectual leadership, particularly by the secretary-general in the 1990s and beyond, do provide some momentum within the organization. The exercise of intellectual leadership, particularly by the secretary-general over shifting norms of intervention, tends to reinforce Western hegemony. These developments make the exercise of entrepreneurial leadership by middle powers or NGOs much more difficult.

The next three chapters demonstrate how factors introduced earlier have influenced UN political debates over issues of universal values and human rights, peacekeeping, and promoting sustainable human development. Chapter 6 explores the attempt to define and embrace values that are shared by the international community. Because such attempts have always been politically fraught, it was perhaps not surprising that the effort to draft the Universal Declaration of Human Rights was cordoned off from Charter deliberations. This chapter explores the debates that have accompanied efforts to produce consensus by the international community over shared universal values. During the Cold War, these debates about values most often centered on ideological divisions as the Soviets and the United States fought for the preeminence of universal social and economic rights versus universal political and civil rights, respectively. In the aftermath of the Cold War, the world witnessed the fall of communism, the spread of democratization, and the entrenchment of free market economic systems as the new liberal orthodoxy that seemed to suggest a new universalism to which the UN could be hand maiden. This liberal illusion was shattered at the 1993 World Conference on Human Rights held in Vienna. There, strong claims were made in support of cultural relativism rather than universalism in the area of human rights. Liberalism and the universality of individual human rights came under siege as proponents of values embedded in different cultures and traditions suggested that Western notion of rights were not in fact universal. At the UN, the politics of culture continued well into the 1990s with the Dialogue Among Civilizations initiative that was launched by Iran and strongly supported by the governments of several Islamic countries. The "dialogue" was interpreted by Western governments as another attack on liberal conceptions of universal human rights, whereas the Islamic world perceived the protection of cultural diversity as a vital issue of international security. These intercultural debates over universal values reveal active resistance to dominant Western conceptualizations as well as the lack of consensus on universal values.

Chapter 7 takes up the question of UN peacekeeping and enforcement operations in the 1990s to show the relative unpreparedness of the UN to deal with problems of peace and security in the post–Cold War environment. Reform in the area of peacemaking is progressing, although effectiveness remains hampered by interstate politics. The end of the Cold War has seen the nature of threats to international peace and security transformed. Today, such threats are more likely to involve conflict within states rather than between them. Outbreaks of violence are rooted in communal, ethnic, and religious tensions, the anarchic consequences of failed states, and activities of terrorist organizations. During the 1990s the UN was called on to respond to intrastate conflicts, and the results were generally less than successful. Attempting to learn from unfortunate experience, the secretary-general, supported by key member states, initiated a thorough assessment of UN peacekeeping activities, animated by the *Brahimi Report* and aimed at reform. Progress toward improving the peacemaking and peacekeeping capacities of the United Nations has been made. But reform as well as performance in the field remains constrained by politics among member states, whose differing interests elevate factional goals and rivalries above commitments to improve the effectiveness of the UN.

How best to promote human well-being has long dominated discourse and practice at the United Nations. Development fads and fancies have come and gone. Each has consumed a rather inordinate amount of UN attention, provoked heated politics, and then given way to some new thesis about how to confront global poverty. While UN members have debated about "development strategies," the gap separating the very rich and the extremely poor has been getting larger and larger. Chapter 8 explores the tensions between efforts to further a globalist agenda focused on enhancing human well-being and the political aims and ends of UN member states and factions that tend to sidetrack the collective uplifting of humanity.

In the opening years of the twenty-first century, a sense of growing consensus—at least in relative terms—seems to have emerged about the best means to foster human well-being. Development has come to be seen as sustainable human development and is closely linked with the evolving concept of human security. This synthesis bears little resemblance to the development discourse promoted during much of the 1960s and 1970s by the Third World majority of UN member states under the rubric "New International Economic Order." To the contrary, since the end of the Cold War, the UN system has become increasingly free to function in the economic realm as it was designed to function, that is, in the service of promoting a liberal capitalist order. Of course, from the beginning, many players and forces have opposed such an agenda and have moved to transform it. Not everyone is content with the liberal design and its hobbled, hampered, and somewhat haphazard implementation. The main argument of the chapter is that three factors converged during the 1990s to underpin an acquiescence among member states in the efforts of the United Nations Development Programme and other parts of the Secretariat to promote sustainable human development. The UN system's underlying normative liberal ideological foundations were largely accepted, and the evolution of multilateral processes since the end of the Cold War strengthened the hands of the UNDP and the secretary-general. Changes in the global political economy also elevated the urgency of trying to do something about poverty. But what is to be done and whether the UN is capable of doing it remain open questions. Events at the World Summit in 2005 underlined these questions and cast new doubts on the UN as a development-promoting institution.

The concluding chapter assesses the capacity of the UN system to respond to twenty-first century challenges. Our conclusion, perhaps not entirely welcome, is that the United Nations is unlikely to respond very well to foreseeable challenges because the political environment within and without the organization will probably remain inhospitable to enhanced global governance. In this context, the kinds of reforms discussed and debated today are unlikely to change much in terms of outcomes. Institutional tinkering is unlikely to result in the changes that UN supporters argue will make the organization more effective. But even these are likely to go farther than member states that seek to protect national sovereignty are willing to allow. The 2005 reform project is unlikely to succeed because the proposed changes do not resolve the contradictions between Westphalian and liberal approaches to global governance.

Following the elaboration of the context of UN politics and the salient political debates in the twenty-first century, it is clear that a reconsideration of the UN is in order. While pessimists argue that the debate over the war in Iraq reveals UN irrelevance and optimists forever want to engage in institutional reform to make the UN more effective, we conclude that both sides have got it at least partly wrong with regard to the UN's role in international politics. The UN does not particularly need to be reformed (at least not in the ways proposed for the past fifteen years), nor is it moribund. The reality is that intergovernmental politics and political interests obstruct effective multilateral responses in the United Nations. In our final chapter we detail the limits to UN multilateralism in providing international peace and security, promoting human welfare, and articulating universal norms and values. The UN has been weak in dealing with terrorism because there is little consensus on defining terrorism. The UN cannot react quickly to threats to international peace and security. The UN cannot develop national economies. The UN has not been capable of producing consensus in the international community over universal norms and values. These conditions, constraints, and incapacities are not likely to change in the foreseeable future.

However, the United Nations does several things rather well, some of which we highlight in the volume, and we argue in our concluding chapter that these multilateral activities should be encouraged and supported. The UN has rather successfully adapted its peace operations to address challenges from failed states by improving its capacity for civilian administration. The cultivation of a talented pool of special representatives operating under the auspices of the secretary-general has been critical in conflict prevention and mediation. The UN is a source of intellectual ferment where new and frequently unorthodox concepts and perspectives reflect and redefine the changing nature of international relations. New thinking that is as often as not UN thinking reorients approaches to global problems. The UN has proven adaptable in opening political space for international civil society to participate in addressing pressing global challenges. Even more important than the missions that it can successfully undertake is the pivotal role that dialogue in the UN can play in confronting some of the central political questions of twenty-first-century world politics. And although consensus on universal values and world order may prove illusive, the UN remains a critical forum for providing hegemonic accountability. It is perhaps only within the United Nations that there exists capacity to question the legitimacy of Western hegemony. Such confrontation at the UN has not, and likely will not, constrain the exercise of power, but its value should not be under-estimated.

CHAPTER 2

The Evolution of an Institutional Form

From birth, the United Nations was part vision, part ideology, part war weariness, and, in part, a realistic response to the state of world affairs at the time. A new more stable, peaceful, and prosperous world order was to be forged out of the old. The Westphalian state-based, self-help system was to be tempered and tamed by institutional forms that seemed to be possible given the conditions of the day. The world was on the verge of a unipolar moment, and leaders of the emergent superpower and its closest ally were ready for change. The United Nations system that resulted represented the firm conviction that a new world order, built on the political, economic, and moral foundations of liberalism—the ideology—was essential for maintaining world peace. However, this new order was plagued from the beginning by the tensions inherent in two often contentious, if not contradictory, globalizing paradigms: the European interstate diplomatic-legal order that we here call the *Westphalian* order and ideological liberalism.

As a cluster of intergovernmental organizations with the national state as the primary unit of membership, the UN system was established as a set of forums where representatives of self-interested states could pursue their diverse and often conflicting policies and intrigues. These were first and foremost sovereignty-based institutions where rules, norms, principles, and procedures reflected and reinforced traditional Western statecraft. On the other hand the United Nations system was also an institutional form founded on classical, liberal ideological tenets, assumptions, and goals. Markets, perhaps guided by invisible hands although certainly not by governmental manipulations and interventions, were to generate the wealth that would catalyze peace. These markets needed to be free, open, and global. International institutions would ensure their smooth functioning: they would set the rules for commerce but refrain from interfering, conducting, or otherwise entering into it. Because liberal thought embraces individuals, people were to be protected from abuse and uplifted in their well-being because they had "rights," which were inalienable and universal. Although scant attention was actually paid to human rights during the founding moments, some of those involved in establishing the United Nations system strongly believed that international institutions should secure these rights, even perhaps in disregard of sovereignty. Ultimately, this aspect of the liberal vision was also realized and institutionalized, and when it was, tensions between the intertwined Westphalian and liberal assumptions underpinning the UN system were exacerbated. The Westphalian assumptions that informed the founding of the UN system championed sovereignty; the liberal assumptions, which were also constitutive, questioned it. The history of the UN system might be looked upon as a half-century-long faltering attempt to paper over the contradictions between the particularistic principles of sovereignty and the cosmopolitan norms of liberalism.

RECREATING WORLD ORDER ANGLO-AMERICAN STYLE

The UN system was born at a particular moment in the *longue durée* of contemporary world order. Twice in a generation the world had been engulfed in horrendous warfare that erased tens of millions of lives, ruined much of the infrastructure of the planet, and cast humanity backward into primeval barbarism. If the American and British leaders of the wartime alliance that called itself "The United Nations" could have their way, history was not to repeat itself, and "succeeding generations" would be saved "from the scourge of war" because world peace after 1945 was to be institutionalized—and policed. The postwar planners were far more pragmatic realists than dreamy idealists. As they designed the postwar order, they were also fighting an apocalyptic war against forces propelled by irrationalist ideologies of fascism and totalitarianism. This was hardly a time when anyone could envision a postwar world wherein power would no longer condition international outcomes. In President Roosevelt's vision, the new world order would be policed by the major powers—the "Four Policemen," acting through a new institution when needed and as appropriate.[1] Beyond legitimizing collective action by the major powers, the Unite Nations was to be more of a "town meeting of the world."[2] It was to serve as a center for harmonizing national policies and as a facilitator that, in Roosevelt's words, would "assist the creation, through international cooperation,

---

[1]Townsend Hoopes and Douglas Brinkley, *FDR and the Creation of the UN* (New Haven: Yale University Press, 1997).
[2]John F. Dulles, "The General Assembly," Foreign Affairs (October 1945), p. 165.

of conditions of stability and well being necessary for peaceful and friendly relations among nations."[3] In other words, at least in Roosevelt's thinking as best we can tell, the United Nations was to be at once a vehicle for the exercise of major power hegemony, assumedly benevolent, and a club of governments. The UN would possibly tame the Westphalian state system, but it would not transform it.

Although the Westphalian vision underpinned much of the design for the United Nations *organization*, that is, the deliberative organs housed largely in New York, it was the classical liberal vision that underpinned much of the rest of the United Nations *system*. The United Nations organization that came to be headquartered in New York was not the first or the second or even the third or fourth international institution established by the victorious allies of World War II as part of the UN system. The Food and Agricultural Organization (FAO) was established following the allies' meeting at the Hot Springs Conference in 1943. In November 1943, forty-four countries met in Washington and established the United Nations Relief and Rehabilitation Administration (UNRRA) to assist liberated peoples in Europe and Asia. About the same time the International Civil Aviation Organization (ICAO) was formed. In April 1944 the International Labor Organization, making an effort to revitalize itself, met for the first time since the outbreak of the war. The Bretton Woods Conference in July 1944 gave birth to two complementary institutions. The International Bank for Reconstruction and Development (The World Bank) would assist in restoring the devastated economies of the war-torn world, and the International Monetary Fund (IMF) would assist in maintaining orderly exchange arrangements among members and work toward a multilateral system of payments that would promote commerce and therefore global economic growth. As primary objectives of economic policy, the Bank and the Fund were expected to contribute to the promotion and maintenance of high levels of employment and real income and to the development of the productive resources of all members. U.S. postwar planners also envisaged the establishment of a trade organization that would complement the financial institutions created at Bretton Woods. This agency would deal with restrictions on trade by governments or cartels and monopolies, cyclical fluctuations in production and employment, and adjustments in the production and trade of primary commodities. After the failure of the International Trade Organization (ITO) to gain congressional approval in the United States, a General Agreement on Tariffs and Trade (GATT) was accepted as the international vehicle for removing barriers to trade. The United Nations Educational, Scientific and Cultural Organization (UNESCO) was formally established in 1945 and assigned the responsibility of promoting democratization through mass education, mass media, scientific cooperation, and cultural preservation. Then, finally, in the

---

[3]Cited in Cordell Hull, *The Memoirs of Cordell Hull*, 2 vols. (New York: Macmillan, 1948), pp. 1646–47.

spring of 1945, the United Nations organization was established as a result of the San Francisco Conference.

Underlying the creation of the UN system of organizations with economic and social mandates was a logic that sprang from a liberal capitalist vision originating in England in the eighteenth century and dominant in American thinking after World War II. U.S. policy makers were convinced that a stable and enduring world political order rested on sound socioeconomic bases and in particular on a viable and expanding international economy and the promotion of full employment. Growth and prosperity within countries in a liberal capitalist world were directly linked to growth and prosperity in the larger global political economy. Peace was a prerequisite for economic growth and prosperity because war stifles international commerce, wastes resources, and destroys real value. Democracy and the promotion of human rights were prerequisites for sustainable peace. In turn, creating and sustaining democracy required social and economic stability and growth. Therefore, it might be reasoned that not only did the Bretton Woods institutions and the first set of functional agencies precede the UN in their founding, but as institutional components of the liberal world order that American leaders envisioned, they and not the United Nations organization were this order's core.

Tenets of classical liberalism had as early as 1941 made their way into the operational provisions of the Atlantic Charter and were reflected in its fourth and fifth principles. Similarly, Article VII of the Lend Lease Agreements between the United States and recipient countries called for "agreed action. . . . directed to the expansion, by appropriate international and domestic measures, of production, employment, and the exchange and consumption of goods, which are the material foundations of the liberty and welfare of all peoples, to the elimination of all forms of discriminatory treatment in international commerce, and to the reduction of tariffs and other trade barriers."[4] In a 1943 radio address, U.S. Secretary of State Cordell Hull further elaborated the liberal worldview:

> We know that political controversies and economic strife among nations are fruitful causes of hostility and conflict. But we also know that economic stagnation and distress, cultural backwardness, and social unrest within nations, wherever they exist, may undermine all efforts for stable peace. The primary responsibility for dealing with these conditions rests on each and every nation concerned. But each nation will be greatly helped in this task by the establishment of sound trade and other economic relations with other nations, based on a comprehensive system of mutually beneficial international cooperation, not alone in this respect, but also in furthering educational advancement and in promoting observance of basic human rights.[5]

---

[4]See, for example, "Mutual Aid Agreement Between the United States and the Union of Soviet Socialist Republics: June 11, 1942," *Department Of State Bulletin, June 13, 1942* (Washington, D.C.: U.S. Government Printing Office, 1942).

[5]Cited in Clive Archer, *International Organizations*, 3rd ed. (London and New York: Routledge, 2001), p. 5.

The new UN system that emerged after World War II, then, represented a blend of realpolitik, ideological liberalism, and pragmatic functionalism. It was designed to be a highly decentralized yet coherent system of independent international agencies. Each was comprised of its own autonomous membership, governing bodies, administrative apparatus, financing, and so forth. Yet collectively they were to function as a more or less coherent system of cooperating agencies. Within this system, the primary purpose of the UN organization headquartered in New York would be to deter aggression and respond to threats to international peace and security. But building the conditions necessary for promoting and maintaining peace and security would be the responsibility of the specialized agencies and the Bretton Woods institutions, with the UN organization playing a supplemental role of standard setter and town meeting of the world. Strong U.S. leadership and American guidance would ensure that things functioned as designed—or so the logic went.

TAKING THE EDGE OFF ANARCHY

One interesting way in which we might look at the United Nations system as it took shape after World War II is to envisage it as an assembled jigsaw puzzle. Historically, the many pieces of this puzzle had been scattered about in international political and economic affairs for some time—indeed for considerable time. But it was only in the aftermath of history's greatest war that conditions afforded an opportunity for finally assembling the puzzle. The picture that comes into focus as the pieces fell into place is a depiction of a world largely created by Europeans because from the sixteenth to the twentieth century, Europeans dominated world affairs. Americans entered this European world as colonial subjects in the seventeenth century, participated in it as autonomous but peripheral players for much of the nineteenth century, and then rose to shape it in the mid-twentieth century. The international order largely created by the United States after World War II did not transform traditional European international relations. Instead, it institutionalized them by assembling various processes and practices of global governance that were already aspects of European statecraft.

European statecraft in the nineteenth century had established a number of international norms and institutional forms that found their way into an evolving system of global governance, all these amounting, if you will, to a taming and tempering of Westphalian international politics by rendering realpolitik somewhat subject to international law and international behavior somewhat constrained by accepted norms. For example, the Congress of Vienna that ended the era of the Napoleonic Wars brought together the representatives of the four major victorious powers of the Quadruple Alliance—Austria, Great Britain, Prussia, and Russia—plus France, the defeated foe, to attempt to reconstruct the European political landscape and to deter future aggression. The Congress gave rise to the Concert of Europe wherein the powerful states of Europe appointed themselves custodians of the global order. The notion that a directorate of powerful states acting in concert can and should assume responsibility for international stability was thus born. Between 1815 and the end of the century, the major European powers met well over two dozen times to sort issues of continental and colonial concern in multilateral fashion. As Concert members perceived themselves regulators not only of European but of global affairs, it was at the Berlin conference in 1878 that they acted to confirm the European imperial status quo and to divvy up the remaining uncolonized parts of Africa among themselves.

By the latter nineteenth century, the notion of concert still was still in place, but it became elusive in practice as newly arrived revisionist powers—Germany and the United States, for example—sought influence commensurate with their capabilities and challenged the status quo. Concerts do not coalesce when major powers disagree. A broader system of international conferencing consequently emerged and congealed around the somewhat idealistic notion that potentially disruptive issues are better handled by talking rather than fighting. Between 1850 and the outbreak of the First World War, more than 100 international conferences, most of them European in scope, were held to sort diverse issues. Some of them actually did this, and many of them resulted in the formation of more permanent bodies that began to look like modern international organizations. As concern over the increased lethality and costliness of war grew, the multilateral conferences came to include such weighty topics as war and peace itself. Most notable in this regard were the peace conferences in The Hague in 1899 and 1907, where attendance included not only the great power core but also a cluster of smaller states. By the time of the second Hague Conference, membership had expanded far beyond Europe. To the emergent norm of multilateral dialogue in the interest of peace was added the principle of universal inclusion. "Assembly" was added to "Concert."

The public international unions must also be added to the evolving pattern of international institutionalization. These were also European innovations. From the mid-nineteenth century onward, the spread of the industrial revolution and associated technological advances in transportation and communication rapidly compressed social time and space and increased transnational interactions and exchanges. In response, a new and revolutionary form of international social organization emerged on the continent—the international public union. Building on the precedent established by the Central Commission for the Navigation of the Rhine that was established as a result of the Congress of Vienna, European governments subsequently set about founding permanent international organizations to deal with a variety of shared problems relating mostly to managing the international impacts of industrial age technologies. More than 30 such intergovernmental organizations were established between 1864 and 1914, including the International Telegraphic Union (1865), Universal Postal Union (1874), International Bureau of Weights and Measures (1875), the World Meteorological Organization (1878), International

Union for the Protection of Industrial Property (1886), International Union for the Publication of Industrial, Literary and Artistic Work (1890), and the General Office for International Transport by Rail (1893). A number of institutional norms evolved along with this new form of permanent international institution. These included: the sovereign state as unit of membership; treaty-based constitutions; universal membership; conferences or congresses as primary policy-making organs; executive councils to oversee the administration of policies; parliamentary diplomacy; egalitarian voting principles; permanent secretariats to implement actions; financing by some formula such as ability to pay; and scope limited to particular functional problem areas. The majority of these organizations were tasked to smooth the workings of the global market, and thus to render the international environment more accommodating to capitalist expansion, which was another aspect of European global domination that we take up in a moment. Nevertheless, the public unions proved useful: this nineteenth-century international institutional form took hold, as did the norms that underpinned the organizations' operations.

The progress of a century of institutional innovations and normative thrusts toward finding cooperative ways to deal with issues of war, peace, and world order was all but cancelled by World War I, and they might have been erased from European and perhaps world history were it not for the efforts of American president Woodrow Wilson. Upon taking the United States into the war, President Wilson made it clear what he wanted coming out of the war. His famous Fourteen Points included establishing a "general association of nations" that would guarantee the "political independence and territorial integrity to great and small states alike." This proposal for a permanent international organization that would deal with issues of peace and security was one among the fourteen points that Wilson refused to negotiate away during the peace settlement at the Great War's end. In one of the outstanding ironies of contemporary history, the United States, mainly for domestic political reasons, refused to join the League of Nations, making the organization a distinctly European affair and also a rather feeble one. The League ultimately failed to keep the peace, not only because the United States shunned it but more precisely because the political-ideological environment of the 1930s invited aggression and mocked international cooperation.

Nevertheless, the League did help firmly embed a number of enduring norms and institutional forms. The tradition of the concert of great powers, for example, influenced the creation of the League Council, and the tradition of congresses to promote dialogue among nations was rehearsed in the establishment of the League Assembly. Membership was theoretically universal and one state-one vote was the principle of participation. In signing the Covenant of the League, member states agreed to respect the territorial integrity and independence of all other member states and to strive to settle their disputes by peaceful means, that is, to resort to diplomacy before they resorted to war. A Permanent Court of International Justice, that was in a way an elaboration on early twentieth-century attempts to devise instruments for international arbitration, was established alongside the League to facilitate the adjudication and peaceful settlement of international disputes. The idea of an international civil service, realized to some extent in the international public unions, was elaborated under the League. Building on the model of the public international unions and his own work in the British civil service, the League's first secretary-general, Sir Edmund Drummond, strove for an international civil service that would be impartial, nonpartisan, and independent. International civil servants would owe their loyalty to the international institution and not to any government of which they may be citizens. The tradition of the international public union itself created political space for the creation in 1919 of yet another one, the International Labor Organization (ILO). It appears that securing humane conditions for working men and women had somehow been left out of assignments to the international public unions of the latter nineteenth century.

The League also added the notion of "collective security" to the inventory of norms and practices underpinning world order. States would respond collectively to deal with those who violated the peace in breach of agreed norms and rules. Aggressors, in effect, would find the world united against them and, in theory at least, would be invariably either deterred or defeated. At the center of this collective security system was the concert of major powers that constituted the League Council. The League's collective security system was flawed because it required unanimity for action, but the blueprint was drawn: collective security would be multilateral diplomacy's strategy for peace, and it would be managed by major power elites, with the rest of the world more or less obliged to cooperate. The League also established a mandate system to deal with areas and peoples that had either been parts of the Ottoman Empire, destroyed in World War I, or colonies of the defeated German Empire. Some would say that the mandate system simply shifted colonies from those who were defeated in World War I to those who were victorious, but it is also the case that the mandate system nurtured the new norm of national self-determination, which was to become very important during the great sweep of decolonization that would occur three generations later.

MAKING THE WORLD SAFE FOR GLOBAL CAPITALISM

In the heyday of their global dominance, Europeans not only imposed the Westphalian state system on the rest of world but the capitalist economic system as well. Accordingly, their self-interested efforts in the nineteenth and early twentieth century to manage the anarchy of politics among sovereign units were paralleled by equally self-interested efforts to keep markets expanding, commerce flourishing, the favorable global division of labor intact, and returns on overseas investments robust. Let us recall that Wilson's vision of world order as embodied in the Fourteen Points included "absolute freedom of navigation upon the seas" and the "removal, so far as possible, of all economic barriers." In his thinking, widely shared in liberal circles, commerce related to peace, and peace in turn promoted commerce. European governments also understood that commerce produced wealth, and wealth produced power. Making the world safe for capitalism was a European project of the nineteenth century, an American project of the twentieth century, and a Western aspiration thoroughly intertwined with the evolution of international organizations.

Historically, the origins of the capitalist world system can be traced to Europe in the mid-fifteenth century, not coincidentally to the time of the early glimmerings of what would become the Westphalian state system. The dominant characteristic of this newly emergent political-economic order was its basis in a capitalist mode of production, that is, the production of goods for sale for profit in markets. The capitalist economy had its foundation in a system of private ownership and control over processes of production. Owners first of land and later of mills, factories, and companies combined capital and raw materials and employed labor to create products having market value in excess of the costs of inputs. Exchanges on the market therefore yielded profits. Aspirations to maximize profits, the symbol of success and the key to growth in capitalist affairs, combined with pressures from competition, made it imperative to minimize the costs of inputs, particularly raw materials and labor. As a result, European capitalism, born as economic activity on local markets, expanded with the consolidation of nation-states to economic activity on national markets and later, in close conjunction with European power, became a worldwide quest for raw materials at their lowest cost, labor that would work for the lowest wages, and consumers available and willing to purchase goods and services. From earliest times in their history, Americans were very much a part of the world capitalist system, and in our time, of course, they are the system's chief advocates. Through the centuries, and particularly during the last two, the world capitalist system has produced unprecedented wealth, although this has always been, and continues to be, dramatically unequally distributed both within and between countries. The rewards from this mode of production accrue to owners of the means of production and the countries wherein they reside; the penalties accrue to workers compelled to sell their labor at lowest prices and countries able to export only low-priced raw materials while being obliged to import higher-priced manufactured products. Needless to say, the unequal exchanges that accompany capitalist economic modes reverberate politically through countries and throughout the world.

The story of European overseas expansion from the fifteenth through the twentieth century is familiar. What needs to be underlined in this narrative is that what was expanding during those centuries was not only international politics in a distinctive European mode but also European capitalism. The colonization of most of the world was all about this. There was no meaningful separation of the political realm from the economic as Europeans used political and military power to organize the world for purposes of furthering European trade. Beginning around the last quarter of the eighteenth century, the coal-based industrial revolution in British production served to elevate the British national economy to a preeminent position in the capitalist world economy. But sustaining this new mode of production required access to markets of a nature, size, and quantity that could not be satisfied within the confines of the British imperial order, extensive as it was. The nineteenth century therefore witnessed the rise of Britain as a hegemonic power on the seas, if not on the continent, bent on opening the markets of the world to the products of the (British) industrial revolution while also procuring the resources required to keep its mills in operation. "Free trade" is always a boon to the most competitive traders. In the late nineteenth century these were surely British traders, and "free trade" became the norm of world economic affairs that Her Majesty's government tried enthusiastically to persuade reluctant others to accept. So much the better that British intellectuals of the day found in liberalism the philosophical key to human progress, and in free trade the economic essence of liberalism.

It was again no coincidence that the capitalist world system that flourished to Europe's advantage during much of the nineteenth and early twentieth century came tumbling down approximately at the same time that the European state system nearly destroyed itself in the cataclysm of World War I. But whereas the European state system was superficially repaired after 1919 and limped along for another decade and half, the European-based capitalist world economy did not recover from the jolts of the Great War, the ensuing Great Inflation, the following Great Depression, and the foolhardy policies of national governments that either eschewed intervention into national or global economic affairs because of classical liberal convictions or intervened so dramatically and nonsensically as to strangle world trade. Deteriorating economic conditions within countries during the 1920s and 1930s also abetted the spread of anticapitalist ideologies of both the political left and right, making it even more difficult for national governments to respond usefully to the crisis of capitalism engulfing the world. Importantly as well, *there were no international organizations available and assigned to managing the international economy* because, as the economic historian Karl Polanyi observed, classical liberal theorists believed that markets, both national and international, were essentially self-regulating and therefore would correct themselves, albeit somewhat painfully for many concerned, as long as public authorities pursued policies of "hands off."[6] Although it is not entirely certain that a flourishing international economy contributes to peace, it was fairly clear that the failure of the global economy during the 1930s contributed to the outbreak of World War II. For this reason, as well as from their liberal ideological convictions and their self-interest in maintaining an advantaged economic position, American statesmen, with British support, were determined to reconstitute the capitalist

---

[6]Karl Polanyi, *The Great Transformation: The Political and Economic Origins of Our Time* (Boston: Beacon Press, 1957), p. 139.

world economy after the war. They no longer believed, however, that this economy could be left to function without international management.

ASSEMBLING THE PIECES AND CREATING THE UNITED NATIONS

U.S. political leaders, as they entered the Second World War, set about planning a world order that would keep the world peaceful, make it safe for democracy, and allow America, as well as others, to prosper within a reconstituted world capitalist system. U.S. president Franklin D. Roosevelt had been a strong supporter of Woodrow Wilson and the League of Nations and therefore looked to resurrecting the form, if not the content and operating code, in a new world organization mandated to promote peace and security. Although taking an active personal role in postwar planning, Roosevelt depended heavily on trusted subordinates and advisers, like Secretary of State Cordell Hull, Treasury Secretary Henry Morgenthau, Secretary of War Henry Stimson, Assistant Secretary of Treasury Harry White, and presidential adviser and personal confidant Harry Hopkins. Within the U.S. government were two centers of planning for the postwar era: the Department of State and the Treasury Department. Harry White served as the special liaison linking Treasury with the State Department. Internationally, meetings, negotiations, and agreements among the Big Three—Roosevelt, Churchill, and Stalin—were also crucial for mapping out the contours of the postwar order. Yet too much stress is often placed on the formal negotiations concerning the creation of the United Nations, and indeed on the novelty of the UN organization, with relatively little attention paid to diplomatic and political-economic traditions, with their associated assumptions and norms, within which the institutions of the UN system are embedded.

The UN agencies being constructed were first and foremost to be intergovernmental organizations with the national state as the principal unit of membership. The norm underpinning this membership was, of course, state sovereignty or the notion that the national state and those controlling it have supreme authority within the territory claimed. Beyond the claim of absolute authority by an established national government over the people and territory therein, the political-legal conception of the state rests on those claims being recognized by others who have previously been granted such status by similar recognition. Once granted, this legally entitles the "bearer" to claim freedom from interference by others in domestic affairs. Article 2 of the UN Charter was unambiguous in this regard as were the treaties and international agreements that served as the constitutional foundations of the other related functional agencies of the United Nations system. Although members agreed to conduct their affairs by peaceful means and to join collectively to deal with threats to the peace, they also pledged to respect the political independence and territorial integrity of fellow members and the sanctity of the norm of noninterference in others' domestic affairs. American delegates at the

San Francisco Conference insisted on having inserted into the records a provision stating that none of the responsibilities assigned to the United Nations in economic and social affairs should be construed as giving authority to the UN to intervene in the domestic affairs of its members. The UN Charter also contained an intricate set of institutional and constitutional devices designed to prevent the organization from getting into areas that might be construed as infringements on national sovereignty.

The political entities that emerged from the collapsing European world empires during the thirty-year period after the end of World War II invariably assumed the form of states because after five centuries of Europeanization, this was the only political form acceptable for participation in international relations. All of the new states claimed rights to membership in the United Nations in accord with their newly acquired sovereignty. A good many were admitted to the UN in the context of begrudged bargaining between the United States and the Soviet Union, where seats for clients of the West were traded for seats for clients of the East. In reality, in many instances UN membership actually *bestowed* statehood because many of the postcolonial entities hardly qualified as states by conventional standards of control over territory and population, effective government, and capacities for self-reliance. Several later failed outright as states. As a result, the notion that the United Nations is an organization of *states* is somewhat of a fiction—"club of governments" is a better description—and the idea that the UN is an organization of "peace-loving" states is a greater fiction still. Without these fictions, however, there would be no organization.

Following on the practice of the League, the General Assembly was made a primary organ of the UN organization. It would be the only primary organ comprised of all member states, and it would function in accord with traditional principles of universality and sovereign equality. As we saw, the institutional model of the multilateral conference originated in the European diplomacy of the nineteenth century, and for the sake of legitimacy such an "assembly" of governments representing the peoples of the world had to be a cornerstone of the United Nations. Universal membership in the General Assembly and one state-one vote majoritarian decision making lent auras of inclusiveness and democracy to the emergent UN organization that, symbolically at least, necessarily had to offset the elitism and exclusiveness of the Security Council. The General Assembly was ostensibly made an authoritative and influential body empowered to consider any and every matter its members may wish to discuss, to direct the UN Secretariat, to create subsidiary bodies, and to "consider and approve the budget of the Organization." In a very Wilsonian way and very much in accord with the Assembly of the League, the UN General Assembly also gained apparent authority from its performance as the "voice of world opinion."

But the drafters of the Charter allotted the General Assembly no means to compel the compliance of member governments. In so doing they defined the body as a forum for dialogue rather than a rule-making center. The General

Assembly could never, either in conception or evolution, be more than a "place to talk" because it too is founded on fictions. For one thing, sovereign equality does not translate into equality of influence: regardless of the symbolism of one state-one vote, it makes a great deal of difference who casts the vote, and cumulated political weakness might add up to majorities in the General Assembly, but it does not add up to political strength. Even the General Assembly's attribution as the voice of world opinion has fictional quality because it cannot be realistically claimed that governments, particularly nondemocratic ones, reliably represent the sentiments of their citizens.

The drafters of the Charter located the power of compellence by the UN in two places, the Security Council and the Bretton Woods Institutions. Here, power within the UN was made to coincide with power outside the UN, and this was as it had to be, for otherwise there would have been no United Nations. It is reasonably clear from the historical record that reestablishing a concert of great powers in the form of the Security Council was of foremost interest to Americans planning the post–World War II order. What Franklin Roosevelt envisioned and pursued, for example, was an arrangement whereby the four major powers of the victorious alliance of powers that defeated Nazi Germany and imperial Japan would continue in the postwar world to police the other nations of the world and enforce world peace. Unlike Woodrow Wilson, Roosevelt sought to balance collective security notions with traditional European norms having to do with spheres of influence. Each major power would look after affairs in its part of the world, and, when necessary, the powers working together would collectively enforce world peace. The American president also seemed unbothered that the core element of the UN's security enforcement mechanism would include five states, only one of which was at the time a liberal democratic nation state in the strict sense of the term. The Soviet Union was a totalitarian dictatorship bent on the ultimate destruction of the capitalist world order. China was ruled by an authoritarian government suffering the pangs of a civil war against a strong communist insurgency. Great Britain was a functioning world empire built around the core of an island-based national state. During most of the planning for the postwar era, France was partly occupied by Nazi Germany and partly governed by a fascist regime. But in the throes of the war to end all wars, there was little room for Wilsonian idealism or probing questions about the nature or intentions of one's friends. Preserving peace after the war was the objective, and a credible concert of great powers was the chosen instrument.

The Security Council, which amounts to the contemporary rendition of the concert of great powers and operates under the principle of collective security carried over from the League, was given the authority to commit all member states to join in the enforcing of its binding resolutions. Article 48 leaves little room for contrary interpretation: "the action required to carry out the decisions of the Security Council for the maintenance of peace and security shall be taken by all the Members of the UN or by some of them, as the Security Council may determine." The only states that the Security Council cannot compel are the five permanent members of the Security Council, each of whom can stop the Council from acting, and then of course the Council cannot compel compliance from any other government that one or more of the permanent members might seek to protect. For most intents and purposes, the so-called veto power that the Permanent Five bestowed on themselves renders "collective security" unattainable because the Permanent Five almost never agreed during the Cold War and seldom agree even today.

The Bretton Woods institutions are also empowered to intrude on national sovereignties. Painful experiences of the 1930s convinced the planners for the post–World War II era that allowing the world economy to "regulate itself" was a flawed notion. The capitalist world economy needed to be transformed in to a "liberal capitalist world system," which is to say the world economy needed to be institutionalized. Although ascribing to the general norm of laissez-faire, American and British planners were nevertheless convinced that some degree of governmental involvement in economic affairs was needed at the international level. U.S. secretary of treasury Harry White warned that "the absence of a high degree of economic collaboration among the leading nations will . . . result in [economic] warfare that will be but the prelude and instigator of military warfare on an even vaster scale."[7] This conclusion was well in line with the thinking of the noted British economist John Maynard Keynes, who was also among those deeply involved in postwar planning. The notion of governmental *intervention*, however, would seem to overstate the nature of the international order envisaged. *Management* comes closer to the mark. The major governments of West therefore committed themselves to the "regulation of the liberal system by removing barriers to trade and capital flows and creating a stable monetary order," and the institutional manifestations of their commitment were the World Bank, the International Monetary Fund, and the stillborn International Trade Organization, that was at first replaced by the General Agreement on Tariffs and Trade and then later resurrected in the World Trade Organization.[8]

The World Bank and the International Monetary Fund are able to provide considerable assistance to economies in crisis, but their assistance has always come with conditions attached. As a rule, receiving assistance from the Bretton Woods institutions, and also today receiving consideration from the World Trade Organization, requires that national policies conform to international standards, and to a significant extent they must also embody economically liberal perspectives and approaches. Framing and formulating *national* economic policies thereby shifts from state governments to international institutions, and sovereignty over economic matters, at least, diminishes greatly. Because the Bretton Woods institutions were established largely by

---

[7]Quoted in Richard N. Gardner, *Sterling-Dollar Diplomacy in Current Perspective: The Origins and Prospects of Our International Economic Order* (New York: Columbia University Press, 1980), p. 8.
[8]Joan Edelman Spero, *The Politics of International Economic Relations*, 3rd ed. (New York: St. Martin's Press, 1985), p. 28.

the United States and the United Kingdom, and because the size of American financial contributions and the sheer weight of the U.S. economy simply make it implausible for either the Bank or the Fund to embark on policies colliding with American views and interests, the policies of these institutions have consistently underwritten American preferences for preserving, protecting, or otherwise managing the world capitalist system. The Bank and the Fund would help regulate the world economy by assisting countries whose problems might disrupt trade and finance or otherwise slow growth. But inviting assistance from the Bank and the Fund has always implied supporting the goals of these institutions by embedding them in national economic policies.

The legacy of the international public unions remained very much alive during the founding of the UN as the preexisting specialized agencies, plus newly created ones like the FAO and UNESCO, in juxtaposition to the UN organization, in effect became the United Nations system. In addition, the League's practice of turning so-called non–self-governing territories into mandates to be administered by various major powers reemerged as the UN's practice of granting trusteeship. But the UN also nurtured the Wilsonian notion of national self-determination and thereby contributed notably to decolonization during the 1950s, 1960s, and 1970s. Otherwise, all of the traditions of political-ideological neutrality, loyalty to the international organization rather than to any national government, and professional dedication to accomplishing assigned tasks that had evolved through earlier experiments in the public unions, functional agencies, and the League were invested in the newly created Secretariat of the United Nations. The professional standards of the international civil service, however, were always ideals, faithfully pursued but never fully attained, even in the UN Secretariat. Political sensitivities among member governments about equitable representation of their nationals within Secretariat ranks forced some trading of equity for efficiency. Perceived entitlements regarding Secretariat posts on the part of various governments forced considerable trading of patronage for competence. The Secretariat building in New York also seems to have been built to include numerous glass ceilings through which qualified women could peer and wonder why career movement upward for them was so elusive. And, there is little question but that during the Cold War years the UN Secretariat was infiltrated by both the CIA and the KGB, and, for that matter, by every other major intelligence organization in the world. It still is.[9] Nevertheless, the UN Secretariat in the broadest sense has done great service to the organization and to the international community over the course of more than a half century. If one seeks truly dedicated citizens of the world, many of these continue to toil in Secretariat offices and to serve the UN around the world.

---

[9]Warren Hoge. "On Bugging News, Annan Had Low-Key Response to Old Practice" *New York Times*, February 28, 2004.

The office of the secretary-general was not an innovation under the UN; the League had one as well. It is unclear what the founders of the United Nations expected of the secretary-general, although we would likely be closest to correct in assuming that he (and probably he rather than she), like the general secretary of the League, would serve as chief executive officer, heading the Secretariat, administering the budget, managing mandated operations, and the like. The evolution of the political role of the secretary-general was not anticipated, even though a glimmering of autonomy was embedded in Article 99 of the Charter. But it has been the evolution of the UN secretary-general as a political actor that is one of the most innovative developments in the twentieth-century international organization. Partly because of the outstanding quality of all but one or two of the individuals who have held the office, and partly because our deeply divided, contentious world has opened political space for a neutral mediator, a sane voice and a moral spokesperson, the secretary-general has acquired autonomous influence. His power is "soft power." He can and does exercise moral and intellectual influence in ways that few others can, and effective secretaries-general have heightened the influence of the UN is world affairs. None of this, however, should be exaggerated. Even the most effective among these respected statesmen have been but bit players in the geopolitical dramas of the last sixty years. Indeed, the effort to expand the Secretary-General's autonomous management capacity was a casualty of the 2005–2006 reform effort when member states from the developing world feared this might erode their authority at the UN.

When all is said concerning the founding of the United Nations, the single most noteworthy international organizational innovation of the immediate post–World War II era had to do with involving the world collectively in the protection of human rights. In a real sense, this represented the completion of the international institutionalization of the classical liberal agenda. At the center of the liberal universe lie human individuals and concerns for their individual well-being. As noted, individuals have "rights," and governments are assumedly obliged to protect these and never to deny them. But human history is in one aspect a very dark narrative of governments trampling on the lives, liberties, and well-being of citizens and subjects, oftentimes in absolutely atrocious ways. Because planners designing the United Nations in the early 1940s were living amid one of the darkest episodes in government-directed inhumanity the world has ever known, we might expect they would have placed the protection of fundamental human rights at center stage. But this was not the case.

For one thing, there were no precedents: even Woodrow Wilson had opposed placing human rights language in the League Covenant because of the racial situation in the United States. Two-and-a-half decades and a major world war later, the situation had changed somewhat. In the face of the Nazi Holocaust, fascist totalitarianism, and Japanese militarism, Roosevelt forcefully articulated his famous "four freedoms" speech in January 1941, and in 1944 he presented Congress with his proposal for an "economic bill of rights" that would guarantee individuals "economic security, social security, moral security—in a family of nations."[10] The U.S. delegation at the San Francisco Conference was lobbied by nongovernmental organizations (NGOs) and by several Latin American delegations to push forward on the human rights front. Charter drafters were able to insert human rights language in the Preamble, which emphasized that a principal purpose of the UN was "to affirm faith in fundamental human rights," and other sections of the Charter called on member states to promote "respect for human rights and for fundamental freedoms for all without distinction as to race, sex, language, or religion." But for reasons discussed at some length elsewhere in this volume, the UN Charter established no international machinery for the protection of human rights.

Despite the predilections of the Roosevelt administration, considerable opposition to empowering the United Nations to promote human rights came from within the United States, which spilled over to temper the American position at the San Francisco conference. The domestic situation in the United States was still quite delicate regarding the issue of race and racial equality, and U.S. immigration policies also had racist overtones. America was not alone in its sensitivities about allowing an international organization to scrutinize domestic doings, as the positions of the European imperial powers at San Francisco reveal, nor was there any lack of concern about possible infringements of sovereignty that might accrue from examining internationally how governments treated their citizens. There was also, even at this early phase of international organizational involvement in human rights, an undercurrent of dissent about the nature, origins, and cultural compatibility of the supposed inalienable and universal entitlements that liberals championed.

Advocates for human rights, among them Eleanor Roosevelt from the United States, were nevertheless relentless in their efforts to create international mechanisms for their promotion and protection and to center these within the United Nations. In February 1946, roughly a year into the workings of the newly chartered UN, a Commission on Human Rights was created under the Economic and Social Council and charged with drafting an international bill of human rights. The Universal Declaration of Human Rights was adopted as a General Assembly resolution in 1948, and this widely approved document represented at least a minimal agreement about rights shared by all humanity. The United Nations Commission on Human Rights therefore had an agenda. With the Universal Declaration, the later adoption of protocols on civil and political and economic, social, and cultural rights, and the activation of the Human Rights Commission, the Human Rights Committee, and the High Commissioner for Refugees, the classical liberal agenda with regard to individualism and rights was fully institutionalized within the UN system. Nevertheless, protecting and promoting human rights proved difficult from

[10]Franklin D. Roosevelt, *Nothing to Fear: The Selected Addresses of Franklin Delano Roosevelt, 1932–1945*, (Cambridge, Mass.: Houghton Mifflin, 1946), p. 112.

the beginning. The UN never got very far beyond setting standards that it could not enforce. But even this represented an international organizational advance.

THE ORIGINS OF POLITICS AT THE UNITED NATIONS

In broadest overview, then, what was institutionalized in the UN was the European-born Westphalian state system, universalized over several centuries, and then tamed and tempered in the course of European statecraft in the nineteenth century. This tamed and tempered system of sovereign states is one part of the structural core of the United Nations system. The other part, as explained, is the world capitalist system, also tamed and tempered by international management through international institutions that are components of the UN system. If sovereign equality and managed laissez-faire are the operating principles of the UN system, classical liberalism is its philosophical milieu, the substance of its vision and the source of its goals.

Yet the problem in all of this is that the United Nations institutionalized European international relations at a point in history when European ascendancy had already passed its zenith and Western hegemony, founded on the residual power of Europe and the superpower of the United States, was soon to be contested. Relatedly, by the early 1950s, capitalism was already being seriously challenged by critics on the political left almost everywhere. It was being directly confronted by the Soviet Union and its allies, and dissent informed by *dependencia* thinking would soon intensify as many of the third world losers in the world capitalist system became UN members. Liberalism, to be sure, had withstood the lethal challenges of Nazism and fascism, but at the very time that its champions felt they had institutionalized it globally, it was attacked by communists, by fascists holed up in political sanctuaries around the world, and by theocrats, antimodernists, and cultural relativists whose ideological assault on everything Western intensified when the Cold War ended. Creating the United Nations in 1945 institutionalized Western hegemony in the world. But the central narrative in the history of the UN, and therefore a primary source of politics at the UN, is the conflict-ridden story of much of the world struggling against Western hegemony in all of its institutional manifestations.

Much can be explained by the dramatic expansion in UN membership during the 1960s and 1970s. From the original 51 members in 1945, membership in the United Nations more than doubled to 104 in 1961, and then increased to 152 by 1979. In 2006 it stood at 192. The new members were for the most part states created as a result of the disintegration of the great European empires, and it became quite clear from early on that most were also the antithesis of everything European. They were on the whole culturally non-Western, racially nonwhite, religiously non-Christian, philosophically nonliberal, politically nondemocratic (at least by European standards), and economically noncapitalist as well as poor and geopolitically weak. They resented their experiences under colonialism and condemned Europeans for having imposed alien rule on them. Even though the United States supported decolonization and made it known that keeping the European empires afloat was not an objective of its foreign policy, in the eyes of many from this emergent Third World, Americans were as culpable as Europeans for past wrongs perpetrated on non-Western peoples. In this they were egged on by the Soviet Union because Leninist ideology prescribed that capitalists had to be imperialists by definition.

Because the peoples of the Third World saw themselves as victims of European capitalism, liberalism, and hegemonic imposition, they could hardly be expected to enter the UN as champions of many of the ideals that the Western founders had embedded in the Charter. Their priority was to undo the discriminatory status quo that the Americans and Europeans wanted the UN to preserve. Their aspiration was to use the United Nations to transform world affairs, which was in direct contradiction to the Western desire to use the organization in ways that would buttress hegemony. Many of the political lines that today sharply divide the members of the UN were therefore already drawn during the organization's first decades:

Economically, the poor peripheral South, was set against the wealthy dominant North, and the crucial issue was whether to keep the world capitalist system intact and meting out rewards and penalties in accord with market conditions or to transform it into a redistributive system that would oblige the rich to uplift the poor. In contemporary thinking, particularly in the South, economic justice is still the central issue, although as discussed later is this book, the North–South debate has shifted. Although still a critique versus a defense of the world capitalist system, North–South controversy today largely is about access to the benefits of globalization, the bulk of which flow northward to the great consternation of the South.

Politically, from the beginning the stronger and more influential West was set against the weaker and marginalized non-West. Latin Americans here found themselves in a position of being Western but weak, and their UN diplomacy was also complicated by fact that during the Cold War they tended to be both anticommunist and anti-American. Eventually, however, on almost all save cultural issues, most Latin American countries fell into line with the non-West. Naturally, the Soviet Union and its clients were not only non-West but emphatically anti-West, but their unsuccessful assault on Western hegemony has passed into history. The West remains comprised mostly of North Americans and Western Europeans joined by a few others entangled in Washington's global alliance network. But all too frequently these days, "the West" reduces to the United States of America, and the "non-West" becomes almost everybody else. The significance of the West has rested, and continues to rest, in the fact that it constitutes the hegemonic bloc that for most of the last half century has run the world politically and the UN along with it. Principal issues along the West–non-West political divide naturally concern power and influence: the West seeks to preserve its preeminence, and the non-West seeks to dilute it, perhaps undo it. Within the UN organization, such clashing aspirations render the Security Council controversial, especially regarding the prerogatives of the Permanent Five. Concerts of great powers are almost always suspect among those who can do little to stave off arbitrary applications of their collective power. But issues surrounding the power of the Security Council, or for that matter the impotence of the General Assembly, symbolize broader and deeper issues stemming from the dramatically unequal distribution of power and influence in the world. Power in the world today has to do less with making things happen than with stopping things from happening, and much to the dismay of the non-West, in contemporary world politics, as played out both within the UN and without, the West collectively, and oftentimes the United States alone, can stop almost anything from happening.

Culturally and ideologically the world was divided along West–non-West lines well before the drafting of the Charter and the creation of the UN. But within the European imperial systems, the non-West had only a very muted cultural and ideological voice. During the Cold War, the non-West was in effect the communist East, as neither of the superpowers paid very much attention to Third World voices. But just as world poverty gained a political voice with decolonization, non-Western cultures and political-ideological expressions gained political voices with the end of the Cold War. The symbolic cultural-ideological battleground within the UN lies in the realm of human rights, about which we will have much to say in this volume. Yet the broader issues symbolized in the debates between "universalists" and "cultural relativists" in forums such as the Commission on Human Rights, UNESCO, and in the committee rooms and on the plenary floor of the UN General Assembly fundamentally concern the acceptability of classical liberalism as the philosophical foundation of social and political life the world over. During the Cold War the West insisted on both the moral superiority and the utilitarian virtue of liberalism as a way of social and political life. Since the Cold War, the West has been insisting that ideologically competitive history has ended and there are no alternatives to liberalism. As if to belie this Western conviction directly, the non-West is presently entertaining a variety of alternatives to liberalism while vehemently resenting having Western ways foisted on them again.

By the turn of the twenty-first century, even the principle of sovereignty was coming under assault at the UN. This was not only, or even mainly, because the fiction of sovereign equality was grating for the governments of weaker and poorer states who immediately on joining the UN discovered that "some states are more sovereign than others." In fact, it was mainly the weaker and poorer states that continued to champion sovereignty and to insist on the privileges and immunities traditionally associated with it. Sovereignty for weaker states is a valued form of protection against intrusion by powers from without, so that they rather enthusiastically encourage the United Nations to uphold it. Ironically, the principal challenge to sovereignty at the UN is coming from the very Western governments who originally determined to make the UN an association of sovereign states and who sponsored the Charter's prohibitions against intruding into the domestic affairs of UN members. From the hegemonic perspective, others' sovereignty can be inconvenient when one is attempting to keep order, liberalize economies, spread democracy, and promote human rights. Sovereignty, some are saying, should be conditional rather than absolute, with conditions to be determined by hegemonic actors.

Even while sovereign immunity is being questioned by hegemonic interventionists and defended by fearful targets of intervention, the very idea of the UN as an organization of sovereign states is rendered problematic by an increasingly robust and active international civil society. Today, more than twenty thousand NGOs are operating in the same world political and economic issue areas as national governments. The major ones among these command greater resources than a fair number of national governments, and in certain problems areas like global environmental affairs or human rights they wield influence comparable to national governments. By institutionalizing the Westphalian state system, even in tamed and tempered form, the founders of the UN may have locked that system—and the UN itself—into an historical time warp. The global politics of the twenty-first century are structurally different from the international politics of the nineteenth and twentieth centuries. Why then, many are asking today, should not nongovernmental international organizations occupy official seats at the tables of world diplomacy? In the United Nations today, this is not simply a question; it is a highly divisive political issue.

CHAPTER 3

The UN Charter and Beyond

Those governments who initially signed the Charter of the UN, and all others who subsequently joined, made specific commitments to promote the goals of the organization. As explained in Chapter 2, the UN was largely an American-inspired project. It was conceived during the Second World War and therefore reflected the temper of its time in its preoccupation with peace and security and its assumptions about the political and economic causes of war. War results from humans' predatory motives, from political settings that permit tyrants to act on their aggressive designs, from the imbalance of power among states, and from physical and spiritual degradation in the human condition. The UN Charter establishes an international organization aimed, as its preamble announces, toward saving "succeeding generations from the scourge of war," which twice in the lifetime of the founding members, "brought untold sorrow to mankind."

As a treaty under international law, the Charter is a rather conservative restatement and summary of the principles and norms of the Westphalian state system. The privileges and immunities of sovereignty fundamentally condition relations among states, and sovereign states are the only entities entitled to enjoy these privileges and immunities. Yet in accord with the essentially Grotian international legal tradition that is carried over into the Charter, governments representing states are also obliged to seek order in international society.

Philosophically, the Charter is a testimonial to liberalism, a kind of nineteenth-century liberalism centering on the value in human freedom and the related expectation that free persons individually and free peoples collectively who rationally pursue their own interests can achieve harmony in their relations and peace among them.[1] Capitalist corollaries to liberal thinking, where prosperity follows the free-wheeling pursuit of self-interest, are also accommodated in the Charter. There is as well in the ideology of the Charter a strain of thinking that Americans would identify as Wilsonian international-ism.[2] It stresses the normalcy of harmony among peoples, but at the same time acknowledges that aberrant behavior does occur in human relations, and to deter, contain, and constrain this, law and organization are imperative at all levels of social intercourse, including the international level. Wilsonianism modifies the laissez-faire liberalism of the nineteenth century by qualifying notions of "invisible hands" and inevitable harmony and stressing instead the necessity of purposeful intervention to build and maintain order in human affairs. Those gathered in San Francisco in the spring of 1945 well understood that not only aberrant, but frightfully abhorrent behavior all too frequently occurred in human affairs, so that Wilsonian thinking readily resonated. It goes almost without saying that there is also a good deal of utopianism embedded in the Charter: the vision, for example, of the moral unity of humankind, exhilaration in the triumph of democracy over tyranny, and the hope that eventually world governance in substance might emerge to occupy the legislative, executive, and judicial institutional framework that the Charter builds.

Historical hindsight makes clear that not all the governments that signed the Charter in San Francisco, or that have signed since that time, share in the progressive thinking that inspired the treaty writers of 1945. Yet there is no question but that the Charter established a rather remarkable international legal entity both in terms of the scope of commitments undertaken by member states and regarding the organization's capacity to act. The purposes of the UN as set forth in the first article of the Charter are fourfold. First, the organization is to maintain peace and security among the states of the world,[3] and from very early on the meaning of this purpose expanded through practice to include maintaining peace and security among peoples as well as states. Second, the UN is tasked by its Charter "to achieve international coop-eration in solving problems of an international economic, social, cultural or humanitarian character," in effect a rather monumental end that has in prac-tice involved the organization, again from early on, in the countless plights of the Third World.[4] Third, the organization is chartered "to promote and encourage respect for human rights and freedoms," a historically innovative assignment, and, as it turned out in practice, a controversial one because it sets the organization on the shaky fence between protecting people and

---

[1]Edward Harlett Carr, *The Twenty Years' Crisis, 1919–1939* (New York: Harper Torchbooks, 1964), pp. 41–62.

[2]Daniel Patrick Moynihan, *On the Law of Nations: A Historical and Personal Account of the Role of International Law in Foreign Policy* (Cambridge, Mass.: Harvard University Press, 1990), pp. 33–54.

[3]United Nations Charter [hereafter Charter], Article 1, Paragraph 1.

[4]Charter, Article 1, Paragraph 2.

offending governments.[5] Fourth, the UN is directed by its Charter to "support the principles of equal rights and self-determination of peoples," a carryover mission from the League of Nations, but again a monumental one as it turned out, because few present in San Francisco could possibly anticipate that the first decades of UN activity would coincide with the final decades of the British, French, Belgian, Dutch, and Portuguese overseas empires.[6]

COMMITMENT AND CAPACITY IN THE UN CHARTER

Constitutionally speaking, the UN Charter grants substantial authority to the organization and endows it with considerable capacity to act. This capacity is greatest in the area of peace and security where the Charter endows the Security Council with supranational capabilities. In the areas of economic and social cooperation, the Charter envisions a wide scope of coordinative capacity across a range of institutions and programs. Within the area of human rights, the Charter is less explicit in the authority and capacity endowed, but it opened the door for member states to subsequently develop such capacity. Regarding self-determination, the drafters of the UN Charter were explicit in their commitment to use the new organization as a vehicle for promoting the political independence of the peoples who remained in the trust territories and protectorates established as a result of the two world wars of the twentieth century. As it turned out, members of the UN found in the Charter the capacity not only to catalyze the end of the trusteeship system but the end of colonialism altogether.

The Maintenance of International Peace and Security

In the realm of preserving and promoting peace and security, the charter-sanctioned authority of the UN is rather impressive. For one thing, member states that sign and ratify the Charter commit themselves in Article 2 to refraining from "the threat or use of force against the territorial integrity or political independence of any state." In Article 33 they make this commitment again by pledging to settle disputes peacefully, and once more in Article 94 the member states commit themselves to complying with decisions of the International Court of Justice, which the Charter establishes in Article 92.

Should member states fail to honor their commitments to nonaggression and peaceful settlement, the Charter projects the UN organizationally into situations involving the disturbance of the peace by creating a substantial amount of institutional capacity to intervene and act. Article 7 creates the UN General Assembly; Article 10 allots this assembly of the governments of the world the prerogative to discuss any question or issue it chooses to discuss; Article 11 specifically authorizes the General Assembly to take up matters of peace and

[5]Charter, Article 1, Paragraph 3.
[6]Charter, Article 1, Paragraph 4.

security, including questions of disarmament, and Article 14 invites the General Assembly to "recommend measures for the peaceful adjustment of any situation, regardless of origin, which it deems likely to impair the general welfare of friendly relations among nations."[7] Article 22, furthermore, empowers the General Assembly to "establish such subsidiary organs as it deems necessary for the performance of its functions," and the Assembly has done this with frequency and determination in many issue-areas including peace and security. The United Nations Conference on Disarmament is a creature of the General Assembly, for example, as is the United Nations Conciliation Commission for Palestine and the recently established United Nations Peace Building Commission.[8]

Although the chartered powers of the General Assembly acting in the area of peace and security, as in others, are recommendatory rather than binding, this is not the case with the Security Council, to which the Charter assigns primary responsibility for UN intervention into matters threatening international peace and security. Article 7 of the Charter creates the Security Council; Article 23 gives the Council fifteen members, and seats five of these— China, France, Great Britain, Russia, and the United States—permanently. Articles 24 to 51, the most detailed section of the UN's constitution, assign powers to the Security Council and spell out procedures. The authority assigned to the Security Council under the Charter is supranational, which is to say that its decisions are binding on all members of the UN. Keys to the supranational authority of the Security Council are to be found in Articles 25, 43, 48, and 49. In Article 25, "Members of the UN agree to accept and carry out the decisions of the Security Council in accordance with the present Charter."[9] Then, in Article 43, in instances when the Security Council has decided that the use of force is required to deter or resist aggression, "All Members of the United Nations . . . undertake to make available to the Security Council . . . armed forces, and facilities . . . for the purpose of maintaining international peace and security."[10] Article 48 again obligates all members to take "action required to carry out the decisions of the Security Council," and Article 49 reaffirms this obligation.[11]

Procedurally, the Security Council is authorized under Article 36 to involve itself, and the UN, in any dispute that it views as threatening international peace and security. In stepwise procedures outlined in Articles 36 to 40, which are the stuff of the Charter's Chapter VI, the Council is authorized to seek the peaceful resolution of disputes by first recommending and prescribing settlement to contending parties. Should Security Council intervention under Chapter VI fail to bring settlement, the Charter authorizes the Council to consider measures under Chapter VII (Articles 39 to 51), which may culminate

---

[7]Charter, Article 14.
[8]UN General Assembly, Resolution 60/180 (2005).
[9]Charter, Article 25.
[10]Charter, Article 43, Paragraph 1.
[11]Charter, Article 48, Paragraph 1; Article 49.

under Article 42 in the UN taking "such action by air, sea, or land forces as may be necessary to maintain or restore international peace and security."[12] Finally, under Article 29, the Security Council is also empowered to "establish such subsidiary organs as it deems necessary for the performance of its functions." In practice, these "subsidiary organs" have become bodies such as the Sanctions Committee, the Counter-Terrorism Committee, the United Nations Monitoring, Verification and Inspection Commission [for Iraq], the International Criminal Tribunals for Rwanda and the Former Yugoslavia, and, most recently, the Peacebuilding Commission, as well as the dozen or more of UN peacekeeping missions presently in the field—for example, UNMIK in Kosovo, UNFICYP in Cyprus, MONUC in the Congo, UNAMA in Afghanistan, and several others—and many more established in times past whose work has been completed.

The charted-allotted capacities of the UN to maintain peace and security do not end with the empowerment of the deliberative or monitoring bodies. Chapter VIII (Articles 52 to 54) urges the establishment of regional arrangements or agencies for purposes of maintaining peace and security, and it invites coordination between these organizations and the UN Security Council. Chapter XIV establishes the International Court of Justice, and although the institution has been seldom used as an arbiter on decisions of peace and security, it remains available as one more UN instrument for legal interpretations on the peaceful resolution of disputes.

Article 99 directly involves the secretary-general in matters of peace and security by inviting him to "bring to the attention of the Security Council any matter which is his opinion may threaten the maintenance of international peace and security."[13] In practice, secretaries-general from Dag Hammarskjöld to Kofi Annan have used their powers under Article 99 with some effect by prodding negligent, reluctant, or politically paralyzed Security Councils into action. Article 97 creates the UN secretariat, the international civil service under the secretary-general that houses the people and the planning for UN peacekeeping activities. Practically speaking, they *are* the UN's capacity to act, and international civil servants most involved in the UN's peace and security operations are presently organized into the Secretariat's Department of Peacekeeping Operations (DPKO) and Department of Political Affairs (DPA). Article 101 of the Charter gives the secretary-general the authority to appoint staff, and secretaries-general have used this authority to assign deputies oversight responsibilities as Special Representatives of the Secretary-General during UN field operations. From the very beginning of the UN's efforts to promote peace and security the Special Representatives of the Secretary-General have played key roles as negotiators, mediators, and conciliators.[14] They too must be

[12]Charter, Article 42.
[13]Charter, Article 99.
[14]Donald J. Puchala, "The Secretary-General and His Special Representatives," in *The Challenging Role of the UN Secretary-General*, Benjamin Rivilin and Leon Gordenker, eds. (Westport, Conn.: Praeger, 1993), pp. 81–97.

included as important elements of the UN's capacity to act in the area of peace and security. Not least important regarding the UN's capacity in matters of peace and security, and indeed much more generally, are the provisions of the Charter's Article 17. Here in one short second paragraph rests the material resource base of the UN: "the expenses of the Organization shall be borne by the Members as apportioned by the General Assembly."[15] Although the UN has no authority to finance itself, it is nevertheless regularly financed. Under the Charter, member states are obliged to pay for UN operations, and they do pay, albeit often reluctantly, sometimes only partially, sometimes late, and generally inadequately. Yet without the money provided by member states through mandatory assessments under Article 17, the UN would have no capacity to act to promote peace and security or, indeed, no capacity to act at all.

International Economic, Social, and Humanitarian Problems

Although UN activities in the area of peace and security typically capture the greatest amount of public attention, the major portion of attention within the UN remains fixed on social, economic, and humanitarian issues. These comprise the sprawling domain labeled "development," and promoting development is a top priority among upward of two thirds of UN member governments. During the era of the Cold War, which began soon after the UN's establishment and continued for the first four decades of the UN's existence, the organization's efforts in the area of peace and security were curtailed by East–West disagreements. The UN was therefore far less than the "peace and security" organization its founders anticipated. But because the early years of the UN also coincided with the collapse of the European colonial empires and the independence of scores of poor and troubled countries, the organization was pressed to respond to the development needs of the emergent Third World. As a result, between roughly 1960 and 1980, dealing with matters of Third World development became the UN's preoccupation. This development orientation in UN affairs remains significant even today.

The drafters of the United Nations Charter endowed the organization with considerable capacity to work at solving "international problems of a social, cultural, or humanitarian character." Article 55 directly connects enhancing the well-being of peoples to promoting peace by looking on such enhanced well-being as "necessary for peaceful and friendly relations among nations."[16] This key article also projects the United Nations directly into the field of development by giving the organization a mandate to promote:

    a. higher standards of living, full employment, social health, and conditions of economic and social progress and development; and

---

[15]Charter, Article 17, Paragraph 2.
[16]Charter, Article 55, Paragraph 1.

b. solutions of international economic, social, health, and related problems; and international cultural and educational co-operation;[17]

Article 56 then commits the member states of the UN "to take joint and separate action in cooperation with the Organization for the achievement of the purposes set forth in Article 55."[18]

Regarding institutional mandates, Article 13 gives the General Assembly specific prerogative to initiate studies and make recommendations regarding the "economic, social, cultural, educational and health fields."[19] Practically from the start of the UN's operations, and emphatically during the 1970s when Third World membership swelled, the General Assembly has used its power to "make recommendations" to focus the attentions of the organization on development issues. The grand debates concerning the New International Economic Order (NIEO) that occurred between 1972 and 1974 and are taken up in Chapter 8 of this book were Third World initiatives played out in the General Assembly. The General Assembly, acting under Article 22 of the Charter, has also used its authority to "establish such subsidiary organs as it deems necessary" to create numerous agencies in the development field. The UN Development Programme is perhaps the best known among these, but others include the United Nations Conference on Trade and Development (UNCTAD), the United Nations Fund for Population Activities (UNFPA), the United Nations Children's Emergency Fund (UNICEF), the World Food Programme (WFP), the World Food Council (WFC), the United Nations High Commissioner for Refugees (UNHCR), and several more.

Article 7 creates the United Nations Economic and Social Council (ECOSOC), and Chapters IX and X center the economic, social, and cultural activities of the organization in this council. The extensive empowerment of the ECOSOC is elaborated in Articles 62 to 72, where, among other things, the Council is given prerogative to conduct studies, issue reports, and make recommendations to the General Assembly and to member states regarding development matters. Unlike the Security Council, however, the ECOSOC has no authority to make binding decisions that obligate members to comply. But the council is empowered to draft conventions "with respect to matters falling within its competence" that may become binding upon signatories.[20] More importantly as it has turned out in UN experience, the ECOSOC under Article 62 is empowered to "call international conferences on matters falling within its competence."[21] This is the constitutional basis for the extensive program of world conferences—on population, food, the environment, women, water, development finance, human settlements, science and technology for

---

[17]Charter, Article 55, Paragraphs 1b and 1c.
[18]Charter, Article 56.
[19]Charter, Article 13, Paragraph 1b.
[20]Charter, Article 62, Paragraph 3.
[21]Charter, Article 62, Paragraph 4.

development, and many more focused on development problems and issues—over several decades of UN operations. Increasingly, calls for such conferences are also emanating from the General Assembly. Many would agree that by mobilizing world attention and focusing it on development issues, these conferences have been among the UN's more productive undertakings.[22] Article 68 entitles the ECOSOC to establish commissions to deal with specific problems of development, and the council has acted on this grant of authority to establish commissions on economic and social development in all of the major regions of the world as well as commissions on refugee affairs, population problems, sustainable development, and other matters. Article 57 asks the Economic and Social Council to establish relationships with the specialized agencies of the UN system, and Article 63 then tasks the ECOSOC with coordinating the work of the autonomous specialized agencies with the UN organization "through consultation with and recommendations to such agencies."[23] Here, the apparent intent of the authors of the Charter was to use the ECOSOC to bring coherence to the full range of social and economic development activities of the UN system. However, given the independent mandates, bureaucracies, and budgets of the specialized agencies and programs, the Economic and Social Council never actually emerged as the systemwide coordinator for social and economic development. Nonetheless, the Charter created this capacity and the means for oversight. Finally, Article 71 empowers the ECOSOC to "make suitable arrangements for consultations with non-governmental organizations" and willy-nilly opens thereby the pathway for the participation of NGOs in UN affairs.[24] Overtime this pathway has become a highway as NGOs have capitalized on "consultative" status to wield increasing, and increasingly controversial, influence at the UN.[25]

Needless to say, through its Department of Economic and Social Affairs, the UN Secretariat, established under Article 97, constitutes the core of the UN's capacity actually to administer the development programs that the deliberative bodies initiate. Economic and Social Affairs continues to be the largest of the Secretariat's departments. Ever since 1961 when U Thant succeeded Dag Hammarskjöld, the UN, with only one exception, has adopted the norm of selecting as its secretary-general a distinguished statesman from the Third World, and these Third World figures have been strong advocates of development and of benign UN intervention into the social and economic problems of the poorer countries of the world. Boutros Boutros-Ghali, who served as secretary-general from 1992 to 1996, and his successor, Kofi Annan, have not shrunk from using the bully pulpit of the office of secretary-general of the UN

---

[22]See Michael G. Schechter, *United Nations World Conferences: Focus on Impact and Follow Up* (New York: United Nations University Press, 2001).
[23]Charter, Article 57, Paragraph 1; Article 63, Paragraph 2.
[24]Charter, Article 71.
[25]Thomas G. Weiss and Leon Gordenker, *NGOs, the UN and Global Governance* (Boulder, Colo.: Lynne Rienner, 1996), pp. 17–51 and passim.

to agitate on behalf of the poorer peoples of the world. And again, it must be underlined that Article 17 is as crucial to the UN's capacity in the area of development as it is in peace and security and all other areas of organizational activity. Although it is true that much of the money cycled through the UN and allocated to projects in social and economic development comes from voluntary contributions from member states deposited in earmarked funds, Secretariat operations are paid for out of the UN's regular budget, which is funded by mandatory assessments under Article 17.

Human Rights and Basic Freedoms

By calling for a reaffirmation of "faith in fundamental human rights, in the dignity and worth of the human person [and] in the equal rights of men and women of nations large and small," the Preamble to the UN Charter involves the world organization in the field of human rights. As noted, Article 1 of the Charter makes "promoting and encouraging respect for human rights" one of the UN's purposes. Article 55 makes "universal respect for human rights and fundamental freedoms" one of the preconditions for stability, "well-being and peaceful and friendly relations among nations," and then Article 56 commits member states to achieving purposes elaborated in Article 55.[26] Within the Charter, several of the institutions and agencies authorized to conduct activities in the area of social and economic development are also mandated to promote human rights. These mandates, however, are quite diffuse, and no chartered agencies or organs are specifically tasked to give human rights first priority. As a result, the institutional capacity that the UN has assembled in the field of human rights is rather jerry-built from bits and pieces of constitutional authority scattered here and there throughout the Charter. As we explain elsewhere is this volume, even before the Charter was drafted, there was considerable reluctance on the part of several key governments to involve the world organization in matters concerning human rights. Some felt that such initiatives would cross the line separating domestic and international affairs that is clearly drawn in Article 2, Paragraph 7 of the Charter, and that therefore the means, methods, and modalities of protecting human rights were the responsibilities of national governments and not of the international community.[27] Consequently, the Charter gives the UN the mission of "promoting and encouraging respect for human rights and fundamental freedoms," but it does not provide very much specific capacity.

---

[26]Charter, Article 55, Paragraph 1c; Article 56.

[27]Article 2(7) is presently one of the more controversial parts of the Charter. It states, "Nothing contained in the present Charter shall authorize the United Nations to intervene in matters which are essentially within the domestic jurisdiction of any state or shall require the Members to submit such matters to settlement under the present Charter; but this principle shall not prejudice the application of enforcement measures under Chapter VII."

Whatever institutional deficiencies there were in the Charter *per se*, were rectified during ensuing UN experience, as chartered bodies like the General Assembly, the ECOSOC, and the Security Council, used their various empowerments, to either inject themselves into the field of human rights or to establish subsidiary bodies specifically mandated to promote and protect human rights. This secondary institution building resulted over time in the rather elaborate UN human rights machinery that operates today.

Article 13 provides the General Assembly with authority to make recommendations concerning "the realization of human rights and fundamental freedoms," and one such recommendation came from the General Assembly early on in the form of Resolution 217A(III), *The Universal Declaration of Human Rights*. The declaration, as we explain in Chapter 6, was a crucial first step toward building the UN's human rights machinery because *defining* human rights, particularly universal ones, had to come prior to institutionalizing their protection and promotion internationally. Using its authorization under Article 22 to "establish such subsidiary bodies as it deems necessary," the General Assembly proceeded to establish the Office of the United Nations High Commissioner for Refugees (UNHCR, 1950), the United Nations Children's Fund (UNICEF, 1953), and the United Nations Development Fund for Women (UNIFEM, 1976), and special committees focused on human rights conditions in Palestine, South Africa, and Namibia.

Paralleling the General Assembly and calling on specific powers "to set up commissions . . . for the promotion of Human Rights," contained in Article 68, the Economic and Social Council at its first session in 1946 created the United Nations Commission on Human Rights and the Commission on the Status of Women. In 1947 the Human Rights Commission created its own Sub-Commission on the Protection of Human Rights.[28] Authorizations contained in Article 62 granting the ECSOC prerogative to "prepare draft conventions for submission to the General Assembly" have over the years resulted in a number of international treaties pertaining to the protection of human rights, and these documents in turn have established a number of continuing committees, such as the Human Rights Committee, the Committee on the Elimination of Discrimination Against Women, the Committee Against Torture, and the Committee on the Rights of the Child, charged mainly with monitoring signatories' adherence to the terms of the treaties.[29]

Most recently, as part of the relaunched UN reform process, the General Assembly embarked on negotiations to create a Human Rights Council directly under its own authority to replace ECOSOC's Commission on Human Rights, whose deliberations over time became politicized to the extent of rendering the commission less than effective. Largely through the intensive

---

[28]The sub-commission was originally called Sub-Commission on Preventing Discrimination and Protection of Minorities.

[29]In the UN table of organization, these monitoring committees are technically subsidiary organs of the General Assembly.

diplomatic efforts of the European Union, the Human Rights Council was established in 2006 to replace the maligned Commission. The General Assembly agreed to a simple majority vote for election of members to the new Council which was less stringent than the two-thirds majority proposed by the Secretary-General, and the United States gave this as the reason for voting against the reformed Council. In opposing the Human Rights Council the US was joined only by a handful of non-democratic regimes. It remains to be seen whether the Council will surpass the Commission in providing the United Nations with effective capacity to uphold and advance human rights, but it does indicate the capacity of the United Nations for reform.

Under the UN Charter, the Security Council receives no specific authorization to consider matters having to do with the protection and promotion of human rights. However, under Article 34, the Security Council is authorized to "investigate any dispute, or any situation . . . in order to determine whether the continuance of the dispute or situation is likely to endanger the maintenance of international peace and security."[30] This can be broadly interpreted to mean that the Security Council can take any situation under consideration once the council decides that international peace and security are endangered. Beginning in the early 1990s, the Security Council has brought under its consideration several situations involving widespread abuses of human rights, and it has justified its involvement, and its consequent forceful action, by defining abuses of human rights as threats to international peace and security. Security Council Resolution 688 (1991), for example, addressed the Iraqi government's suppression of its Kurdish population. By agreeing that the suppression of Iraqi Kurds constituted a threat to international peace and security, the Security Council here involved itself in a situation occurring *within a country* having to do with abuses of human rights. But the council stopped short of threatening or authorizing UN intervention. Resolution 713 (1991), regarding the fighting in Yugoslavia, also defined the humanitarian crisis in that country as a threat to peace and security. This resolution authorized UN intervention under Chapter VII in the form of an arms embargo. Later, by way of Resolution 787 (1992) regarding Bosnia, the Security Council made specific reference to "ethnic cleansing," and the deteriorating humanitarian situation, and, acting again under Chapter VII, imposed economic sanctions on Yugoslavia. Then, in Resolution 733 (1992), regarding Somalia, the Security Council reported that it was "deeply disturbed by the magnitude of human suffering" and that "the continuation of the situation in Somalia constitutes a threat to international peace and security." Here the deteriorating humanitarian situation in Somalia led directly to the Security Council's decision to dispatch a UN peacekeeping force to that troubled country. Since first injecting itself into humanitarian crises in the 1990s, the Security Council has come regularly to consider instances of the widespread of abuse of human rights

---

[30]Charter, Article 34.

and has several more times authorized intervention to protect victims and constrain abusers.

The involvement of the Security Council in matters of humanitarian crises and abuses of human rights has led to the controversial institutionalization of "humanitarian intervention" by the council acting under Chapter VII of the Charter. This is not the place to analyze the controversy but rather the opportunity to underline that the emergence of the Security Council as an enforcer of human rights significantly enhances the institutional capacity of the UN to pursue its Charter-driven humanitarian mission. As a result of redefining and extending its own prerogatives, the Security Council has become an important human rights body.

Needless to say, as in other operational domains, much of the administrative and intellectual capacity in the area of human rights is the result of the organization, efforts, and talents of the UN Secretariat, created as noted under Article 97. Much of the staffing for UN humanitarian efforts is supplied by the Office for the Coordination of Humanitarian Affairs headquartered in New York and by personnel associated with the Commission on Human Rights and related bodies in Geneva. As with other aspects of UN, much depends on funding, and here again member states' obligations under Article 17 are crucial.

The Equal Rights and Self-Determination of Peoples

For the UN, promoting the equal rights and self-determination of peoples is widely considered to be a mission accomplished. The transformation of the international system from a small collection of European empires to a much larger collection of independent sovereign states coincided with the first four decades of UN operations. Although giving the UN primary credit for the decolonization of the European imperial world is far too simplistic, many would agree that the UN contributed importantly.[31] Part of the UN's effectiveness in promoting peaceful transfers of power from metropolitan countries to newly independent ones followed from the fact that the UN Charter created an appropriate capacity for international organizational action.

In the realm of commitment, a "Declaration Regarding Non-Self-Governing Territories" is written directly into the Charter as Article 73. It is the only such formal statement of collective will contained in this founding document, and by accepting the Charter, signatories committed themselves "to develop self-government, to take due account of the aspirations of peoples, and to assist them in the progressive development of their free institutions."[32] Chapters XI and XII of the Charter establish the UN trusteeship system (Articles 77 to 85) and the Trusteeship Council (Articles 86 to 91). The system involved a series

[31]David Kay, *The New Nations in the United Nations, 1960–1967* (New York: Columbia University Press, 1970), passim.
[32]Charter, Article 73b.

of responsibilities accepted by governments that were administering territories under trust, and the Council was allotted authority to determine and ensure that administering governments acted responsibly. Trust territories mainly included non–self-governing entities that remained under mandates granted by the League of Nations and territories that acquired new administrations as a result of World War II. Articles 87 and 88 obligated administering governments to report on conditions within territories under their trust, and these articles charge the Trusteeship Council with scrutinizing and evaluating such reports, thus, in effect, closely overseeing administering governments' behavior. The trusteeship system never included the greatest parts of the colonial world, but it did include more than a dozen non–self-governing territories, the last of which, Palau, achieved independence in 1994. With this, the Trusteeship Council suspended operations.

The General Assembly was much more important in the promotion of decolonization. Driven by its expanding and largely Third World membership, the General Assembly in 1960 adopted the "Declaration on Granting Independence to Colonial Countries and Peoples" and affirmed therein that "immediate steps shall be taken . . . to transfer all powers to the peoples" of trust territories, non–self-governing territories, and all other territories.[33] On adopting this resolution, the General Assembly, acting under charter authority "to establish such subsidiary organs as it deems necessary," proceeded to establish the Special Committee on the Situation with Regard to the Implementation of the Declaration on the Granting of Independence to Colonial Countries and Peoples.[34] This became the very active and effective "Committee of 24," composed of both colonial powers and newly independent countries. It emerged as the principal UN vehicle for promoting decolonization.[35] The impact of the General Assembly's efforts in bringing about the independence of former colonial countries should not be underestimated. Because of the activities of the Committee of 24 and the doggedness of the Third World members of this committee, as well as specific pressures brought by the General Assembly regarding South Africa, Namibia, East Timor, and other remnants of the colonial system, decolonization proceeded more rapidly and less violently than might otherwise have been the case.

STRUCTURAL RECONFIGURATION AND INSTITUTIONAL EROSION

The Charter remains a remarkable document in the capacities conferred for collective action via the UN. However, to suggest that the UN operates in the manner that the Charter prescribes would be whimsical. Conventional wisdom tends to suggest that the organization is severely limited in its abilities to

---

[33]United Nations General Assembly, Resolution 1514 (XV), December 14, 1960.
[34]United Nations General Assembly, Resolution 1654 (XVI), 1961.
[35]Kay, *The New Nations in the United Nations*, pp. 51–64.

act and to affect world affairs, and this common understanding is correct in the sense that the UN is limited in many ways and hampered in pursuit of its Charter-assigned goals. Analysis through much of the rest of this book paints a picture of an organization operating at considerably less than full potential. However, *the reasons for this stem from factors and conditions other than constraints imposed by the Charter.* We attribute the gap between the promise of the Charter and the performance of the organization to the inhospitable political climate(s) surrounding and deeply affecting the UN virtually since its founding.

Because of the changing configurations of world politics, the balance of initiative, authority, activity, and accomplishment among the UN's major deliberative bodies has been altered in ways that the drafters of the Charter could not have foreseen and probably never intended. Under the Charter, the Security Council was central in the organization because it was charged with matters pertaining to peace and security, because it institutionalized the status of the major states, and because it was granted the authority to make binding decisions. Nevertheless the authority to initiate UN action was fairly evenly distributed among the Security Council, the General Assembly, and the Economic and Social Council. In the post–Cold War era, this situation has notably changed, not because the Charter has changed but because the political significance of the different deliberative bodies has evolved. The Security Council, the General Assembly, and the ECOSOC still have the power to initiate UN action, but from the perspective of most member governments the actions of the Security Council are taken far more seriously, and the actions of the counterpart bodies far less seriously than might once have been the case.

The Ascendance of the Security Council

The centrality of the Security Council within the UN system has become much more marked since the end of the Cold War, due, understandably, to the disappearance of East–West ideological and political-strategic bipolarity. Since the early 1990s, the Security Council has been able to act because paralyzing vetoes are no longer predictable. Indeed, these days they are very seldom cast. Instead, the threat of the veto is at present as much of a consensus-building—or action-blocking—device as the veto itself once was a stultifying ploy. Equally significant is the fact that new conditions in the post–Cold War world continue to generate demands for Security Council action. One American official underlined this by explaining that 70 percent of all UN peacekeeping has taken place since the fall of the Berlin Wall. The Security Council, he said, is the "global 911" and "it is still answering the phone everyday." The Security Council, he reaffirmed, "is not a spent organization." For some among the Permanent Five, Security Council membership continues to have intrinsic value because it bestows and preserves privilege, and this, to them, becomes ever more important as international power diffuses, and even more so as state sovereignty itself comes under challenge. Among the non–Permanent Members, Security Council membership still offers an international "place in the sun" and a two-year opportunity, including at least a month of council presidency, to leave a mark on the world.

In recent years the workload of the Security Council has increased dramatically: taking into account both its daily formal sessions and the literally continuous informal interactions among delegations, the Security Council today is never out of session. So too, as noted, has the agenda of the Security Council broadened to regularly include questions of human rights, human security, and humanitarian intervention that would not have been taken up even ten years ago. Some diplomats working on Security Council affairs, as well as some national delegations as a matter of policy, object to this broadened agenda on grounds of legitimacy or simply sheer workload. But most agree that it is here to stay because, as one ambassador remarked, "the Security Council can pretty much discuss anything it wants." Increasingly it does. Topics that would customarily be taken up by the General Assembly, such as HIV-AIDS, more and more often are being discussed in the Security Council.

But the heyday of Big Five consensus that characterized Security Council activities in the early years after the end of the Cold War is over. The main reason for this, an American diplomat explained, is that "there are significant differences with the Russians." About this, his Russian counterpart was very much in agreement. From the Russian perspective, what happens within the Security Council today is "more realistic and more normal relations." It is not a world, he said, in which the "U.S. can do whatever it wants," despite some thinking to the contrary. And it is not only frequent disagreements between the United States and Russia that today divide the Security Council, but similar disagreements between the United States and China, between the United States and France, between France and the United Kingdom, and between France and the United Kingdom, on the one hand, and Russia and China, on the other. It is now quite clear that the "collective leadership" by the Permanent Five that characterized Security Council operations during the early 1990s is long gone. "P-5 cooperation doesn't exist on most subjects dealt with by the Council," a French official explained. The short-lived era of collectively governing the "new world order" lasted through the Gulf War but then gradually transformed into a new era of bargaining over national interests during the debates over sanctioning Saddam Hussein, acting in Bosnia, dealing with Slobodan Milosevic over Kosovo, and debating America's determination to invade Iraq. Today it is recognized, and accepted, that the political dynamics of the Security Council will be driven by differences in national interest among the Permanent Five (and others as well). When debate brings about a convergence of interests, action can be taken. Otherwise, the Security Council will not act. Yet, unlike what befell the Security Council during the Cold War, today's politics of bargained national interests are not paralyzing. For one thing, divisions and disagreements do not consistently set the United States and Russia apart, nor, for that matter, do they set any of the Permanent Five consistently apart. Issues are considered separately and differences over some do not contaminate considerations concerning others. Pragmatism prevails, and Security Council members appear to welcome this political style.

Although the ascendance of the Security Council is a fact of today's political life at the UN, it is also the cause of considerable tension within the organization. It is probably not very far off the mark to say that the overwhelming majority of the UN's member states resent the dominance of the Security Council, just as they resent the broader dominance of the United States over UN affairs. Criticism ranges from familiar objections to what is perceived as the nonrepresentative character of the council as presently composed, to the council's erratic performance, to the council's perceived biases favoring Western preferences and ideologies. The nonrepresentativeness of the Security Council is, of course, the core issue in the debate over reforming the council, which also raises questions about the veto. Critics tend to make their cases with some vehemence, as did one Eastern European delegate, for example, when he commented that "the Security Council cannot be [an] authorizing body because it is not representative of the power structure or any other legitimating quality present in today's world. It needs to be reformed to make it more representative. Part of this reform also has to involve abolishing the veto." Conceding that the debate about reforming the Security Council is going nowhere at the present time, others complain that the council is unpredictable. "The Security Council is a risky place," one G-77 ambassador reported. "Sometimes it acts too fast; sometimes not at all." He went on to explain that in his estimation the pattern of behavior exhibited by the Security Council is apparently unrelated to the critical nature of situations but seems related to other factors that render the council "unpredictable and undependable." The erratic use of considerable Security Council capacity to address problems undermines commitment to use it at all. Among those who are well aware of the hegemony of the Security Council over the UN's political affairs, there is apprehension that the council is presently pushing the UN, and pulling others, in directions contrary to their interests. One Latin American diplomat explained this rather forcefully by pointing out that when the Cold War ended, "we realized that the UN could begin acting in ways it was designed. But, when we found out how the system worked, we were terrified." After he explained that Security Council decisions had involved the UN in "conflict situations" and in courses of policy that contradicted his country's interests, he concluded that "at this point many of us said oops!"

The Decline of the General Assembly

Another reason for the current ascendance of the Security Council is to be found in the relative decline of the General Assembly. After decolonization, voting majorities in the General Assembly started to run against the United States and its Western partners as the newly independent countries sought to shift UN attention to issues they considered critical. Developing countries after the Bandung Conference in1955 sought to formalize their numerical advantage to press the General Assembly to focus on issues of decolonization and social and economic development. As noted, with regard to decolonization and the exploitation of their majority position in the General Assembly, the new nations in the UN were remarkably successful. Concerning social and economic issues, success was much less the case, but the South nonetheless continued to use its majority in the General Assembly as a political club to batter the North because the wealthier countries were perceived to be insufficiently responsive to the plights of the world's poor. In the heyday of the New International Economic Order, the Group of 77 developing nations sought largely through aggressive politics in the General Assembly to change fundamentally the nature of international economic relations by ameliorating the disadvantaged position that most less developed states occupied in the global economy. This was to be accomplished through the obligatory transfer of resources from rich to poor nations. The South also sought to shift the balance of influence in the international economic institutions by disconnecting voting privileges from capital contributions. The closely associated nonaligned movement (NAM) sought to prevent superpower rivalries from engulfing less developed countries and used the General Assembly as its locus and focus of political action. It is true that during these times and through most of these episodes, the South failed to achieve its goals via the General Assembly. Yet it is certainly also true that during these times and episodes, goings on in the General Assembly were considered very important by both the South and the North.

The overcharged political fireworks in the General Assembly during the heydays of the serious North–South confrontations of the 1970s in some ways contributed to the assembly's marginalization and the centering of attention on the Security Council. But even before this, the vitriolic temper of debates and accusations hurled at northern countries in general, and the United States in particular, persuaded these governments that the General Assembly had become a southern echo chamber. They discounted the institution accordingly.[36] At the same time, from the southern perspective, the futility of the North–South encounters in the General Assembly persuaded these governments to also back away from the institution or at least to expect much less from it. As time has gone on, most delegations to the UN have come to expect less from the General Assembly and increasingly look on the body as a "talk shop in decline."

It is not clear to everyone today that the General Assembly is in fact in decline because some of those to whom we spoke emphatically denied this. The body in fact remains an important negotiating forum for some issues like human rights questions, budgetary matters, and many of the issues of institutional reform presently under consideration. It is also the main arena for the brewing debate over the international community's prerogatives in the area of humanitarian intervention. The General Assembly is also the launching vehicle

---

[36]Daniel Patrick Moynihan, *A Dangerous Place* (Boston: Little, Brown, 1976).

for many of the UN-sponsored world conferences. It remains the principal arena for North–South interaction on issues of development, and, as such, a symbol of southern solidarity and a G-77 target for institutional resuscitation.

Although some deny the decline of the General Assembly, others to whom we spoke perceived the body today as about as effective as it ever was with the implication that perhaps it never was very effective. Closest to the general perception, however, was the commentary of one Latin American ambassador who characterized the General Assembly as "an increasingly anomalous body because there is no longer any consensus possible among a sizable portion of its membership." It is losing its political clout, he said, because there is no consensus and no large majority for almost anything. "The only consensus is on the necessity of the UN." But, the ambassador continued, "the General Assembly is no longer a forum for negotiation," and at this point he asked rhetorically, "What is its contribution? What is its role?" He concluded that it "has to offer more."

Others to whom we spoke characterized the UN General Assembly as a "parliament without party discipline," "a bazaar for the hawking of national interests," or a theater for the playing out of a "politics of personalities." The bloc structure of the UNGA is less distinct and less politically consequential than in times past, although the European Union stands massively and immovably as a powerful exception. Regarding the changing bloc dynamics, one French diplomat noted that "effectiveness in the General Assembly depends upon the group structure; otherwise the organ is nothing more than cacophony." Needless to say, the "East" and "West" of the Cold War are no longer, and even the post–Cold War "West" constitutes a shaky coalition at best. The respective solidarities of the Group of 77 and the NAM have also greatly diminished, and this is also partly due to the ending of the Cold War, which has meant that, as one Russian diplomat observed, "The notion of non-aligned has lost its sense." Coalescing around common interests in development has also become problematic for the full range of the membership in the Group of 77 because economic needs and differences in levels of development within the group are raising questions about group commonality and identity. Economically speaking, in what sense do the flourishing economies of the Pacific Rim, the devastated economies of sub-Saharan Africa, and the premodern economies of the non–oil-producing Middle East constitute a bloc of common political-economic interest? Upon discussing UN development issues with a Southeast Asian diplomat, for example, we were advised to understand that his country "was not Africa." Presently, there is some regrouping of the G-77/NAM countries around perceived cultural commonalities in "non-Westernness." The extent to which this signals an enduring reconfiguration of the General Assembly's bloc structure is a matter we consider later in this volume. It nevertheless remains very much the case that without a reliable bloc structure, the General Assembly cannot serve usefully as the negotiating forum anticipated in the Charter, and today the bloc structure is increasingly inchoate.

The Marginalization of the Economic and Social Council

Although there is some disagreement among participants and observers over the current status and importance of the General Assembly, there is widespread agreement concerning the marginalization of the Economic and Social Council. When the Czech ambassador Karel Kovanada stepped down from the vice presidency of the Economic and Social Council in 1997, he told a correspondent from *The U.N. Chronicle* that "What the Charter says [about ECOSOC] is gray theory. Everybody who has been around the UN for a bit can compare what the Charter says about ECOSOC and what ECOSOC really is. They will see that the congruence is not complete." The Czech diplomat then went on to say,

> The Economic and Social Council is in great turmoil. On the one hand, there are people who think that it should not even exist. There are ambassadors in this town who don't want to have anything to do with it, who don't even want to hear about ECOSOC. On the other hand, there are people who feel that the Council should be the driving force of all economic and social activities of the UN system. Now, I don't know whether either of these extreme positions is one that I would agree with. But the fact is, even after a year of service as ECOSOC's Vice-President, I have not sorted out what its main objectives are.[37]

Under the UN Charter, the Economic and Social Council is assigned the tasks of formulating the international community's policy with respect to promoting social and economic development and coordinating the activities of the myriad agencies of the UN system that are engaged in development-promoting activities. In the standard interpretation of the Charter offered earlier in this chapter, the ECOSOC is assumed to be the institutional hub of the UN's involvement in the international political economy. Yet in practice over the years, the ECOSOC has proven to be neither a policy-making body nor a systemwide coordinator of UN development activities. Instead it has become largely a "talk shop" that annually assembles to routinely consider the reports that the subsidiary bodies and specialized agencies are obliged to submit and in turn to send the results of these considerations on to the General Assembly. "The United Nations," another commentator observed, "has a clear mandate and responsibility to play a major role in international economic cooperation, especially through the Economic and Social Council (ECOSOC) system. Yet from its earliest years, the Council has largely failed to do so."[38]

Reasons for the marginalization of the ECOSOC are manifold. For one thing, the council is too large and unwieldy to function efficiently as a policy-making body. In 1965 its original membership of 18 was increased to 27 and then in 1971 it was increased again to 54. Expanding the membership was a

---

[37] *UN Chronicle*, Spring 1997, http://www.findarticles.com/p/articles/mi_m1309/is_n1.
[38] Julian Disney, "Should ECOSOC Be Reformed?" *UN Chronicle* (Summer 2000); http:www.findarticles.com/p/articles/mi_m1309/is_2_37/ai_66579834/print.

justifiable response to Third World demands for greater representation on a UN body that dealt after all mainly with Third World problems. But deference to representation was at the expense of cohesion. Moreover, once the ECOSOC had a Third World majority, the developed countries shied away, as they also did regarding the General Assembly, preferring to do their international business in more hospitable settings. When the North–South dialogue became a donnybrook in the 1970s, the ECOSOC polarized accordingly, thereby rendering policy discussions unpromising.

Equally significant for ECOSOC's institutional fate was the proliferation of agencies and institutions both within the UN system and without that were granted or otherwise assumed "development" missions. In point of fact, the Bretton Woods organizations—the International Monetary Fund and the World Bank—have become the world's development drivers, joined recently and increasingly by the World Trade Organization. They are largely northern dominated, they control much of the resource flow that supports southern development activities, and until very recently they have exhibited little interest in moving closer to the ECOSOC. Yet even directly within the UN system, the UNDP, the UNCTAD, the World Food Programme, UNICEF, and several other important subsidiary bodies are in fact development agencies, to say nothing of the General Assembly itself and its second and third standing committees. Even among Third World countries there is some preference for working through development issues in the General Assembly's committees, where each member can cast a vote, rather than in the ECOSOC, where voting is for council members only. Then there are all of the specialized agencies with development missions—the FAO, the WHO, UNIDO, UNESCO, the ILO—whose policy-making and programmes proceed largely independently of what goes on elsewhere within the UN system. Prevailing amid all of this as a central policy maker was a challenge that the unwieldy ECOSOC of 54 members could not rise to, and coordinating the cacophony of development thinking and behavior proved practically impossible, particularly because most the agencies involved have resisted being coordinated. Well outside the UN altogether, the Organization for Economic Cooperation and Development (OECD) is certainly as significant a contributor to development policy, activity, and coordination as any single organ within the UN.

During the decade of the 1990s, and continuing at present, efforts have been made to resuscitate the Economic and Social Council, but even Secretary-General Kofi Annan has acknowledged realistically that "decision-making on international economic matters, particularly in areas of finance and trade, has long left the UN and no amount of institutional reform will bring it back."[39] Nevertheless, the secretary-general supported by a number of member governments has proposed a series of reforms that although not relocating ECOSOC at the center of policy making regarding development, might instead endow

---

[39]"United Nations, *A More Secure World: Our Shared Responsibility*. Report of the Secretary-General's High-Level Panel on Threats, Challenges and Change.

the organ with more useful functions. One focus of institutional improvement advocates pragmatic and focused changes such as streamlining ECOSOC debates, concentrating the agenda on selected issues, and establishing an executive board. Kofi Annan also supports turning the council into a global forum for development and the Millenium Development Goals (MDGs), that is, a monitoring and prodding agency that would press for the fulfillment of commitments undertaken by the international community in 2000. In addition, ECOSOC's role, according to Annan, should be strengthened by the assumption of joint responsibility with the Security Council for the Peace-building Commission established after the World Summit in 2005 and by establishing a commission of its own on the relationship between security and development. Periodic ECOSOC-sponsored high-level consultations among UN development agencies and the Bretton Woods institutions are among recommended reforms, and some of these have recently occurred. But whether anything will ultimately come of efforts to reform the ECOSOC remains uncertain. The present status of this council remains marginal.

THE TIP OF THE EXPLANATORY ICEBERG

Although it is certainly true that many of the chartered organs of the UN operate at levels of efficiency and accomplishment short of their chartered potential, we caution our readers not to jump to the simplistic conclusion that the oftentimes unsatisfactory performance of the UN in dealing with global problems results from the deliberative and other bodies not working as intended. The institutions were well intended, and on occasion they have worked as intended and still do. There is no need to rewrite the UN Charter, even if this were remotely possible within the world political climate of our times. We tried to hint in this chapter, and we elaborate extensively throughout the rest of this book, that the shortcomings of the UN have little to do with any flaws in its design. What is centrally important is that most members of the UN some of the time, and some members almost all of the time, have fallen short of honoring the commitments they undertook in signing the Charter. This results from no general malevolence toward the UN, even though some governments may approach this in their extreme indifference toward the organization, but rather from priorities impelled by the imperatives of politics, both domestic and international. Most member governments look on the UN not as an institution or organization, but rather as a "place," that is, a venue for doing their diplomatic and political business. For this reason, and rhetoric to the contrary notwithstanding, *reforming* the UN, that is, fixing the organization so that it works better, tends not to be a high priority for almost any member government. Why reform a perfectly suitable place for doing international business? As a result, the almost continuous theme of UN reform played and replayed over the decades has actually come to very little.

Doing international business at the UN has for any number of governments, and perhaps for all of them on one occasion or another, meant something other than focusing on and trying to resolve the pressing problems of the world. Most of the UN's members some of the time, and some of them all of time, seek to accomplish from their participation in the organization goals that have little to do with the Charter or their commitments to it. All member governments, for example, orchestrate their participation at the UN with an eye to impressing important domestic constituencies, which may sometimes mean publicly bashing the UN rather than supporting it, shunning it rather than embracing it, or withholding from it rather than providing for it the resources required for successful action. When politically expedient, nearly all member states will find the means to ignore their responsibilities under the Charter. Otherwise, member governments may use the arenas of the UN to criticize and embarrass rival governments, to maneuver geopolitically, to score ideological debating points, to legitimize national initiatives and policies, or to scandalize UN officials. Some governments go to the United Nations to constrain the UN itself. Most use their membership in the world organization to procure high-paying Secretariat positions for their nationals. Others seek mainly to obtain economic assistance and other material benefits. Needless to say, not very much of this self-interested national behavior contributes to the smooth and effective functioning of the UN. The Charter established a promising framework for international cooperation, but actually cooperating to effect meaningful collective action is something that has all too often eluded UN members.

CHAPTER 4

The United Nations: The Last Bastion of Sovereignty?

At the dawn of the twenty-first century, the United Nations is being called on more and more to deal with a multitude of issues that cannot be solved by strictly, or even mainly, global or national action. In our world, global policy has to be complemented by national enforcement. The UN's agenda is vast, ranging across complex issues of transnational terrorism, domestic military and civil strife, human rights violations, drug trafficking and other transborder crimes, environmental degradation, poverty, inequality, and HIV/AIDS, to name just a few. In the face of globalization's seemingly complete penetration of every corner of the earth, the walls of Westphalian state sovereignty appear to be crumbling.

Yet are they? And what is the role of the United Nations in this process? Is the UN a procedural and institutional bridge to a world beyond national sovereignty? Or is the organization one of sovereignty's last bastions? Mounting evidence suggests that the sovereign prerogatives of national governments are being challenged and circumvented in a variety of ways. On the other hand, governments of UN member states are well aware that their sovereign prerogatives are under siege, and many are endeavoring to take steps to protect them. The clash between the detractors and the defenders of national sovereignty is one of the principal dimensions of UN politics. The ultimate outcomes of the confrontation will be dialectical, although the form of the synthesis is as yet unclear.

THE LAST BASTION OF SOVEREIGNTY?

In his reflections on the state of the United Nations, former Under-Secretary-General Brian Urquhart calls the UN today, "the last bastion of national sovereignty."[1] Noting this, Thomas G. Weiss, director of the Ralph Bunche Institute at the City University of New York, adds that the UN may not be the last bastion of national sovereignty, "but it certainly is one of the foremost."[2] Yet Weiss goes on to argue that national sovereignty has been rendered "contingent" by forces driving contemporary world politics, and, he says, it is in many ways being circumvented or superseded within the United Nations. If sovereignty maintains a bastion in the UN, this sanctuary, says Weiss, is under assault. And Weiss is not the only analyst who says this. A near preponderance of Western writers on the new international relations of the post–Cold War era depict the transformation of the Westphalian state system into something more complex, more interdependent, more globalized, more networked, more pluralistic, and less state centric than in former times. In this new world order, sovereignty means less because territoriality means less.[3] In the face of complex processes of globalization, national borders have become increasingly, and often necessarily, porous, so that reigning sovereign within them and defending them from without are becoming less important. Sovereignty also means less because transnational forces from below and supranational agents from above frequently disregard the privileges and immunities that traditionally accompanied it.

According to this analysis, the transformation of world politics must also be effecting a transformation of international organizations, so that national sovereignty at the UN has not the meaning or political clout it once had. The UN is no longer an association of its member states only, if it ever was. It is directed, some say, by an increasingly autonomous corps of international officials, who see themselves "coordinating the behaviour of states and other actors" or otherwise managing the networks of interacting organizations and agencies that produce global responses to global problems.[4] An energetic secretary-general can mark out a good deal of autonomous political space to maneuver even if this does not yield greater autonomy for the office of the secretary-general. Using such political space, Secretary-General Kofi Annan in particular has gone so far as to urge world political leaders to disregard sovereignty and to intervene quickly when gross violations of human rights occur.[5] He has

---

[1] Cited in Thomas G. Weiss, "The Politics of Humanitarian Ideas," *Security Dialogue*, 31:1 (March 2000): 13.

[2] Ibid.

[3] John Gerard Ruggie, "Territoriality at the Millennium's End," in *Constructing the World Polity: Essays on International Institutionalization*, John Gerard Ruggie, ed. (New York: Routledge, 1998), pp. 173–98.

[4] Kofi Annan, *We the Peoples: The Role of the United Nations in the 21st Century* [*Millennium Report*] (A/54/2000), p. 6; See also Weiss, The Politics of Humanitarian Ideas," pp. 12–14, 67–69.

[5] Annan notes two competing concepts of sovereignty: state sovereignty with its associations with nonintervention and popular sovereignty that makes state sovereignty subordinate to the demands of protecting individual human life rather than a shield for those who would abuse human rights. See Kofi Annan, "Two Concepts of Sovereignty," *The Economist* 352 (September 18, 1999): 49–50.

also proposed direct connections between the United Nations and private sector associations, thus circumventing national sovereignty. Directors of the United Nations Development Programme (UNDP) have similarly advocated direct relations between international organizations and communities and individuals within countries, again bypassing national governments. Such developments, if realized, would endow the United Nations with a dimension of supranationality that is quite new. The organization is also infiltrated in almost every policy sector by numerous nongovernmental organizations (NGOs) that add a dimension of transnationality, which also has to be taken into account in any present-day characterization of the UN. Alliances between international officials and NGO directors are increasingly common at the UN, and these too render the organization something more than an association of member states only.

Although some observers report the declining prominence of national sovereignty, others are urging this decline along. In particular, many Western liberal writers, and many analysts of the UN among them, do not seem to care much for national sovereignty. By their reckoning, if political trends appear to be moving the world beyond sovereignty, so much the better. Lloyd Axworthy, the former foreign minister of Canada, has written that "there will continue to be instances when conflict prevention diplomacy or the deterrent effect of new international law does not succeed." In these cases, the international community must be prepared to end suffering, apparently by endowing this "international community" with agency and setting any concerns about national sovereignty aside.[6] Some scholars see a "consistent trend emerging" that "has begun to point the way to a more defined legal framework for humanitarian action even where sovereign approval is absent." This trend, they suggest, is to be welcomed.[7]

Whether the weakening of national sovereignty is a welcome development is a fitting topic for discussion among political philosophers. Whether national sovereignty is in fact weakening worldwide is something that can be taken up by political scientists, although this is a very broad and complex issue. Analysis in this chapter is addressed to the narrower question about how and with what implications the issue of national sovereignty is being played out in the political discourse within the United Nations. What we have discovered is that the UN is neither the last bastion of national sovereignty nor its graveyard. Instead the UN is a political battleground where defenders and detractors of national sovereignty are meeting head on. The debates rooted in questions of sovereign prerogative occur almost daily and on many substantive fronts. After examining the evidence available, we ultimately conclude that it is much too soon to tell what is going to come of the clashing between

---

[6]Lloyd Axworthy, "Human Security and Global Governance: Putting People First," *Global Governance*, 7:1 (January–March 2001): 21.

[7]Martin Griffths, Iain Levine, and Mark Weller, "Sovereignty and Suffering," in *The Politics of Humanitarian Intervention*, John Harris, ed. (London and New York: Pinter, 1995), p. 34.

those who would wish to keep the UN a club of sovereign states and those who would prefer more trans- and supranationality. It appears, however, that the news about sovereignty's demise at the UN is certainly premature. Still, the UN is no longer an organization of member states only.

SOME CONTENDING MANIFESTOS

Who are the detractors and who are the defenders of national sovereignty at the United Nations? To some extent this depends on the question being debated. There are, for example, issues like the question of capital punishment, where a number of Western countries that normally object to using national sovereignty as a barrier against outside scrutiny tend to assert their own sovereignty in just this way. But, generally speaking, the battle lines over sovereignty are most frequently drawn in the way that Weiss describes them when he speaks of reactions to the notion of humanitarian intervention on the part of the international community:

> The West (including Central Europe) and much of sub-Saharan Africa are essentially enthusiastic; large developing countries (including Nigeria, South Africa, Egypt, India, and most of Latin America) are lukewarm . . . and Russia, China, pariahs (Iraq, Iran, Libya, North Korea, Cuba), much of Asia and the Middle East . . . are hostile.[8]

Our observations suggest that on several issues where questions of protecting or asserting national sovereignty come to the surface, the sub-Saharan Africans are more cautious than Weiss implies. "Lukewarm" with reference to the positions of India and Egypt may overstate their acceptance of agents and activities that go beyond national sovereignty. To the ranks of those pushing beyond national sovereignty one must add the European Union collectively, elements of the UN Secretariat, Kofi Annan, the secretary-general, and most of the NGO community.

The brief of the detractors of national sovereignty is well known. They say that under early twenty-first century conditions of interdependence, national sovereignty is rapidly becoming an anomaly. Appeals to sovereignty, therefore, can only be obstacles to essential projects of international cooperation. Moreover, say the detractors, sovereignty is frequently a screen that governments erect to hide their internationally questionable behavior, particularly in matters of human rights and human security. To the extent that this legalistic sanctuary shelters unacceptable behavior, it should be swept aside. During interviews that we conducted at the United Nations in the spring of 2000, one European ambassador reacted to the notion of using national sovereignty as

---

[8]Weiss, "The Politics of Humanitarian Ideas," p. 12.

a sanctuary by observing that some governments would like to prohibit any and all UN interventions into member states' domestic affairs. These governments, the ambassador disapprovingly commented, "are most interested in establishing procedures that would effectively make such interventions impossible." Over the last several years, Secretary-General Kofi Annan has maintained on numerous occasions that appeals to sovereignty cannot be allowed to either stifle international cooperation or to shield internationally unacceptable behavior.[9]

But the defenders of national sovereignty also have a case. One aspect of this is their conviction that sovereignty protects against unwelcome outside interference in matters that governments wish to consider domestic, *and that under traditional tenets of international law are in fact domestic.* National sovereignty, Algerian president Abdelaziz Bouteflika told the UN General Assembly, is "our last protection from the rules of an unjust world."[10] Respect for national sovereignty, as written into Article 2, Paragraph 7 of the United Nations Charter, should therefore remain an "unchallenged principle of UN activity." Others are more specific. National sovereignty, they say, protects against unwanted political and cultural incursions from coalitions bent on imposing Western values and institutions. Such protection is especially important when Western coalitions identify themselves as "the international community" and claim to speak and act on behalf of the world. Or, even more specifically, keeping domestic affairs sacrosanct by invoking sovereignty protects against American political cajoling and ideological proselytizing. It combats what many label as "neoimperialism." The common theme is *noninterference,* a venerable principle of international law deeply associated with state sovereignty. The goal is to maximize governments' autonomy; the legal and political guarantee is sovereignty. For its defenders, sovereignty is too valuable a political and ideological asset to surrender blithely, whatever the globalizing tendencies of the postmodern world.

There is another aspect to the question of national sovereignty at the United Nations. A number of member governments worry that their exclusive privileges as UN members are today being eroded. They look on the UN as their organization—a club of nationally dispatched diplomats—and they are increasingly sensitive about other actors vying for or usurping roles reserved for sovereignties. This sensitivity has especially to do with the presence and activism of NGOs. But it also affects governments' perceptions of the UN Secretariat and the secretary-general. The United Nations was founded as an intergovernmental organization. Many of its members prefer that it should remain a strictly intergovernmental organization.

---

[9]See also, for example, Kofi Annan's commentary in the *Financial Times,* January 10, 2000.
[10]Peter Ford, "Few Sacred Borders to the New UN" Christian Science Monitor, Sept 29, 1999.

BATTLING ACROSS MANY FRONTS

There is more to the national defense of sovereignty at the United Nations, but rather than expounding abstractly, looking into the substantive debates places sovereignty issues in concrete context. Three sets of highly contentious issues illustrate the extent to which the sides are opposed. There are many more than three such issues being debated today, although, for the argument attempted here three illustrations should suffice. There is first the issue of *humanitarian intervention*, which raises the question of whether the international community may on occasion sweep aside national sovereignty and assist suffering people. Then, there are related, but differently approached, questions of *human rights*, where the issues have to do with whether all national governments are obliged to accept and uphold standards established by a self-defined international community with which they do not identify. Third, there are the so-called NGO questions where the issues have to do with whether nongovernments may enjoy privileges customarily reserved for sovereign states.

Humanitarian Intervention

Reactions to Kofi Annan's opening speech to the 54th General Assembly in 1999 were rather dramatic. Almost every member state that participated at this meeting entered into the debates that followed on the secretary-general's questioning the "absolute and exclusive" status of national sovereignty. Many, mostly Western, delegations spoke in support of Mr. Annan's rather bold initiative. The British, for example, argued that new rules were necessary to allow intervention against sovereign states when "an overwhelming human catastrophe" demands it.[11] American president Bill Clinton, speaking on the day following Annan's address, declared that the secretary-general "spoke for all of us . . . when he said that ethnic cleansers and mass murders can find no refuge in the United Nations [and] no source of comfort or justification in its Charter."[12]

But many delegations also raised objections. In the two weeks of opening debates in the General Assembly, for example, China, India, Malaysia, Iraq, North Korea, and Libya all argued that respect for sovereignty should remain an unchallenged principle of UN activity. Algerian president and then chair of the Organization of African Unity Abdelaziz Bouteflika, quoted earlier, went on to argue that "we do not deny the right of public opinion in the Northern Hemisphere to denounce breaches of human rights where they exist. And we do not deny that the United Nations has the right

---

[11]John Tessitore and Susan Woolfson, eds., *A Global Agenda: Issues Before the 55th General Assembly of the United Nations* (New York: Rowman & Littlefield, 2000), p. 3.
[12]Weiss, "The Politics of Humanitarian Ideas," p. 13.

and duty to help suffering humanity . . . . [But] we firmly believe that interference in internal affairs can only take place with the consent of the state in
question."[13]

In his *Millennium Report* issued in anticipation of the 55th session of the
General Assembly in 2000, Kofi Annan himself acknowledged the raft of critical reactions to his position regarding national sovereignty, saying that
humanitarian intervention could become "a cover for gratuitous interference
in the internal affairs of sovereign states." Still, he contended that "no legal
principle—not even sovereignty—can ever shield crimes against humanity."[14]
About the time that the *Millennium Report* was issued, a Russian diplomat
remained skeptical about the evolving conceptualization and reminded
us during an interview that "the secretary-general is not a decision-making
institution."

The contradictions and contentions between advocates of humanitarian
intervention and defenders of national sovereignty were surely not new at the
time that Annan crystallized the debate. Sides were drawn as early as 1991
when the Security Council debated Resolution 688, which authorized international intervention to protect Kurdish populations in northern Iraq against
repression by the Iraqi government. This resolution passed ten votes to three,
with two abstentions, and the debate surrounding it was largely about the
international community's right to intervene into the affairs of a sovereign
state, in this instance Iraq. Here, for example, the Yemeni government in the
minority contended that "the draft resolution sets a dangerous precedent that
could open the way to diverting the Council away from its basic functions and
responsibilities for safeguarding international peace and security and towards
addressing the internal affairs of countries."[15]

The sides divided again in 1992 when the Security Council authorized
the intervention into Somalia. On this occasion some defenders of national
sovereignty contended that the precedents set by Operation Restore Hope
undermined the credibility of governments all over Africa, and the Egyptian
opposition newspaper *Al-Shaab* concluded that by letting the UN into their
country, "the Somali commanders have handed their country over to the
Americans on a golden platter."[16] Reflecting on Third World negative reactions to the intervention into Somalia, one group of Western analysts concluded that "although the intervention was justified as being an initiative to
save life in the face of the complete collapse of the Somali government, and
effectively of the state, it was seen by many . . . developing countries as the last
stage in a continuum of intervention and interference by Western countries
in the developing world."[17]

---

[13]Robert Holloway, *Agency France-Presse*, September 21, 1999.
[14]Annan, *Millennium Report*.
[15]Griffiths et al., "Sovereignty and Suffering," p. 49.
[16]Ibid., p. 62.
[17]Ibid., p. 62.

The debate continued in the context of the situation in Bosnia, where the Indian government restated its "long held stance that territorial integrity and state sovereignty are overriding goals to which (by implication though never stated as such) human rights and humanitarian concerns should be subordinated."[18] On the same issue, one Indian delegate told us that during the debates over UN involvement in Bosnia, his government was compelled to remind the Security Council that "the Council's consideration of this matter related not to Yugoslavia's internal situation as such, but specifically to its implication for peace and security in the region." Later, lines were drawn again over Kosovo, where much of the world condemned NATO's military intervention as "aggression" against a sovereign state—Yugoslavia. Here, even the UN's humanitarian follow-up, the Interim Administration Mission in Kosovo (UNMIK), remains controversial as member governments complain that the international community is illegally trampling on Yugoslavia's sovereignty. In August 2000, for example, the Russian Foreign Ministry sent a letter to the president of the Security Council, complaining that when the head of the UNMIK defined the status of UN personnel in Kosovo without the agreement of the Yugoslav government, the action ran "counter to the norms of international law and constitutes another gross violation of UN Security Council Resolution 1244 (1999), which expressly reaffirms the sovereignty and territorial integrity of Yugoslavia."[19] Since the NATO attack on Yugoslavia, the Russian Federation has become increasingly less enthusiastic about humanitarian intervention on behalf of the "international community" and increasingly outspoken in defense of national sovereignty, thereby moving closer to China and thus dividing the Security Council on questions of humanitarian intervention.

A Latin American diplomat interviewed in 2003 confirmed for us that the question of humanitarian intervention was "one of the principal issues before the UN." He went on to explain that from his government's perspective it was both a cultural issue and a legal one. On the one hand, UN humanitarian intervention was looked on as "injecting alien values in societies." But he indicated that what was more important to Latin Americans was that those who are championing humanitarian intervention are "aiming at limiting the principle of nonintervention" in international law. The Permanent Five on the Security Council, he said, are leading the rest of the members of the United Nations insensitively and unwisely. The secretary-general, furthermore, "was well meaning, but wrong on this issue."

At a Third World mission we were told that "reactions to Kofi Annan's endorsement of humanitarian intervention were quite negative across the Third World." On the specific issue of the secretary-general's initiative at the 54th General Assembly, one UN official observed that Annan "is increasingly

---

[18]Radha Kumar, "Sovereignty and Intervention: Opinions in South Asia," *Pugwash Occasional Papers*, 2:1 (January 2001): 2.
[19]S/2000/824.

perceived as having sold out to the West, the U.S. in particular." He is perceived, this official said, "as having championed all of the ideological themes favored and promoted by the West," humanitarian intervention included. Another UN official reported that "Kofi Annan's call for humanitarian intervention has not gone down well" and it is only because Annan himself is from the Third World "that he has not been more openly criticized." An African respondent explained that his government was not as negative as some others. But he nevertheless agreed that "humanitarian intervention amounts to a really capricious policy of the West." An Indian diplomat offered that in authorizing humanitarian interventions "the Security Council has taken over issues and operates in domains that are really not its business," and a Russian diplomat concurred, offering that "the Security Council is today getting into a number of things it was not constitutionally mandated to get into." Humanitarian intervention in defiance of national sovereignty is one of these. Another Latin American respondent said that his government was opposed to intervening against the wishes of sovereign states because humanitarian intervention was too often used to cloak the foreign policy ambitions of powerful countries. This, he said, was clearly the case regarding the United States forcing the UN's intervention into Haiti. He added, however, that his country's position was mild compared to others, like India, "who don't even want to talk about it."

Support for humanitarian intervention and for the secretary-general's urging for movement beyond national sovereignty was voiced by one highly place Secretariat official who explained that "the split [over humanitarian intervention] was not strictly North/South." There is nowadays "a sensible corps of Third World countries like South Africa, Bangladesh, and Senegal" that support the concept and practice of humanitarian intervention even when it challenges national sovereignty. However, he also said that "the natural leaders" of the Third World, like India and China, were not among the "corps of the sensible." Discussing his country's position, an American official explained that "there was no U.S. position" because "nobody wants to open that Pandora's box." He volunteered, however, that he saw such intervention as "fundamentally inconsistent with international law," although at times "moral imperatives require it." Washington also remains significantly limited by national legislation as to where, when, and how American forces may actually participate in UN-sponsored peacekeeping, including humanitarian interventions.[20]

Weiss appropriately summarized the debate about humanitarian intervention when he wrote that "non-intervention is affirmed in Article 2(7) of the UN Charter . . . . This construction is increasingly contested, but its staying power is evident from the language of Security Council resolutions, which habitually stresses the exceptional character of each UN intervention. It is also

[20]Thomas G. Weiss, David P. Forsythe and Roger A. Coate, *The United Nations and Changing World Politics*, 3rd ed. (Boulder, Colo.: Westview Press, 2001), p. 92.

evident in the hostility of two permanent members of the Security Council, China and Russia, as well as a host of developing countries."[21]

The debate, therefore, is far from over, despite the conclusions of the Intergovernmental Commission on Intervention and State Sovereignty that presented its report, *The Responsibility to Protect*, in 2001.[22] This commission was established to reconcile the competing norms of state sovereignty and humanitarian intervention. The commission concluded that sovereignty remains the ordering framework for international relations, but that the nature of sovereignty, and freedom from intervention, are contingent on the ability of a state to provide and protect individuals according to international obligations and human rights standards. This responsibility to protect lies primarily with the state itself, but the principle of this new approach is that "where a population is suffering serious harm, as a result of internal war, insurgency, repression or state failure, and the state in question is unwilling or unable to halt or avert it, the principle of non-intervention yields to the international responsibility to protect." Thus not only do states have a responsibility toward individuals within their jurisdiction, the international community has a responsibility to act when states fail in this regard. Intervention has thus been couched in the terms of accountability that provides a new litmus test for sovereignty. States are accountable to citizens as well to the international community for upholding certain standards. This capability component to sovereignty is fairly new in explication, but historically of course any governing system that was incapable of controlling its territory and population was likely to fall prey to the advances of others. This redefinition of contingent sovereignty may face practical rather than normative challenges, not least by apparent prolonged unwillingness of the international community, represented by the UN Security Council, to take its responsibility to react seriously in cases such as the Liberian civil war and its aftermath as well as in the humanitarian catastrophe in Sudan in 2004.

Human Rights

The story of the Vienna Conference on Human Rights is well known. We are, moreover, going to dwell on it at some length later in this volume, so here we focus only on the sovereignty implications of the Vienna proceedings. By adopting Resolution 45/155 in 1990, member governments of the UN believed they were voting themselves a celebration. They were going to meet in Vienna in 1993 to talk about progress made since the adoption of the 1948 Universal Declaration of Human Rights. But Vienna instead became a debate, mainly between the First World and the Third World about universal standards

---

[21]Weiss, "The Politics of Humanitarian Ideas," p. 18.
[22]See *The Responsibility to Protect: Report of the International Commission on Intervention and State Sovereignty*, Ottawa, Canada: International Development Research Center, 2001 and especially the supplementary volume which includes the research essays, bibliography, and background papers.

for human rights and about intervention into the domestic affairs of sovereign states. Not only was there no consensus on the universality of the Universal Declaration, but there was also no longer any clear agreement that anyone had the right to set human rights standards with which anyone else need necessarily comply. At least this was the conclusion that some observers of the Vienna Conference drew, and, more significantly, it was also the conclusion reached by many of the participating governments.

Questions of human rights have always been highly politicized within the UN, although such politicization customarily took the form of hurling accusations about abuses at ideological enemies while protecting ideological friends. This still occurs. But nowadays the more hotly contested political lines are drawn between those who would wish to hold all governments to international standards and those who reject international standards and opt for regional or national ones partly out to keep the outside world from interfering in their domestic affairs. This new debate is sometimes identified as a contest between *universalists* and *cultural relativists,* although in the political context of the United Nations it is really about the right of the international community to set standards and the obligations of national governments to comply. Those who oppose such standards assert that the international community must bear "in mind the significance of national and regional particularities and various historical, cultural and religious backgrounds" and therefore refrain from interfering in national affairs.[23] Commenting on Chinese behavior at the UN, for example, one European ambassador observed that the Chinese do not usually do very much at the UN except intermittently to react strongly to issues that they perceive as very close to their national interest. "Their reaction is always one of don't touch us!" Human rights issues usually provoke such a response from Beijing, but not from China only.

The mix of convictions underlying various national stances in the human rights debates is complicated, and one must be cautious about attributing motives. Among those promoting international standards, among the Europeans in particular, there appears to be considerable concern for maintaining the global human rights regime embodied in present-day international law. Since the end of the Cold War, the Russian government also has been making strong stances in favor of international standards and enforcement, as have many of the new democracies of Central and Eastern Europe. For example, since the transition to democracy, the government of Croatia has supported universal human rights forcefully and most eloquently through a very able ambassador in New York. The U.S. government appears similarly concerned, although trying to embarrass ideological and political foes remains a part of the American repertoire. Latin Americans stand quite squarely behind the global human rights regime, but they are ambivalent about international intervention to enforce it. Cuba's stance against outside

---

[23] *The Bangkok Declaration,* Asia Intergovernmental Meeting, Bangkok, March 29–April 2, 1993, p. 1.

interference dominates both its policies and its participation in the UN's debates. In addition, Cuban representatives point to the futility of trying to promote human rights in a world engulfed in poverty. African governments are divided, and their reluctance to criticize other Africans often places them in awkward positions. Strongest support for noninterference comes from Islamic and Asian governments, but again not all of them. There can be no doubt that some of the protests against outside meddling and many of the invocations of national sovereignty are devices employed by abusers to screen their abuses. But there are also genuine convictions on the part of some that valued aspects of their culture are being jeopardized by a self-appointed international community bent on imposing alien ways. The wall of sovereignty is then a bulwark of national defense.

Since Vienna, the debate in the UN between those promoting international standards and those invoking national sovereignty to block international inference has intensified and broadened. Again, the current secretary-general has been at the forefront of this debate. Five months prior to his controversial 1999 General Assembly speech, Annan told the members of the UN Commission on Human Rights that "emerging slowly, but I believe surely, is an international norm against the violent repression of minorities that will and must take precedence over concerns of State sovereignty . . . . As long as I am Secretary-General, the United Nations as an institution will always place human beings at the centre of everything we do. No government has the right to hide behind national sovereignty in order to violate the human rights or fundamental freedoms of its peoples."[24]

There are many ways to show that the political divide between those promoting international standards and those invoking national sovereignty to block international inference has intensified and broadened. One rather telling source of documentation is to be found in the proceedings of the Third Committee of the UN General Assembly, where human rights issues are annually sorted on their way to the plenary floor. The debates in the Third Committee during the 54th session of the General Assembly were exemplary of these emerging divisions. It is true that these proceedings may have been particularly charged because Annan's provocative statements on humanitarian intervention were in the air. But our research suggests that examining the Third Committee's workings during any of the recent sessions of the General Assembly would have told a similar story.[25]

First, there was in the Third Committee what one might call the *stylized debate* about international standards versus noninterference. Defenders of noninterference annually introduce a cluster of draft resolutions that assert and affirm the privileges of sovereignty and the international illegality of interference in domestic affairs. At the 54th session these included a draft resolution titled "Strengthening United Nations activities in the field of human

---

[24]UN Press Release SG/SM/6949, HR/CN/898, April 7, 1999.
[25]See, for example, A/52/644/Add. 2, and A/C.3/52/SR 44–50.

rights through the promotion of international cooperation and the importance of non-selectivity, impartiality and objectivity" (A/C.3/54/L.73), introduced by Cuba on behalf of a group of Third World countries. Another such resolution was titled "Respect for principles of national sovereignty and non-interference in the internal affairs of States in their electoral processes" (A/C.3/54/L.74), also introduced by Cuba on behalf of an even larger group of Third World countries. Yet another was the draft resolution titled "Human rights and unilateral coercive measures" (A/C3/54/L.79), introduced by South Africa on behalf of the Non-Aligned Movement and China. Iran, joined by a sizable number of Islamic governments, but also Cuba, China, El Salvador, and Kenya, introduced a draft resolution titled "Human rights and cultural diversity" (A/C.3/54/L.62). All of these resolutions voiced essentially the same theme: human rights are culturally defined, and every country should promote human rights as its culture prescribes *free from interference by outside agencies.* Or, in the terminology of the draft resolution, on "respect for the principles of national sovereignty and non-interference in the internal affairs of states in their electoral processes," the United Nations,

> *Recalling*. . . the principle enshrined in Article 2, paragraph 7, of the Charter of the United Nations, which establishes that nothing contained in the Charter shall authorize the United Nations to intervene in matters which are essentially within the domestic jurisdiction of any State . . . . ,
>
> *Reiterates* that by virtue of the principle of equal rights and self-determination of peoples enshrined in the Charter of the United Nations, all peoples have the right, freely and without external interference, to determine their political status and pursue their economic, social and cultural development, and that every State has the duty to respect that right in accordance with the provisions of the Charter, [26]

Rather sizable, though entirely predictable, majorities adopted all of these resolutions. In favor: most of the Third World, most of the Islamic countries, a number of Asian countries, about half of the Latin American and Caribbean countries, and about half of the African countries, seventy-six altogether. Against: all of Europe, Russia, Japan, South Korea, Australia, New Zealand, and the United States, totaling fifty-seven countries.

From the other side came the draft resolution entitled "Strengthening the role of the United Nations in enhancing the effectiveness of the principle of periodic and genuine elections and the promotion of democratization" (A/C.3/54/L.83), introduced by the United States on behalf of a coalition largely composed of Western countries, but also including Russia, some African countries, and a few Asian states. The resolution endorsed the role of the United Nations in promoting democratization. It was adopted without dissent, but only after the initiatives assigned to the UN were greatly limited and after wording was inserted to underline that UN assistance in national

---

[26]A/54/605/Add .2, p. 50.

elections would be offered only upon the request of national governments. Even then, a fair number of governments abstained, including China, Cuba, North Korea, Malaysia, Singapore, Syria, and others.[27] The stylized debate over these "politically coded" resolutions was revealing to the extent that it defined the issues in contention and roughly divided the sides. As a rule, however, very little give-and-take occurred in these contexts because the outcomes were predictable, and most governments seemed inclined to reserve their attacks and defenses for more specific contexts.

There were many such contexts, and in this short presentation, we are able only to offer the flavor and flag the sensitivity of the clashes. The tone of the Third Committee's deliberations on human rights is readily grasped by comparing two keynoting interventions at the 54th General Assembly. Speaking specifically on the issue of East Timor, but more generally about the international community and the promotion of human rights, the representative for Australia observed, "It was reassuring to note that the international community was increasingly active in the promotion of human rights, particularly where it involved intervening across national borders." She went on to say that "human rights violations were no longer sheltered inside territories," and she continued that this "concept sometimes sat uneasily with notions of sovereignty and national interest." The United Nations, she urged, "should impress on States the idea that the adoption of policies that conformed with universally accepted human rights norms served . . . national interests."[28] Then, seemingly in direct rebuttal to the Australian peroration, the representative from China explained that it was the view of his government that "state sovereignty was the prerequisite for the protection of human rights . . . . Any interference in another country's internal affairs entailing the use or threat of force in order to change that country's social system or values . . . was a grave violation of the purposes and principles of the United Nations Charter and the fundamental norms of international law."

"Some countries were trying to dictate to others how they should behave," the Chinese delegate complained. This, he said, is not acceptable.[29] These Australian and Chinese positions could not have been farther apart.

Early on in their 1999 deliberations, the Third Committee received a report from Mary Robinson, the UN High Commissioner for Human Rights. In her presentation Ms. Robinson stressed the universality of human rights as codified in the conventions and commitments of the UN human rights regime. She dwelt largely on civil and political rights and urged the Third Committee to "consider human rights from a world perspective" and to work toward embedding "a culture of respect for human rights in the societies,

---

[27] Ibid., pp. 15–17.
[28] Note that quotations in our text from UN documents cited as "SR" are quotations from the summary record of debates and not quotations verbatim from actual speeches. In this instance, see A/C.3/54/SR.40, p. 4.
[29] A/C.3/54/SR.38, p. 9.

institutions and cultures of the planet."[30] The West and others who endorsed the universality of human rights defined as civil and political rights welcomed Robinson's report. However, the high commissioner was also attacked, by Libya, for example, whose representative argued that "certain states used human rights as a pretext to legitimize interference, often under the umbrella of the United Nations, in the internal affairs of other countries."[31] The Chinese delegate then wished to know "whether the High Commissioner viewed the protection of human rights and the need to respect the sovereignty of States as being complementary." He also wished to know "how her Office managed to maintain a balance between services it provided to States and the imperative to avoid interference in their internal affairs."[32] The Chinese government was also interested in where the money came from to fund Ms. Robinson's activities. Later in the debate over the high commissioner's report, the Cuban delegate let it be known that in his government's view "democracy and universality could be based only on true respect for the rights of nations to adopt the political, economic and social system which their peoples chose in a free and sovereign manner. "Interference and intervention," he continued, "were being disguised as 'humanitarian' action for the alleged protection of human rights [and] upholding the principles of national sovereignty, political independence, and non-interference internal affairs of other States was the only way for developing countries to counter attempts at intervention . . . by the major centers of power."[33]

Lest anyone conclude that the entire defense of national sovereignty and noninterference is emanating from Libya, China, Cuba, and others noted for their outspoken positions, the debates concerning the death penalty should provide a corrective. For some time the governments of the European Union, and the European Union collectively, have been attempting to build support for an international convention that would universally prohibit capital punishment. This issue appeared on the Third Committee's agenda at the 54th session of the General Assembly as draft resolution A/C.3/54/L.8/Rev.1: "The Question of the Death Penalty." As it had many times previously, this issue deeply divided the governments of the world. But the division was not about capital punishment as much as it was about the right of the international community to intervene into matters that states considered to be domestic affairs. Ambassador Kishore Mahbubani of Singapore framed the debate quite precisely when he explained to the Third Committee that "the question of the death penalty would be the defining issue of the current session." The debate, the ambassador said,

> was not about the merits of the death penalty, which was too complex an issue to be resolved in seven-minute speeches, no matter how passionate and morally

---

[30]A/C.3/54/SR.32, p. 2.
[31]Ibid., p. 4.
[32]Ibid., p. 6.
[33]A/C.3/54/SR.37, p. 6.

self-righteous they might be. Ultimately, it was for each society to determine the matter for itself . . . . The real issue was whether a small group of States should raise the question of the death penalty in a divisive manner, attempting to 'bludgeon' others in accepting their view . . . . [T]he move showed tremendous cultural and religious insensitivity.[34]

The draft resolution was introduced by the representative from Finland who announced that "the European Union was determined to oppose the death penalty with the aim of abolishing it, which would enhance human dignity and the progressive development of human rights."[35] Many delegations, again mostly Western ones, spoke in favor of the draft resolution. But the measure immediately generated heated debate. A Japanese intervention was rather mild, with the country's representative explaining that "a worldwide consensus on the abolishment of the death penalty did not exist" and that therefore his government would "oppose the draft resolution . . . submitted by Finland."[36] The reason that this worldwide consensus did not exist was that many governments resented the outside world telling them whether or not they could impose capital punishment. For example, the representative for Qatar intervened to say that "It was the sovereign right of States to enact their own laws without external interference, as provided in Article 2, paragraph 7, of the Charter of the United Nations."[37] The representative from Jamaica said essentially the same thing, reporting that her country "believed the imposition of that penalty was one to be decided by each country in consultation with its citizens."[38] Ambassador Lewis from Antigua and Barbuda, speaking on behalf of the countries of CARICOM, said that "small developing states had become members of the United Nations on the understanding that their sovereignty would be respected and their integrity preserved." It was thus particularly disturbing, the ambassador said, "that more powerful countries were seeking to use the institution to which they had entrusted the protection of their sovereignty as a tool to undermine their constitutions and national legislation."[39] The Philippine delegate explained that her country had in fact abolished the death penalty, but that the Philippines would oppose the Finnish resolution nonetheless because "it was unfair for some States to impose their will on others."[40] As would be expected, the Libyan government rejected the European initiative because it "violated the sovereign right of States and peoples to apply that form of punishment . . . in accordance with their laws."[41] On this issue even the U.S. government came rather outspokenly in public

---

[34]A/C.3/54/SR.30, p. 5.
[35]A/C.3/54/SR.29, p. 4.
[36]A/C.3/54/SR.30, p. 2.
[37]A/C.3/54/SR.29, p. 8.
[38]A/C.3/54/SR.35, p. 2.
[39]A/C.3/54/SR.42, p. 8.
[40]A/C.3/54/SR.31, p. 2.
[41]A/C.3/54/SR.29, p. 7.

defense of sovereignty. Speaking for his government, Ambassador Southwick explained that "the decision of many countries that had abolished capital punishment . . . deserved respect." But in the United States, he said, "an open and democratic process had led to different results."[42] After approximately a month of debating the "Question of the Death Penalty," the European Union withdrew its draft resolution.[43]

Many other issues on the Third Committee's agenda divided the political sides. For example, the European Union introduced a draft resolution titled "Human Rights Situation in the Islamic Republic of Iran," which followed the report of the secretary-general's Special Representative on the Situation of Human Rights in the Islamic Republic of Iran.[44] Both the report and the resolution took note of improvements in the protection of human rights in Iran, but they both also spoke of continuing abuses and the need for further improvement. The Iranian government rejected the criticisms, claiming that "the traditional sponsors of the draft resolution sought to perpetuate a confrontational approach."[45] Several other delegations came to the Iranian defense, some raising questions about monitoring by the UN. In response, the Jordanian delegate explained that the "international monitoring of human rights standards touched upon a sensitive issue relating to the principle of sovereignty of States." That principle, he said, "could not, however, be used to legitimize coercive treatment of human beings." Nevertheless, the Egyptian delegate who next took the floor affirmed that "human rights should not be used as tool to apply pressure on particular States or to interfere in their internal affairs." Libya too was predictably opposed to international monitoring, and upon taking the floor, the Libyan delegate said that his government would vote against the European-sponsored resolution on Iran because it ignored the state's "right to defend its official religion and enact legislation that was in keeping with the cultural and religious characteristics of its society."[46] During this same session there was also a classic locking of political horns between the United States and Sudan. Offering his government's view of the situation in Sudan regarding human rights, the delegate from the United States said that there "continued to be regular reports of slavery in Sudan," that "religious freedom was not respected," that "Christians and animists continued to be persecuted," and that "Christian leaders were arrested on spurious charges."[47] To this, the Sudanese delegate replied that "it was regrettable that certain countries . . . had decided to take upon themselves that task of defending human rights worldwide."[48]

---

[42]Ibid., p. 5.
[43]A/C.3/54/SR.50, p. 3.
[44]A/C.3/54/SR.46, p. 2.
[45]A/C.3/54/SR 52, p. 11.
[46]Ibid. [For Jordanian, Egyptian, and Libyan statements].
[47]A/C.3/54/SR.36, p. 7.
[48]Ibid., p. 12.

Within the United Nations, the debate over the continuing prerogatives and immunities of national sovereignty is real and intense. It appears not to be tending toward climax and certainly not toward compromise. It is surely jeopardizing the international human rights regime that the UN has put in place over several decades, although its more profound effects could be in exposing "the international community" as a myth, a fiction, or a synonym for "the West." To raise questions about the agency of the international community would be greatly to constrain the UN's capacity to act. Reflecting on these matters, one UN official among our interview respondents remarked that "if sovereignty continues to be used as a defense, the UN is going to have to scale down its programs."

The Political Situation Surrounding NGOs

Then there is also the question of NGO representation in UN governing bodies. In terms of the politics of national sovereignty at the United Nations, this is a somewhat different kind of issue because it involves tensions between the members of the UN and the international civil service much more than it involves difference among member governments. The NGO issue, however, is not completely different from the others discussed in this chapter because it centers in national governments' concerns about sovereignty. An edition of the UNA/USA's annual publication *A Global Agenda* makes clear that, "recent years have seen a backlash, calling into question whether governments intend to strengthen or roll back the UN's partnership with NGOs."[49] Whereas as little as a decade ago, nongovernmental humanitarian organizations were widely appreciated by national governments, these sentiments appear to be changing. This is for several reasons. For one thing, many more NGOs are operating transnationally today than there were even a decade ago. They are also more resourceful, certainly better financed, and both more obtrusive and intrusive than even a decade ago. More importantly, as this chapter has shown, there are among national governments today mounting and politicizing concerns about their sovereignty, *and NGOs challenge national sovereignty.* For example, these organizations tend to be looked on in many places as instruments that are forcing open societies that governments prefer to keep closed. NGOs are often the spearheads of Western-inspired, but UN-sponsored, campaigns promoting "democracy," "good governance," "civil society," and other political conditions that are today being demanded by the UN in exchange for development assistance. For many governments, accepting such political conditionality means adopting alien values and institutions and setting aside national sovereignty. Admitting NGOs means—almost literally—opening national political space to herds of Trojan horses full of Western liberal values. Some resentment here is perhaps understandable, and all the

---

[49] Tessitore and Woolfson, *A Global Agenda,* p. 171.

more so when political conditions are met but no development assistance follows.

But there is more. Within the United Nations, NGOs are increasingly perceived as seeking influence over the making of international public policy or, in UN terminology, "wanting a seat at the table." This in the estimation of not a few member governments means changing the UN from an intergovernmental organization into some other kind of organization where sovereignty accords no particular distinction or exclusive privilege. The UN Secretariat, moreover, is seen as encouraging the influence of NGOs, inviting them to the table in effect, and relying on them for policy advice at headquarters as much as for the implementation of policies in the field. The rhetoric of "partnerships," "compacts with civil society," "building international civil society" "managing transnational networks," and the like, pouring forth from the Office of the Secretary-General, from the upper echelons of the UNDP, and elsewhere in the House does little to mitigate national governments' apprehensions about the growing influence of NGOs at the policy table. Converting these slogans into programmes, like the secretary-general's Global Compact or the variety of other undertakings aimed at "partnerships" with civil society adds to the discomfort of many national governments. When some of these programs operate by circumventing national governments, discomfort readily becomes displeasure.

But there is still more. Governments wary about losing their privileges in international policy making to intruding NGOs are also concerned about NGOs operating within their own countries. Because of their contact with publics, and the influence that can accompany their charitable and technical activities, transnational NGOs are able to influence national policies. Many do so, albeit usually within the bounds of the law in host countries, and this tends to happen as pervasively in industrialized countries as in developing ones. Governments, therefore, see themselves politically hemmed between NGOs that are able to press their agendas both within the UN and within host countries. For their part, the leaders of the NGO community frequently contribute to governments' alienation by announcing far and wide that national sovereignty is the major obstacle to solving global problems and that delinquent governments ought to be denied their sovereign sanctuaries.

Hard evidence concerning the backlash against NGOs is rather difficult to come by, partly because resentment about the activities of the NGOs is much more an attitude than a pattern of documented behavior. In addition, there are often discrepancies between governments' public behavior toward NGOs and their private preferences. This situation was emphasized during an interview with a Third World diplomat. "Most governments have objections to the increasing influence of NGOs," the respondent said, "but many governments are constrained by the fact that NGOs are able to pressure them from inside their own countries." This diplomat went on to explain that the "industrialized countries have their hands tied" too because most NGOs come from these countries, and "a good many could make life difficult for national governments." As concerns developing countries, this diplomat continued,

> The Egyptian government is no great supporter of NGO influence, yet they must be very careful because NGOs are very active in Egypt. India and Pakistan hate NGOs! But they can't speak loudly or publicly against them since the NGOs are able to exert considerable pressure in these countries. What the Indian and Pakistan governments say in private about NGOs is quite different from what they say publicly.

There is nevertheless cumulating evidence of NGOs being closed out of international conferences like the Vienna Conference on Human Rights, or restricted in numbers as in preparations for the follow-up to the 1995 Women's Conference in Beijing, or in access as in the NGOs' failure to gain a formal relationship with the General Assembly. Other episodes also evidence the growing annoyance that national governments are displaying toward NGOs within the UN system. For example, in her piece titled "Reality Check: Human Rights NGOs Confront Governments at the UN," Felice Gaer, herself a member of the NGO community, cites a number of instances of tension between national governments and NGOs over questions of sovereign prerogative.[50] In one episode, for example, the UN Secretariat servicing the Vienna Conference encouraged governments to adopt a document expressing appreciation for the work of NGOs in the field of human rights. Here, a number of governments specifically requested that "monitoring" be omitted from the list of appreciated NGO activities because monitoring compliance with human rights standards was in some quarters not widely appreciated. Gaer also reports that the government of Bangladesh insisted that the word "tribute" be dropped from the document because to pay tribute to the NGOs was uncalled for.[51] National governments on the NGO Committee of the UN's Economic and Social Council have of late become increasingly hesitant in accrediting new NGOs and increasingly willing to withdraw existing accreditations.

Our interviews at the UN were especially revealing concerning the NGO question. Elaborating on the notion that the NGOs are instruments for imposing political conditionality and conformity with Western standards of "good governance," one Middle Eastern ambassador told us that the most active NGOs operate in areas like human rights, and most of these operate by opposing governments. "Governments," he said, "are rather upset about this transnational phenomenon." Non-Western governments, he continued, are also upset about Western governments encouraging the NGOs in their oppositional activities in

---

[50]Felice Gaer, "Reality Check: Human Rights NGOs Confront Governments at the UN," in *NGOs, the UN and Global Governance*, Thomas G. Weiss and Leon Gordenker, eds. (Boulder, Colo.: Lynne Rienner, 1996), pp. 51–66.
[51]Ibid., p. 65.

other countries. "They get lots of doses of human rights, civil society, good governance, and democracy but less and less resources to implement changes." A UN official who monitors NGO relations with the UN said much the same thing: "The West is rather aggressively imposing political conditionalities . . . to democratize, to liberalize economy and society. It is a governance language that calls for the opening of the private sector. It's an opening to the activities of the NGOs." This official went on to explain that the governments that may not object to the services that NGOs perform nevertheless "resent pressures to open up societies, to liberalize, and so forth."

The issue of the growing influence of NGOs in UN policy making was forcefully raised during an interview with a Latin American delegate. "Now there is a real confrontation among governments about NGO participation," this diplomat said. What governments are resisting, she explained, is admitting NGOs into intergovernmental decision making. "These are realms reserved for governments and governments don't want NGOs there. Earlier the participation of NGOs was no big deal . . . . But today they clearly want access to policy-making . . . and governments are resisting. The Cubans are livid about this!" When we posed the question about cooperation between the United Nations and the NGOs, one UN official acknowledged that "the secretary-general is using NGOs to further his agenda and bilateral donors are using NGOs to circumvent governments they don't want to deal with." But, this official said, "There is still considerable reluctance to give the NGOs any direct access to international decision making." Another respondent noted that the cooperation between the UN Secretariat and the NGO community has "at the very least created some tensions between the member states and the UN agencies."

One of our respondents volunteered that today the NGOs were actually exerting less influence over UN policies and processes than was once the case because governments are increasingly sensitive about their growing influence. This may well be the case, although we doubt it. What is more certain is that as the influence of NGOs grows, so too will the resistance of governments, particularly within the UN. From all that we have been able to observe, the NGO community remains set upon finding a seat at the UN policy-making table because the NGO leadership is convinced that it has something important to offer. But national governments remain determined to keep the United Nations an exclusive association of sovereign states. Such an incompatibility of views and aspirations neither bodes well for the UN nor the world.

NATIONAL SOVEREIGNTY AT THE UNITED NATIONS

What do debates discussed here tell us about challenges to sovereignty at the United Nations? Is the UN a bastion for protecting the sovereign privileges of member states or an institutional mechanism that is eroding them? This is not an easy question to answer because the ultimate outcomes of the confrontation will be dialectical, and the form of the synthesis is as yet unclear.

Stepping back analytically from the highly politicized fray is revealing, however, in a number of ways. For one thing, when a national delegate told us that sovereignty is a "phony issue," he was correct in one important sense. More important than *whether* UN member states are sensitive about their national sovereignty are the questions of *why*, and *why now* in the post–Cold War era. From all that we have been able to discern, the discourse of the defenders of national sovereignty, replete with the vocabulary of "noninterference," "nonintervention," "domestic affairs," "internal matters" "cultural integrity," and the like, is in considerable measure a coded protest against perceived—and unwelcome—Westernization, liberalization, cultural globalization, Americanization, and American hegemonism. To assert national sovereignty in UN settings is to signal rather deep displeasure with, and anxiety over, the extensive diffusion of Western cultural, and particularly political-cultural, values and institutions. Such diffusion has certainly accelerated in the post–Cold War world. So too, therefore, have responses, reactions, and resentments. We expect that in issue-areas where cultural differences are breeding political reactions, as, for example, over questions of human rights, ideological confrontations coded as questions of sovereignty will predictably escalate in the UN. These may well cripple the organization in some policy areas in the future, much as East–West ideological differences crippled the UN regarding security issues in the past.

The present-day debates over questions of national sovereignty are also raising serious questions about the meaning and/or identity of "the international community." Consensus by the international community can move normative mountains and alter the structural nature of international politics by redefining the principles that guide collective international action, as the case of decolonization demonstrated. "The international community" is of course a myth, but at least for much of the decade of the 1990s (and perhaps before that) it was a useful myth. It identified, and to a considerable extent legitimated, the collective international action in the first Gulf War, early on in the Balkans, and elsewhere. Practically speaking, however, "the international community" was the combined, collective, and consensual will of the UN Security Council or at least the will of the Security Council's Five Permanent Members. In the immediate aftermath of the Cold War, this "international community" was able to act. It acted, and its actions were at least abided by much of the rest of world. But who, today, is "the international community"? Who today is the "international community" that may legitimately intervene, uninvited, into the internal affairs of countries even for purposes of protecting peoples against atrocious behavior on the part of their governments? Who today is the "international community" that may legitimately establish, monitor, and enforce standards of civilized behavior acknowledged almost everywhere? The debates over sovereignty detailed here suggest that there is little consensus among governments that might contribute to redefining these central concepts crucial to global governance. Although the vast majority of resolutions in the General Assembly, in its committees, and even in the Security Council are adopted by consensus, there are a significant number that rather consistently divide the governments of the world into a bare majority and a huge minority that confound consensus and undermine the myth of "the international community." These very close votes also suggest that it is not only the radicals like Cuba and the pariahs like North Korea that are today questioning the myth of the "international community." The politics surrounding issues of national sovereignty are then in some measure about the continuing efficacy of the myth of "the international community." If there is no longer an identifiable and acceptable "international community," but instead an increasingly identity-defensive cluster of national communities at the UN, collective action becomes much more difficult, and as the UN official cited earlier concluded, "The UN is going to have to scale down its programs." Such politics of identity are not new to the UN, but with the politicization of culture in the postcolonial and post–Cold War world, they may be becoming more central to the organization's functioning and more determinative regarding its future.

Then again, issues of identity, coded as questions of sovereignty, may have little to do with the UN's future. Because issue-areas tend to overlap and because discourses entwine, it is difficult, and somewhat artificial, to separate UN concerns into categories like political affairs, social affairs, economic affairs, cultural affairs, and the like. Nevertheless, it is the case that economic discourses are different, and the significance of sovereignty issues is different within economic contexts. In UN shorthand, "New York" and "Geneva" operate in different discursive worlds. "UN New York" is a world of *political* discourse kept in motion by the activities of the Security Council and the General Assembly, whereas "UN Geneva" is a world of *political-economic* discourse animated by the UN's Geneva-based specialized agencies. The world we examined in this chapter is mostly the "New York" world. How central or meaningful it is for the UN overall is, frankly, very difficult to discern, especially since New York–based and Geneva-based agents typically characterize each other as being "out of touch."

Globalization is a fact of economic life in the twenty-first century, and along with integrating the world into a single extensive market comes the recognition that the only thing that enforcing sovereignty can do is to isolate states from participation. Some might consider this desirable, but most see the benefits of participation in the global market outweighing the costs. Privileging sovereignty, some argue, is not necessarily a formula for economic achievement in a globalizing world. Indeed, it could be a principal obstacle achievement. Accepting economic interdependence is the correlate of participating in the global market, and it implies largely erasing the distinction between domestic and international macro- as well as microeconomic thinking, planning, and policy making. Within international networks of economic interdependence, national sovereignty tends to lose its meaning because it loses its utility.

Nevertheless, claims of sovereign privilege by member states still echo through trade, finance, and development debates—even in Geneva. Sometimes the target of concern is national vulnerability to unpredictable economic shocks and crises that appear to be aspects of globalization and which bring with them social dislocation and economic and political instability. Concern is also expressed over the loss of sovereignty in the form of lessening control over domestic resources and policies and, in the case of developing countries, having their economic policy making transferred de facto to the Bretton Woods institutions and much of the policy implementation transferred to international NGOs operating within their borders. Yet in the context of striving to manage economic interdependence in the interest of growth, sustainability, and social justice, even the most dogged efforts to protect sovereign privileges may turn out to be but a dance of dinosaurs. Protectionism these days stifles trade, investment, and development. Ultimately, assertions and contentions about sovereignty may prove be as irrelevant at the United Nations as they are in the international economic relations of a globalizing world. One of our respondents said it better than we could ourselves when he remarked that "in most realms of human affairs today—economics, environmental matters, culture, etc.—national sovereignty is largely irrelevant, as everything cuts across and penetrates national borders." But he nevertheless emphasized that, "in political affairs sovereignty is still invoked, insisted upon, asserted and contested" *at the UN*, which turns out to be sovereignty's last bastion.

CHAPTER 5

In Search of Leadership

Very little happens in multilateral diplomatic contexts unless a national government, a coalition, occasionally even an individual, takes the initiative and steps forward to lead. Yet cynicism about the prospects for exercising leadership via diplomacy abound. Australian diplomat Richard Woolcott once remarked that "apart from a good mind, the two most important assets for a United Nations diplomat are a good tailor and a strong liver."[1] Despite the endless and seemingly inconclusive negotiations that recur in New York, Geneva, and throughout the United Nations system, in spite of the soporific discourse that characterizes UN debates, and irrespective of the countless official reports prolifically produced and seldom read, multilateral diplomacy does produce international action. Results, however, follow from the exercise of leadership. The United Nations acts when somebody leads, but it drifts and fails when nobody leads.

All governance requires leadership for success, and this is no less true in the international context. Leadership involves providing vision, direction, and an effective marshaling of resources to take action. Success is often understood to be the counterpart or outcome of leadership, but it is important to note that leadership does not always result in successful outcomes because the creation of new regimes, laws, and programs within international institutions follows from the interplay of numerous elements in addition to effective leadership.[2]

---

[1]Cited in "Thoughts on the Business of Life," *Forbes*, January 20, 2003, p. 120.
[2]Oran Young, "Political Leadership and Regime Formation: On the Development of Institutions in International Society," *International Organization*, 45 (1991): 281–308.

Nonetheless, leadership remains a necessary condition for organizational action, and because of peculiarities of the UN organization, exercising leadership constitutes a rather formidable challenge.

Leading an organization, for example, requires fundamental consensus about the mission of the organization, and this is one reason why it is so difficult to lead within the UN where, realistically speaking, such consensus does not exist. Different member states harbor varying notions concerning the purposes of the United Nations: most would certainly assign different priorities to the organization's purposes, and almost every member government would agree that the UN is first and foremost an instrument for promoting national interests which vary enormously. For most member governments in some issue-areas, and for some in all issue-areas, arriving at international agreements and engaging in collective action are not matters of high priority in national foreign policy so that cooperating within the UN is of marginal concern. This definitely complicates any attempts to promote collective behavior in the international sphere that goes beyond symbolic resolutions and statements expressing high-minded sentiments. Everything, moreover, is further complicated by varying cultures of negotiation reflected in 192 member states as well as in the aspirations and interventions of the thousands of NGOs.[3]

Where leadership within the UN actually resides is also complicated. One can point to formal *roles* that are understood to be leadership positions within the organization, as for example, the secretary-general, the permanent five members of the Security Council, the president of the General Assembly, and the chairs of the Assembly's main committees and similar chartered offices. But influence flowing from these roles varies enormously through time and across issues and incumbent personalities. In recent years, moreover, and save perhaps in the case of the secretary-general, the declining effectiveness of role holders has reflected the declining legitimacy or status of the roles themselves.

Leadership within the United Nations is more closely associated with the attributes of leaders than with formal roles or offices. The UN, for example, is comprised of member states that are sovereign equals according to international law but vary rather dramatically in the international distribution of power. These structural factors condition the exercise of leadership inasmuch as power, either national or coalitional, tends to be an important attribute of leadership. This is so if for no other reason than the powerful control the resources that permit the UN to act, and these same resources fashioned into carrots and sticks contribute importantly to diplomatic persuasiveness. Various qualities of what some have called "soft power" are also attributes of multilateral leadership at the UN. Governments' reputations for "international community mindedness" invite deference, capturing the "moral high

---

[3]See Chester A. Crocker, Fen Osler Hampson, and Pamela Aall, eds., *Turbulent Peace: The Challenges of Managing International Conflict* (Washington, D.C.: United States Institute for Peace, 2001).

ground" regarding issues of legality and humanity attracts support, and the personal styles, eloquence, depth of experience, and intellectual qualities of particular diplomats also count.

There are also different kinds of leadership. In UN affairs is it useful to distinguish among structural, entrepreneurial, and intellectual leadership. *Structural leadership*, as noted, has to do with power, and it accrues in the UN to representatives of leading powers or blocs. Exercising *entrepreneurial leadership* involves making use of negotiating skills, and capitalizing on soft power attributes to bring conflicting parties together by brokering difficult compromises or otherwise facilitating diplomatic deals. Over the decades of the UN's functioning, entrepreneurial power has accrued rather disproportionately to certain middle powers; Canada, Sweden, Australia, India, Brazil and Mexico for example, are noted for their skilled multilateral diplomacy and respected for their commitments to international cooperation. *Intellectual leadership* has to do with promoting visions and ideas, farsightedness and foresightedness, and designs, plans, and strategies for collective action by the international community. In the United Nations, such leadership has intermittently accrued to the executive heads of agencies, to certain secretaries-general, and to particular individuals or special committees and commissions. Neither of course has the UN been immune to or isolated from intellectual, philosophical, and ideological currents swirling about it in the global environment so that intellectual leadership within the UN sometimes comes from outside the UN.

Leadership requires followership. This mirror component of leadership is less easy to describe or define, although within the UN it is manifestly important. Consent, support, and commitment are key components of followership. Absent these, the exercise of leadership is impossible. Followership is naturally to be accounted for by qualities and attributes of leaders that others respect, but this is not the end of the explanation. In the UN today, identity—historical, cultural, religious, regional, and socioeconomic—seems increasingly to determine who is willing to follow whom. In addition, just as global issues like combating terrorism, stemming environmental degradation, or promoting economic openness are recruiting some especially concerned or affected states into leadership roles, like-mindedness or identities of concern are mobilizing followers. Those who are today opting to lead against American hegemony can count on scores of followers. And naturally, promises of economic and political rewards continue to attach followers to leaders, often producing strange patron–client relationships. Selling support within the UN for economic or political compensation outside the UN is not uncommon.

WHO IS LEADING AT THE UN TODAY?

The prognosis for leadership within the UN in the early twenty-first century is mixed at best. In the new millennium, the long-term implications for UN multilateralism of structural changes in world politics are increasingly manifest.

Structurally, the rather awesome military, economic, and cultural power of the United States, the "only remaining superpower," ought to cast that country as leader of the international community and mentor of multilateral affairs. Yet the United States remains rather indifferent to the UN, a proclivity already in evidence under the Clinton administration and later greatly amplified under the administration of George W. Bush. Preferences for unilateral action combined with ambivalence about multilateralism and a certain amount of distrust regarding the UN have long been signal characteristics of U.S. foreign policy. Onetime U.S. ambassador to the UN, Daniel Patrick Moynihan, described the world organization as a "dangerous place," and succeeding generations of officials and legislators have preserved the perception.[4] Therefore, although power qualifies the United States to lead at the UN and even as this power bestows considerable influence, proclivity and policy render "the only remaining superpower" a reluctant multilateral leader.

This is in stark contrast to the emergent European Union (EU) whose members are individually and collectively committed to the UN and to multilateralism. Leaders of the European Union understand that the United Nations will be the prime setting for the expression and exertion of whatever the collective political and economic power of twenty-five affluent countries amounts to. The EU therefore wants to lead at the UN. At the turn of the twenty-first century, however, the EU remains handicapped by its inchoate common foreign and security policy. Europeans also remained preoccupied with building "Europe," which means giving much higher priority to regional over global concerns.[5] Notably, the two main candidates for structural leadership within the UN, the reluctant United States and the aspiring European Union, have divergent views regarding the organization. The United States tends to embrace a Westphalian notion of the organization as a forum for the pursuit of national interests, whereas the EU has embraced a view of the UN that casts the organization as guarantor of order and conscience of the world community. Some say, however, that these two "visions" of the UN both smack of a Western determination to preserve long-standing hegemony. Meanwhile, the Group of 77 (G-77) and the nonaligned movement (NAM) as alternative aspirants within the UN collectively command very little structural power, which prevents them from providing leadership within the organization or from successfully challenging Western hegemony more generally.

This new geopolitical structure in world affairs constrains entrepreneurial and intellectual leadership in the context of UN multilateralism. The traditional middle powers have been marginalized in the post–Cold War environment. This is in large part because of the structural changes that have taken place with the EU assuming a more important role within the UN.

---

[4]Daniel P. Moynihan, *A Dangerous Place* (Boston: Little, Brown, 1978).
[5]The EU signaled its intention to promote "effective multilateralism" in its first ever European Security Strategy. See *A Secure Europe in a Better World* (Brussels: Secretariat of the Council of the European Union, 2003).

Several middle powers that once provided entrepreneurial leadership are now part of the structural power bloc of the European Union. Although the ranks of the middle powers have broadened to include newer middle powers such as India, Brazil, and others, this ad hoc arrangement of opportunistic middle power entrepreneurialism is not necessarily as good for the institution as it is for the occasional activist middle power. NGOs have become much more involved in multilateral processes in the post–Cold War environment, and they can provide entrepreneurial leadership, but their participation in the UN context is contested by many of the member states, thus blunting their influence.

By contrast, intellectual leadership has been abundant in the post–Cold War environment. The ideas and strategies that have emerged from the UN since the Cold War's end have contributed to shaping an understanding of global governance, to defining challenges to collective action, and to promoting multilateral responses. UN-fostered thinking and planning about sustainable development, humanitarian intervention, and human security are perhaps the most notable, but there are many others.[6] The many commissions and high-level panels convened to explore ideas about global challenges and global governance have been impressive, and their success is measured in how those ideas have been translated into ways that scholars, practitioners, and others think and talk about contemporary international relations. However, the exercise of intellectual leadership, often by Secretariat officials rather than representatives of member states, is problematic because it has been viewed by many non-Western member states as reinforcing Western hegemony over global governance. The intellectual leadership attempted by Secretary-General Kofi Annan to promote democratization or to support shifting norms of intervention to protect human rights has been supported by the structural leadership of the organization, that is, Americans and Europeans, but it has also been resisted by non-Western member states. By the same token, Secretariat-generated ideas concerning sustainable development have not been altogether appreciated by some Western governments, most notably the United States.

STRUCTURAL LEADERSHIP

There are today significant challenges to effective structural leadership at the UN. As noted, the United States has reverted to ambivalence about UN multilateralism. The EU is committed to effective multilateralism, but differences in interest and vision among its members deny it a meaningful common foreign policy, and the EU's coordinative processes make it an inflexible and slow

---

[6]See, for example, the most recent of these: *In Larger Freedom: Towards Development, Security and Human Rights for All*, Report of the Secretary-General, A/59/2005, March 21, 2005; *A More Secure World: Our Shared Responsibility*, Report of the Secretary-General's High-Level Panel on Threats, Challenges and Change, A/59/565, December 2, 2004; *The Responsibility to Protect: Report of the International Commission on Intervention and State Sovereignty* (Ottawa, Ont.: International Development Research Centre, December 2001).

interlocutor. The Group of 77 developing states as well as the Non-Aligned Movement remain disparate, dislocated, collectively weak, and ineligible for structural leadership. Structural power within the international system is not producing structural leadership within the UN today.

The end of the Cold War was accompanied by high expectations that the United Nations would finally function as envisioned after the paralysis of the superpower standoff. First, Soviet leader Mikhail Gorbachev announced his policy of "new thinking" that explicitly embraced multilateralism via a revitalized UN. Then American president George Herbert Walker Bush envisioned a new world order in which the UN would be an integral part. As the Cold War wound down, analysts and onlookers were persuaded that the structure of the international system would allow for an empowered UN to act.[7] It is now quite clear that the "collective leadership" by the Permanent Five (P-5) that characterized Security Council operations in the immediate aftermath of the Cold War is long gone. "P-5 cooperation doesn't exist on most subjects dealt with by the council," a French official explained in an interview. The short-lived era of collectively governing the "new world order" lasted through the Gulf War; but then gradually transformed during the debates over sanctioning Saddam Hussein, acting in Bosnia, and dealing with Slobodan Milosevic over Kosovo into a new era of bargaining aimed as much at promoting national interests as at buttressing world order. The dynamics of structural leadership within the General Assembly are even less clear because as a counterpoint to the Security Council, the assembly has been marginalized. One thing on which almost all member governments agree is that happenings in the General Assembly are of less and less consequence.

American Unilateralism

The *New York Times* reported in 2004 that spirits at the UN were rebounding after a year of bruising abuse heaped on the organization by American officials in the debates surrounding the war in Iraq.[8] A reluctant UN, after being pointedly limited to a consultative role in the aftermath of the Iraq war, was then asked by Washington to play a "vital" and central role in the rebuilding process. This whipsaw effect is a consequence of the complicated relationship between the United States and the UN. "Like any other country," Singapore's ambassador to the UN, Kishore Mahbubani, has said, "the U.S. will handle the UN for its national interests. The UN's problem is that the U.S. is not like any

---

[7]These aspirations were analyzed in our earlier reports on the UN. See Donald J. Puchala and Roger A. Coate, *The State of the United Nations, 1988*, Reports and Papers, No. 2, Academic Council on the United Nations System, 1988; and Donald J. Puchala and Roger A. Coate, *The Challenge of Relevance: The United Nations in a Changing World Environment*, Reports and Papers, Academic Council on the United Nations System, 1989.

[8]Warren Hoge, "After a Hard Year, Signs of Rebounding Spirits at the U.N.," *New York Times*, March 8, 2004.

other country."[9] Ambassador Mahbubani explained that the UN was designed to function with two or more great powers, but the reality is that we live in a unipolar world. Although this has been more or less true since the end of the Cold War, the impact of a unipolar world on the exercise of structural leadership within and without the UN is becoming ever clearer.

The reality of the multidimensional power of the United States today and the immense gap in capabilities between the United States and even the second-ranked powers affects the United Nations in profound ways. The UN largely remains an American-controlled organization, as it has been for the last half century, with the difference being that at present this control is more compelling than ever before. Almost everything the UN does or does not do is greatly conditioned by the will, whims, and resources of the United States. The deference to American power exhibited, grudgingly or otherwise, throughout the House and among the missions is rather remarkable. As one European diplomat explained when discussing the organization of peace-keeping, few operations are likely to move ahead without financial contributions from Washington, so that even after the U.S. administration approves a mandate, "We must simply sit and wait until Congress decides on the money." A similar remark could have been made in reference to many UN programmes. Politically, moreover, the United States looms centrally and massively on the Security Council, and little that is actionable can emerge from the General Assembly or any other organ unless it garners Washington's approval. "Nothing can be done without the concurrence of the United States," a French diplomat acknowledged. "It reflects the reality of the world."

The commonplace notion that the United States has abandoned the UN is wrong. As one diplomat remarked, "The U.S. has not disengaged; it is present and one cannot ignore that." This is precisely the problem. The United States is obtrusively present at the UN, but it is offering little leadership. Although U.S. influence over the operations of the UN is pervasive because of American power, Washington's active involvement in UN affairs is highly selective, episodic, and intermittent. The United States involves itself in the UN only when it deems such involvement to be in its immediate national interest. The American government tends to look on the UN as an instrument of American foreign policy, but from Washington's perspective it is only one of many instruments available. It uses this instrument as it sees fit as, for example, as a police force and welfare agency in Haiti, as a whipping boy to deflect criticism from failures in Somalia, as a battering ram during the period of international sanctions on Iraq, as a cleanup crew in Kosovo, and, more recently, as a pressure valve to lessen Africa's clamoring for greater international attention. At other times, the United States may choose to thwart UN action, as in Rwanda, or to steer clear of the organization altogether, as in its turn to mobilizing NATO and disregarding the Security Council for the

---

[9]Ibid.

bombing of Kosovo. When in the spring of 2003 the UN Security Council would not mandate an invasion of Iraq and the unseating of the Saddam Hussein regime, the United States moved against Iraq anyway. "The UN is a club that if you play it properly it will reinforce your own interests," a British diplomat noted. "Yet it seems that the U.S. does not often view things this way . . . . The U.S. position creates a fundamental schism in that it tends to be unilateral yet other members try to respond to it multilaterally and want the U.S. to respond to their responses multilaterally. The resulting situation is one of confusion and uncertainty among the members."

The view of U.S. behavior in the UN prevalent within the New York diplomatic community is critical. Virtually no one interviewed, save perhaps some officials within the U.S. mission, was able to find much satisfaction in what the United States is doing in and to the United Nations. To be sure, American statesmanship at the UN has registered accomplishments that others appreciate, as for example with Washington's coalition building at the time of the Gulf War, the prosecution of the war itself, the organization of the peacekeeping operation in East Timor, and the efforts to build international will for intervention into the Darfur region of Sudan. The United States can and does act via the UN in the interest of the international community when it chooses to do so. But in the eyes of many at the UN, Washington makes such choices all too infrequently and almost never out of concern for the larger international community.

Criticism of the United States voiced during interviews came from several different directions. "Others want us to show up and to participate, to pay attention, to lead, and we are not perceived as doing that," one U.S. official said during an interview in the spring of 2000. Regarding U.S. behavior in the UN, what many perceived during the Clinton administration was the U.S. government blaming the UN for American casualties in Somalia that actually resulted from unilateral decisions made in Washington, the U.S. government abetting genocide by urging the UN out of Rwanda when it should have been going in with force, the White House issuing Presidential Decision Directive 25 (PDD-25) that all but precluded continued U.S. participation in UN peacekeeping, and the U.S. government rather inelegantly and unabashedly twisting diplomatic arms to get U.S. financial obligations to the UN reduced. The succeeding George W. Bush administration was certainly no kinder to the UN, as reflected in Washington's campaign to undermine the International Criminal Court that was otherwise supported by most of the UN membership, the U.S. government's lambasting of UN weapons inspectors in Iraq, and, most critically, Washington's rejection of the Security Council's authority that resulted in the unilateral U.S. decision to invade Iraq. George Bush's 2005 appointment of John Bolton, a harsh and outspoken critic of the UN, as U.S. ambassador was interpreted by much of the world as a gesture of dismay directed at the world organization. Many, therefore, look on the United States much more as a spoiler than as a leader in UN affairs.

But criticism is also voiced by some who do perceive the U.S. to be leading, but either leading in the wrong direction or dominating in its own hegemonic interest. Much of this criticism, although by no means all, comes from
diplomats associated with member states of the Group of 77 or the NAM,
who perceive the United States to be foisting institutions and values on the
rest of the world, particularly concerning economic liberalism and narrowly
conceived democratization. "The U.S. is using the organization for its own
purposes and interests, which are not necessarily those of the international
community," one Latin American diplomat reported, and "it frequently leads
in directions that others don't want to go." The main problem, a UN Secretariat official concluded, is that "the UN has to get out of the U.S. embrace.
The U.S. is largely running the organization. It has to become the organization
of its members, not the tool of one of its members." This is not necessarily
the conclusion of some American allies and friends who would prefer
enlightened leadership coming from the United States, ideally combined
with multilateral sensitivity, but simply do not see this coming from Washington today. Such sentiments were reflected in the observations of an East
European diplomat, who in a 2002 interview said, "The UN can be an important instrument for shaping the world in the way that the U.S. would like.
But it has to be used sensitively and consistently. Using it abusively and intermittently is harmful to U.S. interests and goals. Unilateralism mobilizes
opposition even among those who might agree with the goals and substance
of what the U.S. seeks."

The United States is the only remaining superpower. Its power will continue to jolt and jar the UN, especially when the organization is pushed by its
members or pulled by its officials in directions objectionable to Washington.
The American foreign policy tradition and, above all, the nation's domestic
politics—under Republican and Democratic administrations alike in the
post–Cold War era—point to continuing recourse to unilateralism. At times
this unilateralism will be played out within the UN, at times in obliviousness to
the UN. Circumstances at the UN in 2003 prior to the invasion of Iraq were
seen by many in the United States at the time to underline the irrelevance of
an organization that refused to enforce its own resolutions. The bloody aftermath and the great difficulty encountered by U.S.-led forces in reestablishing
peace and order in Iraq may prompt American rethinking about the usefulness of UN multilateralism. The most likely prospect, however, is continued
American indifference to the UN and ambivalence about multilateralism.
When in the summer of 2005 a diplomat at the U.S. mission was asked
whether the United States would continue to lead in the UN, he replied in
puzzled fashion, "This is an interesting question; I really hadn't thought about
it." Thus for the UN in the early twenty-first century, the United States will
likely remain a part of the problem, that is, a potentially disruptive force to be
managed, rather than an agent of cooperation and international community
mindedness. Working around American international eccentricities long has
been part of the UN political process. This will have to continue.

The European Union and "Effective Multilateralism"

If the United States is the "bad cop" of Western hegemony, then the European Union is most certainly the "good cop." In an EU-issued report titled *The Enlarging European Union at the United Nations*, the EU's ambitions and position within the UN are explained.[10] The report emphasizes that the EU "has grown into a significant world actor," is "the biggest trading entity in the world," and the "world's largest provider of overseas development assistance." The report says further that "Together, the EU-25 comprises more than one eighth of all votes in the United Nations General Assembly" and EU member states "account at present for a third of the UN Security Council's membership." Notably, too, EU member states together are the largest financial contributor to the UN system. "At present, the EU-25 pay 38 percent of the UN's regular budget, more than two fifths of UN peacekeeping operations, and around half of all UN Member States' contributions to UN funds and programmes." The EU, then, certainly has presence at the UN.

But does the EU also have the capacity to exercise structural leadership? The diplomatic imbroglio that played out in the UN Security Council in February and March 2003 led many observers to conclude that divisions over Iraq had not only deeply damaged the transatlantic relationship but also poisoned relations among Europeans themselves. As the French and Germans took a firm stand against the use of military force to disarm Iraq, Britain, Spain, and several "new" European states, including the Vilnius group that was at the time largely comprised of EU applicants from Eastern Europe, supported U.S. calls for precisely such action. This prompted an angry French president Jacques Chirac publicly to scold the Central and East European applicants to the EU by rather undiplomatically advising them that they were being ungrateful and should know when to hold their tongues. Such a highly publicized display of EU disunity on the world stage and within the UN Security Council suggested that there was no common foreign policy for the EU within the UN.

But, in fact, this very high-profile European divide over Iraq flies in the face of strong and steadily growing EU unity within the UN since the early 1990s. Although consultations among the members of the European Community at the UN have taken place for decades, the EU effort to speak with one voice within the world organization really emerged with the decision to pursue a common foreign and security policy that was confirmed by the Maastricht Treaty in 1993. Maastricht and subsequent treaties have obliged EU member states to coordinate to the greatest extent possible at the UN, without undermining the special responsibilities of France and the United Kingdom in the Security Council. That is, although the member state holding the rotating EU

---

[10]*The Enlarging European Union at the United Nations: Making Multilateralism Matter* (Luxembourg: Office for Official Publications of the European Communities, 2004).

presidency frequently speaks on behalf of the union in the Security Council, the French and British as permanent members are not obliged to defer to the EU position (although they often do). Statements presented to the Security Council on behalf of the EU increased from fifteen in 1990 to eighty-six in 2000. Otherwise, the EU voice is louder, stronger, and more consistent in the General Assembly where there is a common EU position on almost all important issues. Voting cohesion among the members of the EU on roll-call votes in the General Assembly increased from 53 percent in 1990 to 83 percent in 1999, even as the EU grew from twelve to fifteen members over that period.[11] The European Union, then, is emerging as an actor in its own right at the UN.

The European Commission, the executive arm of the EU, has delegations in New York and Geneva, and it represents members collectively in areas in which it has competence, for example, in matters of trade. The EU is itself not a member of the UN, but internal EU negotiations, which are intense and continuous during UN sessions, tend to lock members into common positions across most of the UN agenda. It is through these common positions that the EU registers its presence and its influence in UN affairs. Individual EU member states are free to speak on whatever issue they like, but they may not deviate from commonly agreed EU positions.

Interviews in the UN with both EU and non-EU ambassadors underline that the EU is recognized among the UN membership as a notable force in multilateral diplomacy. A prominent Iranian diplomat, for example, remarked that the UN is increasingly influenced by the Europeans "because the EU attaches more importance to the UN [than the United States]. There is very seldom an issue that the EU is attached to, where the EU does not get its way." Similarly, a Singaporean official noted that the EU is "particularly united within the General Assembly, and when they get the Latin Americans to come along, they are a strong bloc."

According to another EU report titled the *European Security Strategy*, the EU has made effective multilateralism one of its three strategic objectives, so that strengthening and renewing the UN has become a European priority. In recent years, a number of the most innovative efforts to find multilateral solutions to global challenges have been the result of EU leadership. The EU, for example, was central in efforts to bring both the Kyoto Protocol into force and thereby to address, however marginally, the challenges of climate change through reduced greenhouse gas emissions. EU member states are perhaps the most ardent supporters of the International Criminal Court, and all EU members are signatories to the Rome Statute that establishes this judicial body. In the diplomacy of international trade, the EU is a looming presence, and in recent years EU collective preferences and positions have been

---

[11]Katie Verlin Laatikainen, "Assessing the EU as an Actor at the UN," *CFSP Forum* 2:1 (January 2004): 4–10.

proposed in international financial institutions such as the International Monetary Fund (IMF) and the World Bank.[12]

What is the vision behind this EU commitment to the UN and multilateralism? Analysts of contemporary world affairs observe that the EU is a "different kind of power."[13] Member states of the EU have pooled rather than abandoned their sovereignty, and the key to cooperation among member governments of the EU is in defining a distinctive "European interest" that does not contradict separate national interests. Proponents of European integration also believe it possible to project a "European interest" onto the world stage that would both complement the national interests of EU members and give the EU itself a place among powers. Scholars who think about the EU's place among powers have defined "Europe" as a "normative power" or a "civilian power" that acknowledges international interdependence and accepts the challenge of managing it successfully.[14] To date, the EU's interest in the world has been mainly economic, as has been the coalition's collective power and influence, so that "Europe's" aims have been to foster an international environment hospitable to commerce. In the words of British scholar François Duchêne, "The European Community's interest as a civilian group of countries long on economic power and relatively short on armed force is as far as possible to domesticate relations between states, including those of its own members and those with states outside its frontiers."[15]

But the increasing size of the EU, particularly since the end of the Cold War, together with the broadened and deepened complexity of cooperation among members and pressures from the world beyond Europe have been moving member governments to define a common foreign policy for the union, and indeed a security policy as well, that establishes a collective European interest in world affairs beyond the realm of economics.[16] This European common foreign and security policy (CFSP) is presently emerging. Ostensibly, at least, it eschews concepts of power and interests and suggests that the EU is in fact a "postmodern" type of foreign policy presence, where the focus of common stances is on "normative power of an ideational nature characterized by common principles and a willingness to disregard

[12]Lorenzo Bini Smaghi, "A Single EU Seat in the IMF," *Journal of Common Market Studies* 42 (2004): 29–48.

[13]The dismissive neoconservative approach is represented by Robert Kagan, "Power and Weakness" *Policy review* 113 (2002): 3–29. Manners essentially makes the same argument with a more positive spin. See Ian Manners, "Normative Power Europe: A Contradiction in Terms?" *Journal of Common Market Studies*, 40:2 (2002): 235–58.

[14]François Duchêne, "The European Community and the Uncertainties of Interdependence," in *A Nation Writ Large: Foreign Policy Problems Before the European Community*, M. Kohnstamm and W. Hager, eds. (London: Macmillan, 1973).

[15]Duchêne, p. 12.

[16]Katie Verlin Laatikainen and Karen E. Smith, eds., *The European Union at the United Nations: Intersecting Multilateralisms* (Basingstoke: Palgrave, 2006).

Westphalian conventions."[17] EU member states continue to have narrower national foreign policy interests, but what they share as a group are common values and principles that can safely be espoused by "Europe" without undermining national interests.

What values does the EU stand for? According to John Richardson, former head of the European delegation to the UN, the core values that the EU stands for include rule of law; support for democracy and human rights; open, market economics; social solidarity; sustainable development, and tolerance of cultural diversity. Interestingly, these values are very similar to those that the United States purports to stand for, and although cohesion within the UN between Europe and the United States has declined since 2003, the EU and Washington still tend to vote in harmony a great deal of the time in both the General Assembly and the Security Council.[18] To be sure, there is a difference in tone distinguishing European and U.S. behavior within the UN, and this should not be disregarded or undervalued with regard to diplomatic impact. But there is not very much difference in values. The problem, particularly for Europe, is that these values are not exclusively European but constitutive of Western hegemony. Europe's values seem very much in line with the rest of the West, even as European norms of interaction may be different. How distinct, then, can the EU be, if the union shares fundamental values with half the world? And how effective can European leadership be if values underlying EU stances continue to offend the other half of the world? Asking the same question in a somewhat different way, Andrew Clapham, professor of international law in Geneva, wonders how influential the EU can be within the UN if the "EU represents an ideological and powerful bloc," and if "other blocs may have to redefine their identity and ideology in counter-position to the EU?"[19] Although the EU purports to follow a normative or values-based foreign policy and assumes its values to be benign and universal, it is questionable whether the rest of the international community will accept this self-definition given the growing structural power of the EU in the UN system.

Other analysts predict that the EU will increasingly challenge the international balance of power in ways that students of power politics would recognize.[20] That is, the EU's current emphasis on normative influence

---

[17]Ian Manners and Richard G. Whitman, "The 'Difference Engine': Constructing and Representing the International Identity of the European Union," *Journal of European Public Policy*, 10 (2003): 389–90.

[18]See the analysis by Knud Erik Jørgensen and Katie Verlin Laatikainen, "The EU at the UN: Multilateralism in a New Key?" Second Pan-European Conference on EU Politics, Bologna, June 24–26, 2004.

[19]Andrew Clapham, 'Where Is the EU's Human Rights Common Foreign Policy, and How Is It Manifested in Multilateral Fora?' in Philip Alston, ed., *The EU and Human Rights* (Oxford: Oxford University Press, 1999), p. 649.

[20]Charles A. Kupchan, "The Rise of Europe, America's Changing Internationalism, and the End of U.S. Primacy," *Political Science Quarterly*, 118:2 (2003): 205–32, and Charles A. Kupchan, "The End of the West," *Atlantic Montly*, 290:4 (2002): 42–45.

reflects little more than its rather fragile unity in the realm of foreign policy and its lack of military capability. When the EU fortifies its political unity and builds its capabilities, it too will behave as a conventional great power.[21] Most European leaders reject scenarios that elevate the EU to conventional great power status in the twenty-first century and affirm instead that civilian power and normative leadership will remain the union's goals. But in whatever way the EU's policy evolves in the years ahead, there is considerable reason to expect that it will conflict with the United States, both within the UN and without. Either the EU's multilateral and normative approach will contrast with Washington's unilateral focus and preferences for using military force, or EU interests will clash with American interests in the tradition of power politics.

Perhaps, then, the stage is being set for a new period of bipolarity within the UN. If the EU is indeed a different kind of power, then Europe will seek to counter U.S. unilateralism and reliance on military power by embracing the multilateral and cooperative means of dealing with conflict resolution. We might anticipate a future in which the UN remains a Western-dominated institution but with a new bipolarity in which the Europeans dominate in economic and social areas of the General Assembly and ECOSOC while the Americans predominantly focus their energy on peace and security and their attention on the Security Council. If the Europeans manage to elevate the importance of the General Assembly, reestablishing a balance between the assembly and the Security Council, Europe's greater influence in the General Assembly could create a new, more productive period of Western engagement in UN multilateralism and possibly overcome long-standing North–South stalemates. Such a divergence of policy attention between the EU and the United States could then reflect a rather productive division of labor in the exercise of structural power across the UN system. On the other hand, if the EU does come to embrace or reflect realpolitik in the more traditional sense, the UN could become the locus of political disputes and diplomatic loggerheads between the United States and the EU much the same way the World Trade Organization is currently a locus of economic disputes. Clear political differences in the area of protecting human rights and the global environment are emerging between the United States and the EU. Others could emerge. Historically bipolarity has not been very healthy for the United Nations.

With the accession of Central and East European members, the EU's institutional reach will expand from the Western European and Other Group in the UN to include as well the Eastern European Group. The significant financial clout of the EU within the world body further reinforces the very real structural power that the EU holds. If the UN is not to fade into irrelevance in the face of American ambivalence or hostility, it may paradoxically mean that the EU has to embrace power in the traditional sense to promote its normative vision of "effective multilateralism" and provide the structural

---

[21]Charles A. Kupchan, *The End of the American Era* (New York: Alfred A. Knopf, 2003), pp. 119–59.

leadership necessary to do this. Europe's multilateral bent may be more palatable to the rest of the international community than Washington's unilateralism, but European aims and intentions still promote Western liberal ideas and reinforce Western hegemony. That many other members of the UN reject both liberal ideas and Western hegemony does not necessarily disqualify Europe from structural leadership in the organization, but this certainly renders such leadership difficult to exercise.

The Group of 77 and the General Assembly

After decolonization, which was largely over by the mid-1970s, voting majorities in the UN General Assembly started to run against the West as newly independent countries in the emergent Third World sought to shift attention to issues they considered critical. Neither fighting the Cold War nor taking sides in it was of much interest to postcolonial peoples. But rectifying the injustices of colonization was in their interest, and even more so was eliminating their poverty, dependency, and technological backwardness and reviving their cultural distinctiveness. As early as 1955, twenty-nine developing countries meeting in Indonesia at the Bandung Conference sought to consolidate their presence at the UN and to press the General Assembly to focus on issues of development. By 1961 the newly independent countries had organized themselves into the NAM, a coalition committed to staying out of the Cold War, to preventing superpower rivalries from engulfing less developed countries, and to translating their growing numbers into voting power in the General Assembly. Then, in 1964, most of the same Third World countries as well as many other new members of the UN coalesced into the Group of 77 specifically to wield voting power in the interest of economic development. In the heyday of the push for a New International Economic Order in the mid-1970s, the Group of 77 sought to use voting power in the General Assembly and other UN bodies to change fundamentally the nature of international economic relations. This was to be accomplished through obligatory transfers of resources from rich to poor nations, through global price supports for Third World commodities, and through enhancing Third World influence over decision making in the international economic institutions.[22] The thrust toward a New International Economic Order came largely to naught in the 1970s, as did other Third World initiatives like the New World Information Order in the 1980s and successive plans for "decades of development." This is because voting power in the UN General Assembly does not amount to structural power in the UN. Nor does collective weakness add up to strength, no matter how large the coalition, and much to the continuing disappointment of leaders of the NAM and the Group of 77, commanding majorities in the UN's deliberative organs does not bestow leadership in the organization.

[22]See Joan Edelman Spero, *The Politics of International Economic Relations* (New York: St. Martin's, 1985).

The Group of 77 and the NAM remain important components of the political structure of the United Nations, although, if anything, the never very consequential political clout of these coalitions has diminished. Collective weakness still does not add to up to power, particularly in a unipolar world. In addition, the integrity of the Group of 77 is presently in jeopardy for a number of reasons, the principal one being that the group no longer represents an economic stratum in the world or a political-economic condition with which the large majority of countries can identify. As one Western diplomat noted, "The world has moved beyond a time when the solidarity of the Group of 77 was of central importance to the group. Countries are cutting out of the G-77 because their status and their interests no longer locate them with a group of poor developing countries." "Mexico is out; Korea is out. The rationale for the G-77 is spent," one Third World diplomat explained. Added to this diffusion of interest based on diversity of economic accomplishment is a diversity of economic doctrine, where a large number of developing countries have climbed aboard the "liberalization-marketization-structural adjustment-globalization" bandwagon. Others reject this way of thinking and prefer instead to explain the world, their position in it, and their policies toward it in terms of a critique of globalization that pictures them as victims of market forces. Still others, particularly some from the least developed countries as well as some of the most ideologically driven, have never abandoned the notion of a New International Economic Order that would transform the UN into a global welfare state. This position, one diplomat explained, does not "draw the support of other Third World countries." Compounding the fractionation among Third World countries is disagreement over leadership, within both the G-77 and the NAM, where, presently, some of the more radical governments such as Cuba, Algeria, Libya, and Iran, are attempting to speak for the rest of the Third World. They appear, however, to be alienating at least as many governments as they are attracting. The radical position is outspokenly anti-Western, unrelenting in attributing all economic, social, and political maladies in the Third World to malevolent Western motives and influence, and adamant in its call for global revolution whereupon "the least shall be first."[23] "The G-77/NAM remains dominated by extremists," one Latin American diplomat explained. A UN official added that "among the G-77, the radicals—Cuba, Algeria, China—are still active and disproportionately influential because of their tenaciousness. They don't command the respect or the credibility that they perhaps once did. But they are dogged and this counts." When not hijacked by the extremists among them, the G-77 and the NAM often seem like engines for muddling through rather than providing leadership at the UN. The Third World coalitions articulate positions, but exactly whom these positions represent is no longer entirely clear. In 2004 Canadian diplomat and scholar Paul Heinbecker concluded in a thoughtful essay that the G-77 is

[23]Frantz Fanon, *The Wretched of the Earth* (New York: Grove Press, 1963), p. 37.

"outdated" and the NAM is "hoary." Both, he observed, are "holdovers from a bygone age . . . engines of groupthink given to lowest common denominator outcomes."[24]

The reality of the factional situation in the General Assembly is somewhat more nuanced than has been perhaps appreciated. Realities of diminishing political clout and increasing factionalism should not be interpreted to mean that the NAM and the G-77 have lost either all of their cohesion or all of their credibility. The G-77 remains a force, if for no other reason than that its leadership does remain tenacious, even when it speaks only for itself. It is clearly also the case that those who value Third World solidarity have not abandoned their efforts to enhance it. For example, one G-77 leader to whom we spoke described the G-77 and the NAM as currently passing through a period of "rebuilding" because, he said, "we are living in a different period," and "there is a need for concerting political positions among the states that compose the G-77 and the NAM." The NAM and the G-77 also remain important as caucusing groups, where, even if they fail to enforce discipline, they nevertheless provide opportunities for smaller and poorer countries to make their views known. Numbers still make some difference in the General Assembly, and this ability to marshal votes was amply on display during the spring of 2006 during negotiations over UN management reform. The G-77 under the leadership of South Africa managed to reject management reform proposals championed by the United States, Japan, Australia and the EU that would have given the secretariat more authority over hiring and personnel. This was seen as eroding the authority of member states and the G-77 rejected both the proposed reforms and the threats of a spending cap imposed by the largest UN funders.

Even if voting results do not impel compliance with resolutions, they indicate something about where the international community stands on different issues. Third World majorities are no longer as impressively large as they once were. Yet they still embrace many countries and represent, ostensibly at least, vast numbers of people in the world. Still, the weakening of the major factions that once structured the politics of the General Assembly is not a happy development for this UN organ. For one thing, the disappearing blocs and undisciplined factions render diplomacy very difficult. With whom is one to negotiate when one's interlocutor evaporates? As a result, many member governments of the EU as well as other countries like Canada, Australia, and Japan that have traditionally centered their diplomacy in the UN are among those least pleased about the weakening of the NAM and the Group of 77.

[24]Paul Heinbecker, "Washington's Exceptionalism and the United Nations," *Global Governance*, 10 (July–September 2004): 278.

ENTREPRENEURIAL LEADERSHIP

Leadership is not simply a matter of structural capabilities. Bringing multilateral projects to fruition also requires entrepreneurial leaders who use negotiating skills "to frame issues in ways that foster integrative bargaining and to put together deals that would otherwise elude participants."[25] As is often the case in international collective action, participants may reap joint gains by coordinating efforts, but the obstacles to realizing these joint gains are considerable. Entrepreneurial leaders facilitate collective action by effective agenda setting, publicizing the importance of the issues at stake, devising innovative policies to overcome bargaining impediments, and brokering support for particular options. Entrepreneurial leaders are not necessarily mediators, although they resemble mediators in their efforts to make negotiations successful. "They are typically agents of actors that possess stakes in the issues at hand and participate in the relevant negotiations in their own right . . . . Equally important, entrepreneurial leaders do not limit themselves to efforts to assist or facilitate negotiations among the principals. They work to frame the issues at stake and intervene energetically in the substance of negotiations, endeavoring to invent attractive options and persuade others to back the options they espouse."[26] There may be multiple entrepreneurial leaders in any given negotiation. Their efforts are directly primarily toward getting something accomplished.

Where does entrepreneurial leadership come from in the UN? During the Cold War, the so-called middle powers played the role of policy entrepreneurs to facilitate consensus, to find common zones of agreement, and to move negotiating processes along. Traditional middle powers included countries such as Canada, Australia, Sweden, other Nordic countries, the Netherlands, Brazil, Mexico, and occasionally other Latin American states. Middle powers have been strategically important and have enjoyed a great deal of credibility within the UN. It is often easier to identify middle powers than it is to define exactly what they do to broker compromises, but their productive contributions earned them the designation "the good guys club."

Scholars do agree that the modern concept of "middle power" is Canadian in origin.[27] During the Cold War, Canadians pointed out that second-order powers like Canada benefited disproportionately from multilateral agreements and the smooth functioning of international institutions. In addition, because of their relative weakness, the middle powers threatened no one and were therefore often able to broker solutions to protracted and divisive negotiations. Although weaker geopolitically speaking, the middle

---

[25]Young, "Political Leadership and Regime Formation," p. 293.
[26]Ibid., p. 295.
[27]See John Ravenhill, "Cycles of Middle Power Activism: Constraint and Choice in Australian and Canadian Foreign Policies," *Australian Journal of International Affairs*, 52 (1998): 309–27.

powers were not less developed countries without resources to invest in subsidizing promising compromises, and they frequently made such investments. Middle powers sought to bridge the structural divides of the Cold War era, serving as interlocutors between East and West as well as between North and South. According to Dartmouth University's Gene Lyons, middle powers "do not pose a threat to weaker countries, they can run interference for stronger countries whose support for certain policies might be viewed suspiciously as a move for self-aggrandizement, and they can usually provide material and human resources that are required to implement operating programs."[28]

As with many other institutions, processes and patterns in world affairs, the end of the Cold War, and the changed structure of world politics have affected middle powers and middle power entrepreneurship within the UN. For one thing, the ranks of the more-or-less permanent assortment of "like-minded" middle powers that exercised entrepreneurial leadership during the Cold War have been thinned. For example, save for the Norwegians, the other Nordics, the Swedes, Danes, and Finns, are now conducting their diplomacy through the EU. The Dutch, of course, were charter members of the EU, but notwithstanding they managed early on to play a middle power role at the UN. Nowadays, however, strong pressures to maintain EU solidarity have greatly constrained these formerly very active European middle powers. The disappearance of these states has left the traditional non-European or non-EU traditional middle powers, like Canada, Norway, Australia, somewhat adrift. For their part, Canadians appear to be in a period of introspection about their role in the world. Recent books by well-known Canadian authors like Andrew Cohen's *While Canada Slept: How We Lost Our Place in the World* and Michael Bliss's *Right Honorable Men* lament the apparent passing of Canada's tradition of producing visionary world leaders.[29] Historically, Canada's middle power behavior was both diffuse and routine; that is, Canada traditionally emphasized external mediation across a wide range of UN activities.[30] Canada's exposed position next to the United States in North America prompted its embrace of multilateralism on a global level and made it perhaps the most consistent and loyal middle power and a country that "moved well out in front of both the United States and the major Western European countries on a number of environmental and resource issues in the 1970s."[31] Bliss, a noted historian and Canadian internationalist, acknowledges, "I am in almost total

[28]Gene Lyons, "International Organizations and National Interests," *International Social Science Journal*, 144 (1995): 267.

[29]Andrew Cohen, *While Canada Slept: How We Lost Our Place in the World* (Toronto: McClelland and Stewart, 2004); Michael Bliss, *Right Honorable Men: The Descent of Canadian Politics from Macdonald to Mulroney* (Toronto: Harper Collins, 1994).

[30]Andrew F. Cooper, Richard A. Higgott, and Kim Richard Nossal, eds., *Relocating Middle Powers: Australia and Canada in a Changing World Order* (Vancouver: UBC Press, 1993), p. 29.

[31]Ibid., p. 30.

despair. You have a country, but what is it for, and what is it doing?"[32] The Canadian gaze appears indeed to have turned inward, and critics like Canadian scholar and statesman Jack Lawrence Granatstein criticize this inward turn and preoccupation with domestic concerns. "A country is more than just a health system."[33] Nevertheless, Canada's middle power diplomacy within the UN has diminished.

By contrast, since the end of the Cold War, Australia has become more active as a middle power deeply committed to entrepreneurial diplomacy. But Australia's activities have been limited to a few areas only. Insecure in its Asia-Pacific geopolitical environment, and becoming more and more marginalized within the international economy, Australia has tended to focus its activity on a small number of issues, where perceived stakes for the country are particularly high. For example, for all of Australia's declared interest in Third World issues and problems, few of its initiatives have been directed outside the Asia-Pacific region.[34] This narrower regional focus by Australia remains in effect, although the preeminent brokering role that Australia played in bringing the international community into East Timor, as well as the productive middle power contributions that Australia appears to making in ongoing efforts to improve UN peacekeeping capabilities, are very positive.

The Nordic countries for many years coordinated extensively within the UN, presenting common positions on a variety of issues and working collectively to bridge differences among major powers and different coalitions. The Nordic position was a special one within the "good guys club." But the constellation of Norway-Sweden-Denmark-Finland has been sundered by the growth of the EU.[35] Nordic members of the EU experience frustrations from constraints on their flexibility imposed by imperatives to reach and support EU positions at the UN. There is no longer an independent Nordic voice in UN affairs. Even greater difficulties are experienced by Norwegian delegates. As a result of the decline of Nordic collaboration, the Norwegians have had to scramble to find a new identification within the UN and a new role as the EU has increased its voice at the cost of a Nordic one. On this, one diplomat from Eastern Europe remarked, "The EU is more consolidated and integrated. There is a clear disappearance of the Nordic bloc, and Norway, standing alone, is no match for the EU." Norway dances awkwardly and intermittently with the EU in the political bodies of the UN, but it is unable to play a middle power role alone.

---

[32]Cited in Clifford Krauss, "Canada's Prophets of Pessimism (Is It the Weather?)" *New York Times*, September 29, 2004, p. 2.

[33]Ibid.

[34]Cooper et al., "Relocating Middle Powers," p. 31.

[35]See Katie Verlin Laatikainen, "Norden's Eclipse: The Impact of the European Union's Common Foreign and Security Policy on Nordic Cooperation in the United Nations," *Cooperation and Conflict*, 38 (December 2003): 409–41.

In the post–Cold War environment, middle power roles have gone functional, and the entrepreneurial leadership once performed by middle powers is now described as "niche diplomacy."[36] That is, rather than the stable grouping of "like-minded countries" or "institutional loyalists" that provided entrepreneurial leadership on a more or less consistent basis during the Cold War, in the twenty-first century, entrepreneurial leadership emerges from shifting coalitions of multilaterally inclined states in particular issue areas or "niches." No one plays the role of middle power in general. Rather, different entrepreneurs tend to emerge as issues change and interests in "getting something done" change accordingly. The changed political landscape of the early twenty-first century world has invited the emergence of a wider variety of middle powers. India, Brazil, Nigeria, Malaysia, Argentina, Turkey, and South Africa are now frequently seen to be providing intermittent entrepreneurial leadership in specific functional areas. An example of this would be the New Agenda Coalition—Brazil, Egypt, Ireland, Mexico, New Zealand, South Africa, and Sweden—that emerged in the late 1990s to reinvigorate the UN's disarmament agenda that has been languishing because the great powers have been focusing instead on proliferation issues.[37]

This wider assortment of middle powers brings with it a new dynamics of entrepreneurialism. Engagement by the new middle powers is increasingly selective. Many prefer a combative style of confrontation with the United States, the usual outlier on most issues, rather than accommodation and engagement. Some prefer regional instead of global activism. For instance, both Malaysia and Australia have preferred to broker multilateral solutions in the Asia-Pacific region, and their regional focus combined with different interests has culminated in a middle power rivalry.[38] The diversity of interests and behavior of the middle power entrepreneurs in the post–Cold War era therefore poses some threat to the practice of entrepreneurial leadership itself. Instead of brokering in the interest of compromise or conflict resolution, middle power activity begins to smack of competition for influence among "self-interested" middle powers. This, admittedly, is quite different from the diplomatic modes of the "good guys club."

Could it be possible for the multilaterally minded EU to provide entrepreneurial leadership in the UN by taking on the middle power role? True enough, the EU possesses several attributes associated with the entrepreneurial middle power role. These include, for example, strong diplomatic capacity, a capacity for building coalitions of like-minded partners, and resources sufficient to make side payments or otherwise to close deals where financing is a

---

[36]Andrew F. Cooper, ed., *Niche Diplomacy; Middle Powers After the Cold War* (London: Macmillan, 1997).
[37]"Nonproliferation and Disarmament Go Hand in Hand," *International Herald Tribune*, September 21, 2004.
[38]Cooper, *Niche Diplomacy*, p. 19.

stumbling block.[39] However, "Europe" is likely disqualified from the middle power entrepreneurial role for a number of reasons. For one thing, the EU is not a middle power, as our earlier discussion made clear. It commands considerable power both material and normative, aspires to structural leadership, and has an agenda of its own. In addition, brokering compromises requires a flexibility that the European coalition does not easily demonstrate. Once the EU-25 have agreed on a position, there is little flexibility for concessions or compromises. There also remains the rather serious limitation inherent in the disconnect between the universalistic values and principles that the EU espouses—that is, the European agenda itself—and the middle power role in consensus building. There is no doubt that the EU can build consensus because its foreign policy is in fact premised on building consensus among the twenty-five members. However, the values and principles contained in this consensus are mainly shared among the Europeans, or at most among Westerners. Within the broader confines of the UN with all its cultural diversity, building consensus has to mean deemphasizing controversial values. But how is this possible if the objective of the EU's foreign policy is to promote the Western values that Europeans hold dear?

With middle power entrepreneurial leadership in flux, some have suggested that NGOs could fill in the gaps. Secretary-General Kofi Annan, for example, explicitly embraces the growing role of NGOs in providing leadership as he attempts to foster the nascent role of civil society in global governance. He has called them "essential partners . . . not only in mobilizing public opinion, but also in the process of deliberation and policy formation and—even more important—in the execution of policies, in work on the ground."[40] It is true that NGOs are sources of support for a broad range of multilateral undertakings, but this is not the same thing as providing entrepreneurial leadership in the context of UN diplomacy. For one thing, NGOs have a "profound feeling of impatience at forms of diplomacy conducted at a slow speed—or no speed at all—behind closed doors."[41] Rather than a quiet diplomacy behind closed doors, the NGO leaders' impulse is to conduct diplomacy via public advocacy. Appeals are made over the heads of other negotiators and around governments to opinion leaders and mass publics. Instead of the formality of traditional statecraft and bargaining table settings, NGOs prefer informal mechanisms and information technology. Their approach moreover is much more likely to be confrontational instead of conciliatory because their objectives are to push governments to take action. This is a rather far cry from the traditional brokering role of middle power entrepreneurs.

---

[39]Ravenhill cites these as the central characteristics of middle powers. See Ravenhill, 1998, p. 313.
[40]Opening Address to the 50th Annual DPI/NGO Conference, September 10, 1997, SG/SM/6320.PI/1027.
[41]Andrew F. Cooper, John English, and Ramesh Thakur, *Enhancing Global Governance: Towards a New Diplomacy* (Tokyo: United Nations University Press, 2002), p. 7.

That NGOs can serve as entrepreneurial leaders and that they can make end runs around formal diplomacy and international institutional roadblocks was perfectly clear in the case of the Treaty to Ban Landmines. By now, the story is well known: between 1992 and 1997, NGOs united in the International Campaign to Ban Landmines, got the issue on the global agenda, and coaxed, pressured, and provoked scores of national governments into negotiating, signing, and ratifying the Ottawa Convention.[42] This so-called Ottawa Process also involved interesting partnerships between NGOs and conventional middle powers like Canada, Belgium, Austria, Germany, and Norway. The importance of this accomplishment in global governance orchestrated by the NGO community should not be underestimated. But it must be underlined that it largely occurred *outside the UN*, and it gathered impetus only after the UN failed in 1996 to act to ban landmines, in spite of strong NGO prodding. Nor were NGOs anywhere nearly as successful in 1998 at protecting the Rome Statute, which founded the International Criminal Court, from being eviscerated by the United States.

The crux of the problem regarding NGO entrepreneurs and effective leadership within the UN is that regardless of Annan's receptivity, many member governments reject the legitimacy of NGO interventions into formal UN diplomacy. From the point of view of a very large majority of UN member governments, regardless of their political-military power, economic status, or ideological leaning, one of the most important issues facing the UN is whether it is going to remain an intergovernmental organization. Whether the twenty-first century can expect a universal international organization constituted in any other than an intergovernmental way is impossible to predict, although it would be reasonable to assume that some future international organization open to NGO membership would also be open to NGO entrepreneurship. What is clear regarding the UN today, however, is that its member states, astutely aware that the privileges and immunities of sovereignty are under siege, are determined to keep the UN an intergovernmental organization. That NGOs should formally participate in international policy making, or far less lead in this process, is therefore out of the question.

What, finally, of the brokering role of the secretary-general and the Secretariat? Although the secretary-general's job description is rather vaguely outlined in the UN Charter, quiet, emollient diplomacy has become one of the trademarks of the office. It is undoubtedly true that over the years within the private confines of the secretary-general's office numerous differences between governments have been bridged, many conflicts have been resolved, and others have been prevented. In fact, the secretary-general's office is probably the only place in the world where governments can expect impartial hearings and unbiased mediation, and in this sense the secretary-general does

---

[42]William Maley, "The UN, NGOs and the Landmines Initiative: An Australian Perspective," in *Enhancing Global Governance: Towards a New Diplomacy*, Andrew F. Cooper, John English, and Ramesh Thakur, eds. (Tokyo: United Nations University Press, 2002).

exercise entrepreneurial leadership. But this seldom extends to policy initiatives concerning UN affairs more broadly.

Secretaries-general have to tread a fine line between enticing and hectoring because they must remember that they serve the member states. Annan, for example, was very clear in stating and enforcing his reluctance to return sizable numbers of UN officials to the insecure environment of Iraq during the summer of 2004. And this was despite strong American pressures for greater international involvement after the formal return of Iraqi sovereignty. Conversely, when about the same time the BBC reported that British intelligence had bugged the offices of the secretary-general and that transcripts of his meetings with other world leaders had circulated freely within the Blair cabinet, Annan's carefully considered official response was that he was "disappointed if this were true."[43] The point is that secretaries-general account for no structural power within the UN, and their entrepreneurial power is greatly constrained by imperatives to muster widespread major power support for initiatives. Independent policy initiatives by the secretary-general, not vetted through consultations with the Permanent Five, are rare. By reverse token, secretaries-general that cross the great power members often grow to regret it. Mr. Annan's balking at U.S. requests in 2004 did not endear him to Washington and probably contributed to foreclosing his chances for a third term as secretary-general. The American-led ouster of Annan's predecessor, Boutros Boutros-Ghali, is an even clearer object lesson of what happens when a secretary-general crosses the interests of the great powers. The secretary-general's capacities for entrepreneurial leadership are then considerably constrained by his lack of political autonomy within the UN system.

INTELLECTUAL LEADERSHIP

The power commanded by the secretary-general and other high officials within the UN, and hence the leadership they can accomplish, is to be found in the realm of ideas. Intellectual leadership involves producing new ideas, worldviews, or systems of thought that shape the perspectives of those who participate in global governance. The UN has been and remains a wellspring of intellectual leadership, a place where ideas and new perspectives on pressing global challenges are formed. The unique milieu of the UN, wherein individuals and groups, within the international civil service in particular, are compelled to confront and think about the world as a whole can foster integrative, cross-disciplinary, and sometimes very creative thinking about how the world works. It is in this area of creative thinking that the UN has blossomed since the end of the Cold War, and the appeal of ideas generated has reinforced

---

[43]Warren Hoge, "On Bugging News, Annan Had a Low-Key Reaction to Old Practice," *New York Times*, February 28, 2004.

the UN in an intellectual leadership role. In fact, intellectual leadership was paramount even during the Cold War, when innovative ideas emerged from the UN even amid the dulling sameness and intellectual sterility of East–West affairs. Statesmen associated with the UN like Lester Pearson and John Holmes are rightly honored for their important intellectual contributions that shaped UN practices. Nowhere, for example, is peacekeeping mentioned in the UN Charter, but through the intellectual leadership of Dag Hammarskjöld and Lester Pearson, the design for this, the most identifiable among UN activities, evolved. Ideas related to economic development, such as the challenges that economic dependency posed for postcolonial societies, were elaborated by Raul Prebisch, and they emerged from the working experiences of the UN's Economic Commission for Latin America. The Green Revolution, today a reality, was originally a UN-generated idea. The notion that protecting human rights is a responsibility of the international community was originally a UN-generated notion. The vision that economic growth can be rendered sustainable for future generations even in the context of finite global resources is also a UN-generated vision.

Intellectual leadership emanating from the UN survived the disillusionment with multilateralism that characterized the mid-1990s, and it continues to thrive. Special commissions and the regular summits that highlight particular global concerns—population, the condition of women, the environment, human rights, racism, sustainable development—are the focal points of this intellectual activity. Usually appointed by the secretary-general, special commissions are tasked to thoroughly examine particular global challenges. Their findings are addressed by the international community in global conferences, and the intellectual products of global dialogue and debate are diffused by representatives of member states and NGOs. A textbook early example is the Brundtland Commission, which in the late 1980s was charged with analyzing the competing demands of environmental protection and the necessity of economic development. The concept of sustainable development, fully elaborated in the commission's report, *Our Common Future*, sought to reconcile the competing principles of less developed countries' right to economic development with the collective nature of global environmental protection. The resultant concept of sustainable development—that is, development that would not impair the ability of future generations to enjoy comparable or better standards of living—was the basis for the 1992 Earth Summit in Rio de Janeiro that produced Agenda 21, a blueprint for implementing the idea of sustainable development. Most of the global environmental policy initiatives that emerged in the 1990s can trace their intellectual foundation to the ideas first produced by the Brundtland Commission.

The legacy of Secretary-General Annan is likely to be his intellectual leadership. At the opening of the 54th General Assembly, for example, Annan cautioned that "states bent on criminal behavior [should] know that frontiers are not the absolute defense," and that "the time of absolute and exclusive sovereignty . . . has passed."[44] In fact, the secretary-general has maintained on numerous occasions that appeals to sovereignty cannot be allowed to either stifle international cooperation or to shield human rights violations by governments or other internationally unacceptable behavior.[45] In challenging the absolute immunities of sovereignty, Annan injected into international discourse a new way of thinking and talking about relations among states, the citizens within them, and the international community writ large. He added logic and appeal to the legitimacy of intervention by the outside world into the affairs of delinquent states, and he naturally also provoked widespread controversy that continues today. The secretary-general's public reconsideration of sovereignty has nevertheless shifted thinking about humanitarianism and intervention from *rights*, such as the right to absolute sovereignty, to *responsibilities*, such as the responsibility of the international community to act in the face of human rights abuses by governments. This reframing accomplishes two things: it delegitimizes opposition to intervention exhibited by countries that use the veil of sovereignty to hide abuses of human rights, and it creates obligations for an often reluctant Security Council to take its humanitarian responsibilities seriously.

The September 11, 2001, terrorist attacks in the United States crystallized the challenges facing the UN in a new and turbulent world. The institution was designed to provide collective security by protecting states from one another, but by the 1990s it became apparent that the concept of security itself had changed. War now takes the form of communal and ethnic strife within states; human rights atrocities are committed within the boundaries of states or wars perpetrated by governments against their own people; and international terrorism is marked by violence that is transnational although not necessarily international. Although states are reasonably secure today from the overt predations of other states, human societies are under siege in a variety of ways. Because the primary mission of the UN is to provide international peace and security, the question of how to do this in the new contexts of the twenty-first century is of central concern. "How to do this" is first and foremost an intellectual challenge that the UN must meet if collective security is to have meaning in our new age.

Realizing this prompted Annan to declare that the UN was at a "fork in the road" and that the dilemmas of insecurity in our time had to be squarely addressed. Consequently, in November 2003 Annan established a high-level panel on "Threats, Challenges and Change" tasked with examining the challenges of collective security in the twenty-first century. It is likely that this commission will continue the legacy of earlier panels and introduce a new

[44]Kofi Annan, *Secretary-General's Speech to the 54th Session of the General Assembly*, September 20, 1999.
[45]See also, for example, Kofi Annan's commentary in the *Financial Times*, January 10, 2000.

conceptualization of collective security that will shape the debates over multilateral security for years to come. Annan himself published a comprehensive assessment of the challenges facing the UN and his proposed reforms in a report entitled *In Larger Freedom* that framed the 2005 World Summit meeting on UN reform.[46] His report highlights the interdependence of collective security, development, and human rights and attempts to foster broad commitment to the reform project by constituents with widely divergent interests and assumptions about the proper priorities of the world organization.

The intellectual contributions fostered by Annan's leadership have led some to call him the equal of the legendary secretary-general Dag Hammarskjöld. Some have said that when Annan decides an issue is important, the UN system and the world pay more attention and action is more likely than if the UN passes some dreary resolution. Annan and the UN received the Nobel Peace Prize in 2001, and in that same year he was nominated by the Security Council for a second term ahead of schedule. Although widely respected and admired for his intellectual contributions, it is precisely Annan's active and energetic intellectual leadership that has been contested in some quarters. Many of the secretary-general's new ideas about world affairs and the UN role have not been entirely welcome in some national capitals. The idea of qualifying sovereign prerogatives, for example, has been met by national governments' emphatic determination to preserve them. Some suspect the secretary-general of harboring supranational aspirations or of favoring increased autonomy for the UN vis-à-vis member states. In this vein, there was (and indeed remains) a notable uproar over the UNDP's embrace of the notion of "human security," which some interpret as the UN seeking to deliver "security" to people by circumventing governments. Some Third World governments have complained that Annan's ideas regarding democracy and liberal economy are "too Western," and they grumble that the secretary-general, although Ghanian by nationality, has been coopted by the West. There is also considerable suspicion at the moment among member governments concerning the UN's promotion of partnerships with private sector organizations like multinational corporations, another of Annan's new ideas. "Governments simply don't want to mix the public and the private sector," we were told, partly because they do not want their national economic and political spaces penetrated by either the UN or multinational corporations." So even the exercise of intellectual leadership in the UN is greatly constrained, again largely by the attitudes of member states, by rivalries among them, by a jealous clinging to sovereign exclusiveness, and by institutional inertia and a prevailing fear of change.

---

[46] *In Larger Freedom: Towards Development, Security and Human Rights for All*, Report of the Secretary-General, A/59/2005, March 21, 2005.

CONSTRAINED MULTILATERAL LEADERSHIP

It was common at the end of the Cold War to assess leadership in the United Nations through the lens of hegemonic stability.[47] That approach conferred inordinate influence to structural power in determining outcomes, and it worked well for most of the second half of the twentieth century. When the United Nations acted it was because one or the other of the two superpowers wanted to act while the other remained indifferent. Otherwise, when the UN did not act it was because one or other of the two superpowers did not want it to act. Either could block UN action, and both did. Where both superpowers were largely indifferent, usually on questions of development or other issues of North–South relations, traditional middle powers sometimes intervened and managed to broker diplomatic deals that neither helped the South very much nor cost the North very much but at least kept relations between them reasonably cordial. Then, as now, the United Nations produced as many ideas as policies, and many of these were good ideas, although few led to collective action that changed the world in any important sense. UN intellectuals also came up with a goodly number of bad ideas, and some of these, like import substitution as a development strategy, actually did some harm.

In the post–Cold War world, new structural dynamics shape the possibilities for exercising multilateral leadership. For one thing, the Western ideological and material hegemony that structurally defines the early twenty-first century world also structurally defines the UN. However, within the UN, Western hegemony is divided between a United States predisposed toward unilateral action, and hence rather indifferent to the UN, and an emergent European Union committed to multilateralism. Within the UN, the United States is reluctant to lead, although it can and does exert power to block or delay action. The EU, in contrast, is willing to lead but not yet prepared. The evolution of the transatlantic relationship could have important bearing on the exercise of structural leadership within the UN, as this can move toward a newer type of benign bipolarity that reflects a division of labor in the exercise of Western hegemony. Or there may in the future be a real clash of European and American interests, which is not likely to bode well for UN multilateralism. In either case, managing American ambivalence combined with dominance will continue to be a problem for the UN.

Even more problematic perhaps for the UN is the fact that there is much less opportunity today for the exercise of entrepreneurial leadership because there are many fewer credible candidates for entrepreneurial roles. For a variety of reasons, traditional middle powers are no longer able, or willing, to play consensus-building roles. Newly emergent middle powers are either not consistent in brokering roles or are as set on competing with one another as with moving diplomacy toward productive closures. NGOs lack legitimacy and

---

[47]See Robert Gilpin, *War and Change in World Politics* (Cambridge: Cambridge University Press, 1981).

operate most comfortably in confrontational rather than in conflict-resolving modes. The absence of effective entrepreneurial leadership within the UN today is strongly reflected in the extensive inventory of global issues mired in impasse.

The UN remains an important fount for the emergence of new ideas concerning global conditions, challenges, and responses. Although many would contend that the intellectual leadership of today's UN essentially advances a Western agenda, it is actually far more radical. The new ideas percolating out of the special commissions and Secretariat committees envision a UN whose legitimacy transcends intergovernmentalism and Westphalian sovereignty to embrace international civil society, to tame economic globalization, and to enhance human security. That world politics are not yet ready for the UN's "new thinking" is obvious, but grasping the significance of the UN in today's world in large part means understanding the tensions between the world that member governments are trying to hang on to and the world that UN intellectuals are trying to usher into reality.

Perhaps in the end, leadership in the UN comes down to individuals and the personalities and idiosyncrasies that characterize them. UN diplomats like former U.S. ambassador Richard Holbrooke have called the area of midtown Manhattan surrounding the United Nations complex the UN village "with its own language and time zone, where 'demand' means ask, 'strong' means not so strong, 'severe' means not so severe, and 'urges' means begs . . . . Thousands of people live here who have very little interaction with the rest of the city."[48] At any given time, small groups of people within the UN village are central to multilateral governance. David Malone, a former Canadian diplomat and director of the International Peace Academy, has remarked that "at any given time, out of one hundred and ninety-one ambassadors, about thirty-five control the game. Within the Security Council, four or five ambassadors at any given time are dominant, perhaps a few more counting the nonpermanent ones. This is also true in each of the General Assembly Committees."[49] In the Secretariat there are probably 30 or 40 key people on whom the UN centrally depends. For insiders, leadership within the UN has everything to with respectability and credibility within the "village," and these qualities follow most often from combinations of intellect, talent, and humanity.

[48]Cited in Linda Fasulo, *An Insider's Guide to the United Nations* (New Haven: Yale University Press, 2004), p. 91.
[49]Ibid., p. 91.

CHAPTER 6

The Politics of Culture

The UN is an institution in which solutions to global problems are debated and sometimes crafted. But at a deeper level, the UN is also a place where the international community attempts to identify commonly shared values. Actionable political positions and policy choices depend on value consensus, and disagreements about fundamentals like ends and means concerning the human condition are often at the roots of inaction at the UN. Agreeing on universal values in an organization of 192 member states composed of thousands of ethnic, religious, and cultural groups is difficult. Difficulties are compounded by the lobbying activities of countless NGOs that tend to be passionate about promoting singular values. They are compounded even further when questions of values get politically transformed into issues of hegemony, autonomy, privilege, and power.

This chapter details the politics within the UN fought out, rather intensely these days, over defining universal values. There is in the world today a highly contentious politics of culture. This has infected the UN in destructive ways by reinforcing divisions between developing and industrialized countries, sometimes complicating North–South issues by making them also West–non-West issues. Whether or not values are universal or culturally contingent is one dimension of the politics of culture. The intensity of current UN debates about cultural issues was driven home to us in two interviews conducted in New York in 2002. One was with a Latin American diplomat, whose assignment in New York was to represent her government in the General Assembly's Third Committee. The other was with a Central European ambassador. To get the full effect of the information being conveyed, we need to quote at some length from our interview transcripts. First, our Latin American respondent:

> Because Ms. L's. description of her work in human rights opened the way, we asked about cultural relativism in the human rights debates. Her eyes lit up! She said that cultural sensitivity was a real issue. She also said that the nature of the confrontation had changed inasmuch as the opponents of universalism had heretofore been using a defensive strategy of watering down resolutions, or inserting loophole paragraphs into resolutions that otherwise endorse universalism. But today, the opponents are on the offensive and are offering their resolutions, trying to rally support from the international community. She offered as examples an Iranian resolution on cultural diversity, a call for a world conference on dialogues among civilizations, and the resolution on the culture of peace at the General Assembly. The way Ms. L. described it, there is real fighting in the trenches over these issues of morals, values, cultures and traditions, and those engaged in the debates look very seriously on what's developing. She described the atmosphere as "not cooperation, rather confrontational." She acknowledged that a good deal of the dissent was a rejection of Westernism, a defense against the imposition of Western values. But she said that years ago there was a search for common standards that could be agreed. "Not anymore!" The division is not North–South so much as West–non-West. Here, she said, Latin America is very much in the Western value camp.

Then, the Central European ambassador, who officially, and apparently personally as well, suspected and resented the stance and the tactics of those who were attacking international standards in the area of human rights in the name of cultural relativism:

> We asked about the UN debate over cultural relativism. The ambassador did not accept that the issues in the debate were actually very serious. He contended instead that the cultural issues were really covers for political interests. They were employed by governments whose real interest was the protection of sovereignty and the prevention of outside interference in or scrutiny of domestic affairs. Otherwise, the cultural issues were used by those who wanted to attack or penalize other governments for reasons other than their cultural beliefs. The "cultural relativism debate," the ambassador said, "is therefore quite phony."

We could observe that the ambassador's resentment was quite real, but in light of the seriousness surrounding cultural issues, in the realm of human rights in particular, we cannot agree that these issues are phony. Various countries, groups, factions, and coalitions would like to believe that *their* values are universal. Some are insisting on this in the UN today and deeply alienating others as a result.

The current cultural debates should be set in historical context. Over the years, the UN did compile a record of apparent agreement among nations about values that all could share. Values regarding peace, sovereignty, and self-determination are enshrined in the Charter. Values in freedom, individual dignity and human well-being are proclaimed in the Universal Declaration of Human Rights and related documents signed and ratified by a vast majority of states. It is both significant and ominous that in the post–Cold War era some of the historic agreements about the universality of human rights in particular seem to be coming undone, and to the extent that they are coming undone it is largely for political reasons.

THE UNITED NATIONS AND HUMAN RIGHTS

The first effort to define and affirm universal human rights occurred during the drafting of the Universal Declaration of Human Rights (UDHR) between 1947 and 1948. In the long and difficult process of drafting the UDHR, the principles of fundamental, indivisible, and universal human rights were contested, but ultimately the concept of universalism was enshrined. Furthermore, this consensus was understood to be *universal,* not simply an *international* agreement based on political contingencies. What was a human right anywhere was also a human right everywhere, regardless of cultural, political, or socioeconomic context. As the Cold War advanced, the discussion of human rights fell captive to the ideological split between East and West, and the principle of indivisibility of human rights was a primary casualty. During this period, the principle of universalism was accepted by both East and West even as the superpowers disagreed about what rights ought to be universalized. The West, steeped in the wisdom of the eighteenth-century Enlightenment, insisted on the cluster surrounding individual liberty and questioned the universality of rights associated with economic well-being. By contrast, the East, persuaded by the thinking of Karl Marx, questioned individuality and insisted on the universality of rights pertaining to collective well-being. As the Cold War came to an end, however, debates about human rights shifted as universalism itself became the issue. The question was no longer which human rights are universal but rather *whether any human rights are universal.* Are human rights not culture bound? Why should rights embodied in any particular cultural tradition not be recognized and accepted as such? Most importantly, why should rights emanating for one cultural tradition necessarily be accepted and respected in others?

Universalism in the form of beliefs in shared humanity traditionally has been the realm of religion rather than politics.[1] Throughout most of world history, the rights of citizens or subjects were understood to be politically contingent. Rulers dispensed rights to subjects, usually ungenerously. It was not until the eighteenth century in Europe and North America that the conception of human rights was couched in the language of universalism. But the

---

[1] See especially Chapter 9 in Donald J. Puchala, *Theory and History in International Relations* (New York: Routledge, 2003).

universality of human rights was not established by international agreement until the middle of the twentieth century. The barbarism and lethality of the Second World War, the horrendous toll in civilian lives, and above all the gross inhumanities of the Nazi-perpetrated Holocaust, prompted the effort to institutionalize the protection of individual human beings. These efforts were based on an inchoate notion of shared values and standards of civilization common to humanity.

An early effort explicitly to define values universally shared occurred in 1943 as the nascent UN sought to create an International Bill of Rights. The primary driving forces behind the movement to incorporate a bill of rights into the UN Charter were American NGOs and a cluster of Latin American governments. By the autumn of 1943, a coalition of religious groups within the United States joined in a common program to support a human rights component in plans for the UN organization. The American Institute for Law produced a draft International Bill of Rights as did the International Labor Organization, the American Jewish Committee, and the American Bar Association. At the Inter-American Conference on War and Peace held in the waning days of World War II, more than twenty countries in the Americas also called for a bill of rights to be included within the Charter itself. Latin American delegations at the San Francisco Conference led the charge for stronger language on human rights along with more than forty NGOs largely from the United States.[2]

That no International Bill of Rights was actually included in the UN Charter has to be attributed largely to the indifference of the major powers, who were mostly interested in establishing an organization to keep the peace. President Franklin Roosevelt, prompted by American NGOs, raised the issue of protecting human rights at Dumbarton Oaks. But neither to Roosevelt nor to the other major power participants was it "self-evident that the proposed organization ought to be concerned with such matters," particularly since international lawyers were advising that "a state's treatment of its own citizens, with rare exceptions, [w]as that nation's own business."[3] Still, in the environment surrounding the end of the war and the opening of the concentration camps, it was difficult to ignore the issue of human rights. As a result, the universal nature of human rights and their protection appears in the Charter in a number of places. The Charter also calls for the establishment of Commission on Human Rights (CHR), which came into existence in 1946 and included as a high priority on its agenda the drafting of an international bill of human rights.

Between January 1947 and December 1948, the Commission on Human Rights drafted the Universal Declaration of Human Rights (UDHR). At the

---

[2] William Korey, *NGOs and the Universal Declaration of Human Rights: A Curious Grapevine* (New York: St. Martin's, 1998).

[3] Mary Ann Glendon, *A World Made New: Eleanor Roosevelt and the Universal Declaration of Human Rights* (New York: Random House, 2001), p. 9.

outset, many delegates hoped that a declaration on human rights could be accompanied by a legally binding covenant that would establish enforcement mechanisms to oblige governments to protect the internationally stipulated rights of citizens. Some even sought to allow for petitions to international authorities from individuals. However, the idea of a legally binding covenant was strongly opposed by the Soviet Union and the communist bloc, and it garnered only limited approval from a number of other delegations. As a result, the CHR determined that it would not be able to forward both a declaration and a covenant and produced only a non-binding declaration in the form of a resolution placed before the UN General Assembly.

The General Assembly resolution containing the text of the Universal Declaration of Human Rights was adopted by the UN General Assembly on December 10, 1948.[4] The vote was forty-eight in favor and none against. But there were eight abstentions—the USSR, Yugoslavia, Byelorussia, Czechoslovakia, Poland, Ukraine, South Africa, and Saudi Arabia—and these were significant because they signaled that from the very beginning that the UN's venture into the realm of human rights was controversial. Not all UN members wished to go on record as accepting that human rights were universal or in approving exactly which rights were universal. There was also in 1948 the frequently voiced observation that the rights enshrined in the Declaration came out of distinctly Western philosophical and religious traditions, and there was a certain amount of grumbling about this. The specific objections from the Eastern bloc countries were predictable: the communists argued that the Declaration had a biased emphasis on the rights of the individual against the state. In classless societies, they argued, tensions between the individual and the state were ameliorated, and in such societies "there could not be any contradiction between the government and the individual, since the government was in fact the collective individual."[5] The South African abstention was a transparent attempt to protect the racist system of apartheid that its white minority government was in the process of institutionalizing at the time that the Universal Declaration came before the General Assembly. It was thus a political rather than a principled objection to universalism or the idea of human rights per se. The South African government indicated that it favored a minimalist approach to human rights, limited only to those defining conditions necessary for "physical and mental existence as a human being." Such conditions, the South African delegation said, did not include the right to freedom of movement within one's country and between countries or that right of persons to participate in the government of their country.

[4]A/777 (December 10, 1948). Elements of the UDHR not receiving unanimous approval: Preamble adopted with 2 abstentions; Article 1: 45–0, 9 abstentions; Article 2/Paragraph 2: 36–1, 8 abstentions; Article 14: 44–6, with 2 abstentions; Article 19: 45–0 with 4 abstentions; Article 20: 44–7, with 2 abstentions; Article 27: 53–0, with 3 abstentions; Article 29: 47–0, with 8 abstentions.
[5]Johannes Morsink, *The Universal Declaration of Human Rights: Origins, Drafting, and Intent* (Philadelphia: University of Pennsylvania Press, 1999), p. 22.

Saudi Arabian objections were based on cultural and religious interpretations of parts of the draft declaration. The Saudis objected in particular to clauses that called for nondiscrimination in marriage, which, they argued, was contrary to the Muslim prohibition against marrying outside of the faith. They also had difficulties with provisions of the resolution concerning freedom of conscience, thought, and religion leading to the declared right to change one's religion. During the debates, other Muslim countries supported the Saudi position, although some, such as Pakistan, Turkey, Iran, and Syria, did not. It is important to note that the Saudi position and those sympathizing with it directly contradicted the principle of universalism with respect to human rights. By contrast, the Saudi stance endorsed cultural differentiation and cultural contingency, thus previewing a UN debate that was to reemerge fifty years later. Most interestingly, and indeed ironically, during the early debates surrounding the Universal Declaration, one of the clearest statements of the cultural relativist position was offered in a 1947 letter from the American Anthropological Association to the Commission on Human Rights. A human rights document, this letter said, had to "formulate a statement of rights that will do more than just phrase respect for the individual as an individual. It must also take into full account the individual as a member of the social group of which he is part, whose sanctioned modes of life shape his behavior, and with whose fate his own is inextricably bound."[6] The American Anthropological Association conveyed skepticism that such a statement of universal human rights that respected the social embeddedness of individuals could ever be articulated.

It is true that the principle of universalism regarding human rights was widely accepted by the international community throughout the period of the Cold War, even though consensus as to what actually constituted universal human rights was never really reached. The decades of the Cold War were disappointing for advocates of human rights both within the UN and without because universalism fell prey to the politics of ideological posturing. The superpowers used the human rights organs of the UN to indict one another for perpetrating abuses of human rights, and this exploitation of the UN for Cold War purposes transformed institutions like the Commission on Human Rights into political theater. Representatives of the Soviet Union and Eastern bloc client governments pilloried the West, the United States in particular, for condemning Third World peoples to poverty and perpetuating imperialism. But at the same time they ignored the gulags, persecutions, and severe restraints on freedom in their part of the world. The United States and its Western partners harangued the totalitarian "slave states" of the East but conveniently ignored the inhumane practices of the military dictatorships that lined up as Western Cold War clients. Meanwhile, newly independent Third World members of the UN used the human rights organs to heap guilt on

---

[6]American Anthropological Association, "Statement on Human Rights," *American Anthropologist*, 49:4 (1947): 539.

former metropolitan countries for abuses under colonialism. Arab countries, supported by others in Asia and Africa, also readily discovered that UN human rights forums provided excellent platforms for condemning the Israeli treatment of Palestinians. All of this invited a pervasive cynicism in the human rights issue-area that sapped the vitality of UN institutions. This cynicism pervaded and largely paralyzed the International Conference on Human Rights, sponsored by the UN and held in Teheran in May 1968.[7] Despite the intentions of conference convenors to move from promotion to protection of human rights, the Teheran conference quickly devolved into acrimonious debate and politicized finger-pointing. The twenty-odd resolutions adopted by the conference reflect divergent political interests and agendas.[8] The Cold War era did not undermine the principle of universality but subverted the principle for political purposes. Still, from very early on, the issue of cultural relativism regarding human rights that was voiced by the Saudis and a few others in 1948 simmered well below the surface, and the politics of universalism was a function of ideology rather than culture. The issue of culture was largely ignored for forty years because the subsequent era of competing ideological universalisms between East and West subsumed cultural challenges to universalism. But in 1993, after the end of the ideological global division, the cultural challenge to universalism took center stage.

UNIVERSALISM UNDER SIEGE: THE 1993 WORLD CONFERENCE ON HUMAN RIGHTS

Revealingly, there was not another UN-sponsored conference on human rights until 1993. This World Conference on Human Rights, set in Vienna, was convened in a world newly emerged from nearly half a century of superpower conflict. It was convened in the celebratory context marking the end of ideological divisions between East and West. A focus on human rights was understood to have played an important role in the dissolution of the Soviet bloc. The purpose of this world conference was to "arrive at an authoritative statement of the world's consensus on matters of defining and promoting human rights."[9] The conference was also set in the liberal ideological environment of the ascendant West and in the structural context of unapproachable American power, both of which prompted those Western governments and NGOs who were most enthusiastic about the conference to expect that Vienna

---

[7]See, for example, Moses Moskowitz, *International Concern with Human Rights* (Leiden: Sijthoff Publishers, 1974); Morris B. Abrams, "The UN and Human Rights," *Foreign Affairs*, 47:2 (January 1969): 363–74; Roger S. Clark,. "Human Rights Strategies of the 1960s Within the United Nations: A Tribute to the late Kamleshwar Das," *Human Rights Quarterly*, 21:2 (May 1999): 308–41.
[8]A/CONF.32/SR.2
[9]Donald J. Puchala, "The Vienna Conference on Human Rights: Bridge to the Future or Bridge over Troubled Waters?" Unpublished case study used for Central European University Summer Institute courses.

would resoundingly endorse the universality of human rights. It is worth recalling in this context that a widely discussed thesis among scholars in the 1990 to 1993 period was Francis Fukuyama's notion concerning "The End of History," which anticipated that the universal embrace of liberal values was all but inevitable.[10]

In June 1993, 7,000 participants—including representatives of 171 member states and representatives of more than 800 NGOs—met in Vienna to consider progress and potential in the promoting of human rights. But those who presumed this would be a constructive expression of consensus were surprised by the divisive and highly contentious nature of the proceedings. There was no consensus and clearly no global rallying around liberal values. An appeal to cultural relativism with regard to human rights was the rallying cry. Liberal norms—individualism, personal liberty, democracy, and freedom of commerce, for example—prominent in human rights discourse of the early 1990s and assumed to be universally endorsed were assailed.

Vienna turned out to be an early indication that a new divide over human rights, reflecting a new post–Cold War politics of culture, was emerging within the UN to challenge long-standing agreements about universalism in values. We dwell at some length on the Vienna Conference is this chapter because, in our estimation, it was a signal event in the UN experience. For one thing, it was eminently clear at Vienna that the Cold War divide between the East and West was no longer an important axis of world politics. Russia and all of the former communist countries of Central and Eastern Europe aligned at Vienna with Europe, the United States, and most of Latin America. But it was also eminently clear at Vienna that the East–West divide had been replaced by a West versus non-West cleavage riven by politicized sensitivities about cultural differences. Practically speaking, the "non-West" at Vienna was comprised of much of the Arab world, some other Muslim countries such as Iran, China, much of the Pacific Rim (excepting Japan and South Korea), and Cuba. At the UN, on issues at the interface of culture and human rights, the critique of liberalism and universalism emerging from the non-West has persisted since Vienna.

PREPARING FOR THE VIENNA CONFERENCE

By a decision of the General Assembly in December 1990, the World Conference on Human Rights would be organized by regional preparatory committees called PrepComs, which were empowered to make proposals for setting the agenda at Vienna. The plan was that each regional grouping should arrive at a consensus, and then negotiations among regional groupings would reach a higher-level consensus that would become the agenda for the conference. Working through the agenda was supposed to yield a final document in the

---

[10]Francis Fukuyama, "The End of History," *The National Interest*, Summer 1989, 3–19.

form of a declaration that would assumedly elaborate and celebrate global consensus on universal human rights.

The African group met in Tunis in November 1992 and emphasized in their report that acting on economic and social priorities was tantamount to promoting human rights. The "right to development," they said, is a fundamental human right. They understandably also underlined that racism, extremism, and fanaticism represented serious threats to the promotion of human rights. Otherwise, the Tunis Declaration endorsed the Universal Declaration, the facilitating covenants, and the African Charter on Human and Peoples' Rights. But the African report also emphasized that "no ready-made model can be prescribed at the universal level since historical and cultural realities of each nation and the traditions, standards and values of each people cannot be disregarded." In this, it would appear, the Africans were offering a rather ambiguous "yes, but" regarding the universality of values pertaining to human rights. When it came to enforcing international standards, the Tunis Declaration made it clear that although human rights were of "global concern," implementing agreed standards was nevertheless the responsibility of national governments.

The Latin American regional group met in San José, Costa Rica, in January 1993 and produced a regional declaration that affirmed the universal nature of human rights. This placed them comfortably in the Western liberal camp, indeed outspokenly so with regard to their strong endorsement of democracy as "the best guarantee of the effective enjoyment of all human rights." The Latins were somewhat vacillating where it came to economic principles because, like the Africans, they declared that the "right to development is an unalienable human right," and they further observed that "the free market system cannot in and of itself guarantee or promote the enjoyment of human rights." Yet save for this publicly expressed dismay over neoliberal economic doctrines emanating from Washington and London, and the implicit, yet mandatory, kick at the United States for applying double standards in evaluating others' human rights records, the Latin American regional position was altogether Western.

Then there was the Asian group. Their meeting was held in Bangkok, Thailand, in March 1993 and yielded the Bangkok Declaration, which spelled out positions that were viewed by many in the West as deeply subversive to the universality of human rights. Much of the Bangkok declaration focused on issues of national autonomy and sovereign prerogatives, and in a series of strongly worded articles, it rejected intervention by the international community to enforce human rights standards and resisted any elaboration of UN machinery aimed at facilitating international intervention. We discussed the politics of sovereignty at the UN in Chapter 4. More importantly for the purposes of this chapter, the Bangkok Declaration openly questioned the universality of human rights and in so doing questioned the authority of the global regime set in place by the UN over the course of four decades. The preamble to the Bangkok document "expressed concern that these [existing] mechanisms relate to mainly one category of human rights." Later passages paid superficial deference to universality but then contradicted the very idea by arguing that human rights standards "must be considered in context of a dynamic and evolving process of international norm-setting, bearing in mind the significance of national and regional peculiarities and various historical, cultural, and religious backgrounds."

The Asian report also contested Western values, liberal democracy in particular, reiterating that "all countries, large and small, have the right to determine their political systems, control and freely utilize their resources, and freely pursue their economic, social and cultural development." Given cultural peculiarities, and the insistence that these had to be recognized in the area of human rights, the Asian position implied severely restricting the role and authority of the UN in this area. Even though the Bangkok Declaration was criticized by NGOs from the Asian region, the impact of their criticism was apparently minimal.

Interestingly, prior to the Vienna Conference the so-called Western European and Other Group did not produce a declaration or other formal document affirming its consensus. This group included most of the culturally Western countries outside Latin America, and their reluctance to announce positions apparently stemmed from the desire to prevent the world gathering at Vienna from polarizing into the West versus the rest. The group did meet informally in Atlanta in 1993, however, and issued an unofficial statement that strongly embraced the universality of human rights. The document also called on all states to withdraw their reservations to existing human rights treaties in order to universalize human rights standards. It was the most explicit among the regional positions regarding strengthening international mechanisms for the implementation and enforcement of human rights.

VIENNA 1993

What had been planned as a celebration turned out to be a donnybrook. The differences that emerged among the regional groupings during the preparatory phrase reemerged at Vienna. These were somewhat papered over in the final document produced by the World Conference, but what is memorable about the conference is not this bland document but rather the politics of culture and the global falling out that the document disguised. Taken largely by surprise, representatives from the Western European and Other group were apoplectic. The United States and several EU governments were emphatic in their rejection of culturally relative approaches to human rights and decried efforts to introduce this kind of thinking. Taking for granted the philosophical foundation for universalism, their arguments against relativism were legalistic and political. Speaking legalistically, they accused the cultural relativists of reneging on their commitments under the Universal Declaration on Human Rights. Politically, the Western camp argued that the culturally relativistic stance was nothing more than a shield for dictatorship and a false justification for continuing abuses of human rights. Latin Americans admonished that if universal standards could not be agreed on, then the whole machinery for international monitoring and implementation was moot.

The Asians, joined in the debates at Vienna by a number of Middle Eastern governments, some African states, Cuba, and others, were adamant in their efforts to change the nature of the debate. It was not about international law or about good world citizens versus miscreants, they insisted, but instead about whether different cultural traditions validated different interpretations and standards of human rights. "Universality," according to Singapore's Bilahari Kausikan, "is not a static concept. Rights, like all human norms, evolve in response to changing configurations of interests and needs."[11] According to the Asian values perspective, rights, like other entitlements bestowed by governments, are politically contingent. Mostly implicitly, but sometimes quite explicitly, the debate as the Asians and their partners perceived it was about Western preferences for maintaining global cultural hegemony accomplished during the heyday of European colonialism. Why in a postcolonial and post–Cold War era should the world still unquestionably accept the transcendence of Western values? Of course the non-Western stance at Vienna was a dramatic challenge to the apparent consensus forged in 1948 and written into the Universal Declaration, although even here representatives of the Asian group argued that the consensus of 1948 was perhaps more myth than reality. "Most rights are still essentially contested concepts," the Singaporeans instructed. "There may be a general consensus—but this is coupled with continuing and no less important conflicts of interpretation."[12]

The West and the non-West accused each other of obstructing progress at the Vienna Conference. The West criticized its antagonists for dwelling on matters long since settled with the signing of the fundamental documents of the human rights regime that affirmed universalism. Asians and others criticized the West for refusing to acknowledge that the international consensus on human rights was actually far narrower than the founding documents imply. Although the cultural relativists certainly made their presence known, they were a minority among national delegations to the Vienna conference. Their numbers, moreover, were probably further reduced by the strong-armed diplomacy of economic "carrots" and political "sticks" exercised by the United States. The U.S. delegation went so far as to circulate a list of countries responsible for blocking consensus at the conference—China, Syria, Iran, Iraq, Libya, Myanmar, Sudan, Vietnam, North Korea, and Malaysia—implying, rather unsubtly, that these governments were abusers of human rights. In the end there was a final conference declaration. It upheld the existing human rights regime and endorsed universal values in human rights. But it represented

---

[11]Bilahari Kausikan, "An Asian Approach to Human Rights," *Proceedings of the American Society for International Law* (82 ASIL Proc. 70, 1995), p. 148.
[12]Ibid., p. 147.

neither progress in the international promotion of human rights nor even international consensus concerning the nature of human rights. Like the conference itself, perhaps, what the final declaration actually declared was that the UN would be the arena for the new world politics of culture in the early twenty-first century.

A small aside is in order before we move on from this discussion of Vienna 1993. The fireworks at the World Conference on Human Rights were not limited to the official proceedings. After being specifically prevented from participating at the intergovernmental conference, the hundreds of human rights NGOs that descended on Vienna organized a parallel forum called "Human Rights for All." In this, the NGOs were encouraged and supported by the UN Secretariat. The NGO forum was also a raucous affair with more than three thousand delegates participating, who immediately produced a barrage of complaints on behalf of "impoverished peasants, terrorized tribals, embattled ethnic communities" and scores of other causes and human calamities that represented the singular interests of specific NGOs.[13] As a result, the NGO forum erupted into anarchy and militancy as the NGOs threw over the Joint Planning Commission, which originally enabled their participation, and demanded a new one. Delegates stood on chairs and shouted down the invited speaker, former U.S. president Jimmy Carter, because, despite his contributions to human rights, he nevertheless symbolized the United States. Underlining this, a delegate from India explained, "We've struggled for human rights all our lives, for decades. Now that the Cold War is over, are we going to let the United States come here and co-opt us and take over leadership of our struggle?"[14] Like the Vienna Conference itself, the NGO forum amplified the cacophony into which the discussion of human rights had degenerated. It also provided a good deal of grist for the mills of those within and without the UN who look askance at NGO interventions into world politics.

A DIALOGUE AMONG CIVILIZATIONS: THE CONTINUING POLITICS OF CULTURE AT THE UNITED NATIONS

The Asian challenge to the universalism of Western values coincided with the rising prominence of another academic who disputed the Fukuyama thesis. In 1993 the American scholar Samuel Huntington argued that the future of international relations would be conditioned by the fault lines of civilizations because there were and always had been irreconcilable differences among

---

[13]Linda Gail Arrigo, "A View of the United Nations Conference on Human Rights, Vienna, June 1993: From Among the Throng at the Non-Governmental Organization Forum," *Bulletin of Concerned Asian Scholars* 25:3 (1993): 69.
[14]Cited in ibid., p. 70.

cultures.[15] Huntington averred that "Islam has bloody borders," distinctly etched, for example, into the history of southern and Eastern Europe. He agreed with the Asian position that believing in the universalism of values is in fact a product of Western culture. Huntington's work generated a great deal of debate: detractors, mostly in the West, charged that Huntington was wrong and taking him seriously would precipitate the very cultural clashes he predicts. His supporters, mostly in the non-West, agreed that the cultural fault lines, which Westerners refused to recognize because they were liberal universalists, were real and ominous. However, the debate about "clashing civilizations" is not simply academic. Reacting to the Huntington thesis took three years and numerous meetings and generated countless papers consumed by diplomats at the UN. After September 11, 2001, it haunted political discourse within the UN and without, and it still gives many pause to think about fault lines in the world where great cultures intersect.

The drive at the UN to initiate a Dialogue Among Civilizations predated 9/11. Nevertheless, embodying as it did a continuing skepticism about value universalism, the Dialogue project relocated and carried forward the debate about cultural relativism that shook the Vienna Conference in 1993. In his first address to the UN in 1998, Iran's recently elected president Mohammed Khatami told his colleagues and counterparts in the General Assembly that the world needed to have a cultural dialogue among civilizations. Shortly thereafter the General Assembly adopted a resolution, drafted by Iran and cosponsored by more than fifty other governments, that designated the year 2001 as the "United Nations Year of Dialogue Among Civilizations."[16] The resolution invited governments, international organizations, and NGOs to plan and implement the intercultural dialogue, and the Group of Eminent Persons appointed to flesh out the concept of Dialogue concluded that it should be an effort to "find a new way of looking at our neighbors, globally, locally and even individually, and also to understand the significance of the United Nations."[17] Promoters of the "dialogue" viewed the UN not solely as an organization of sovereign states aimed at avoiding war, but "a place where a contract can be consummated that would provide the best recognition of each other's identities and the acceptance of common belonging."[18] The function of the Dialogue, its promoters explained, was essentially to promote cultural forms of peaceful interaction while yet preserving cultural diversity: but inasmuch as the "dialogue" sought universal appreciation for cultural differences rather than the pursuit of universal commonalities, it could be interpreted as a more

---

[15]See the fullest treatment of his thesis in Samuel Huntington, *The Clash of Civilizations and the Remaking of World Order* (New York: Simon & Schuster, 1996).
[16]A/53/22.
[17]Giandomenico Picco et al., *Crossing the Divide: Dialogue Among Civilizations*, Report of the Group of Eminent Persons (2001), p. 41.
[18]Ibid., p. 44.

subtle attack on universalism than the Asian values debate in 1993 where the validity of universalism had been directly rejected.

Between 1998 and 2001, a broad-ranging diplomatic effort, led by Iran, put substance on the skeletal framework of the Dialogue. This prompted the secretary-general to appoint a special representative for the Dialogue Among Civilizations, the experienced mediator Giandomenico Picco, who brought together eminent diplomats, writers, scholars, and artists to explore the concept of civilizational dialogue in an era of globalization. In the UN tradition of "a document that must please everyone and displease no one," this group recommended that efforts ought to be made "to overcome hegemony and exclusion by acknowledging and accepting cultural diversity while embracing universal commonalities and articulating a global ethics."[19] In November 2000 the General Assembly, again at Iranian urging, passed a resolution urging all members of society to participate in programs devoted to the Dialogue Among Civilizations, and to set aside two days in the General Assembly session of 2001 to consider the Dialogue. The government of Iran worked to mobilize the Organization of the Islamic Conference (OIC) to draft a plan of action for promoting the Dialogue that could be put before the international community at the UN. Such a text emerged in the summer of 2001 and was ready for consideration by the 56th General Assembly.

But the terrorist attacks in the United States against the World Trade Center and Pentagon on September 11, 2001, just days before the opening of the 56th session, resulted in a security shutdown of the UN headquarters and threw the scheduling of the General Assembly sessions into disarray. The issue of the Dialogue Among Civilizations was finally taken up in November, where the secretary-general reported that UNESCO exhibited considerable interest in the project. Then two days followed of a largely positive, although largely pro forma discussion, with many delegates remarking that the events of September 11 demonstrated more than ever the critical need for intercultural dialogue. Later the General Assembly unanimously adopted the OIC-proposed Program of Action for the Dialogue Among Civilizations.

Despite the General Assembly's considerations in November 2001, fundamentally speaking there was no "dialogue among civilizations" at the UN. It never really started. Or at least it has not started yet. Picco remains in place as the personal representative of the secretary-general in promoting the Dialogue. Member states have been encouraged to contribute to the trust fund to keep the project alive financially. It remains underfunded because only Switzerland has contributed. Austria, Iran, Ireland, and Qatar helped financially to bring the study groups of eminent persons together, but there have been no allocations to the Dialogue project from the UN's regular budget, which signals marginal interest in the undertaking. The secretary-general was instructed to report on the results of the "dialogue" at the 60th session of the General Assembly, and although mention was made of the dialogue in the

---

[19]Ibid., Introduction.

truncated declaration produced in September 2005, it remained an initiative tied to UNESCO activities and not a program central to the General Assembly or the Security Council. If the proposed "dialogue" was supposed to shift the context of UN politics toward a greater acceptance and legitimacy for cultural modes of political participation, the Dialogue Among Civilizations did not get very far in the primary political bodies of the UN.

Yet its apparent failure is fascinating. Why, especially after 9/11 and after the atrocities of ethnic cleansing in the 1990s, wasn't this appeal for cultural tolerance embraced enthusiastically? The short answer is that Western diplomats who had been involved in the bruising World Conference on Human Rights in 1993 viewed it as a thinly disguised attempt to reintroduce cultural relativity and undermine universality. The meaning of the Dialogue was contested on a fundamental level from the outset, and the skepticism accorded to the initiative reflected the earlier divisions that emerged in Vienna. The Dialogue also looked to be yet another attack on what others kept calling Western cultural hegemony, which of course it was. Iran, after all, was not in Western eyes the most credible candidate to lead a global movement promoting cultural tolerance. Others see the Dialogue as a casualty of the events of 9/11, which, again, it was, inasmuch as few Western governments were interested in talking about intercultural conciliation in the midst of what some were describing as the beginning of a new era of culture wars.

The impacts of 9/11 on the Dialogue Among Civilizations should not be exaggerated because it really appears that the initiative was dead in the diplomatic waters well before the terrorist attacks. Nevertheless, the terrorist attacks did have the effect of sidetracking the Iranian and OIC initiatives within the UN because they consumed the political attention of much of the world and filled the "political space" in New York that might otherwise have been occupied by different issues including the Dialogue Among Civilizations. During the latter years of the Clinton administration, and even more definitively with the coming into office of the George W. Bush administration, the United States had veered onto a unilateral course in its foreign policy. By implication and action, Washington came to take the UN less and less into account. However, for a few months in the immediate aftermath of 9/11, the United States reengaged at the UN, and the international community used the machinery of the UN to express solidarity with the United States. Combating terrorism moved immediately to the top of the UN agenda, and within the world organization almost all attention was focused on the Security Council where responses to 9/11 were being cobbled. This understandable flurry of political activity at he UN in the autumn of 2001 marginalized the Dialogue Among Civilizations, to the point where representatives of the OIC acknowledged that they "could not move forward with the Dialogue after 9/11 because we were preaching the idea of tolerance but this intolerant attack came from the Muslim world."[20] The events of September 11, felt closely at

---

[20]Interview at the OIC Mission to the UN, December 23, 2002.

the UN, became enmeshed in the broader cultural clashes between universalists and cultural relativists.

Regarding the Dialogue more generally, diplomats in New York who were drawn into talking about it were, in some cases consciously and admittedly, cast into a realm of discourse that they were neither trained nor particularly predisposed to deal with. Many UN delegates did not know what to make of the initiative. One diplomat closely involved remarked that "it seemed weird . . . another one of these strange proposals that comes along every year." And a European colleague observed, "It's like apple pie and motherhood. Who could be against dialogue?" One of the reasons that the Dialogue amounted to so little in New York is that many of those engaged wanted to see it as partisan and political because they were conditioned to believe that everything connected with the UN was partisan and political. These people lived in a political world where power and national interests were brokered, where it was always essential to ask about geostrategic motives, to suspect that others' high-sounding rhetoric veiled self-interested goals and to deeply discount conciliatory gestures from political or ideological rivals. That someone simply wanted to talk so that international understanding might be enhanced was, from the perspective of the New York diplomatic community, somewhat incredible. If it actually was what its sponsors said it was, then the Dialogue Among Civilizations should more properly have been an exercise for philosophers, historians, theologians, educators, and artists. The politically battle-scarred diplomats in New York were not the ones most likely to pull off a successful dialogue among civilizations.

In fact, when the Dialogue moved outside the political venues of New York and was actually engaged by philosophers, historians, theologians, educators, and artists, as well as diplomats, it took on a bit of substance. But when considered in the political environment of the UN General Assembly, the dialogue never really became an exercise in shared cultural understanding. The puzzled and skeptical interpretation of the Dialogue by a diplomat from Eastern Europe was typical: "You can usually track (an initiative) backward and see that it's a political agenda from a national leader. . . . The Dialogue initiative was OK. The idea was to promote exchange. But in my opinion it was a miserable kind of initiative. It couldn't and didn't grow up in the UN environment." Instead, the dialogue politicized into a debate reminiscent of Vienna in 1993. Almost everyone agreed that the Dialogue Among Civilizations could amount to a refutation of the Huntington thesis about the inevitable clash of civilizations, and this was probably useful because of the incendiary potentials of the "clashing" notion.[21] It was also broadly accepted that dialogue was preferable to cultural exclusion and division. But beyond such superficial acknowledgments, there was mostly disagreement.

[21]Kofi Annan, "Dialogue Among Civilizations," *Presidents and Prime Ministers* 10 (January/February 2001): 25–26.

For one thing, the international community could not agree on the meaning of "civilization," or whether civilizations were important units of international interaction. A delegate from Singapore argued, for example, that "civilizations are not monolithic entities with fixed borders." There is no civilization in the world, she said, "that can claim to be ethnically, culturally, religiously, or socially homogenous. The civilizations of the world are no longer separate entities but are inextricably linked with each other both culturally and geographically."[22] These realities, she explained (somewhat ironically given Singapore's central role at Vienna), posed problems for a dialogue among civilizations because they rendered it difficult to identify who belonged to a particular civilization and who did not, and even more difficult to agree on who could conceivably claim to speak for a whole civilization. Other delegates, however, accepted a priori that civilizations are important shapers of identity, and problems having to do with who is in and who is outside are less than serious. But among those who affirmed that civilizations were worth talking about, there was little agreement on the question of what distinguishes one civilization from another. Is it religion, race, artistic and literary modes and traditions, or other cultural or historical attributes?

Westerners argued that even if there were such cultural entities as civilizations, commonalities among them, associated with the fundamentals of the human condition, overshadow civilizational differences. About this, Vaira Vike-Freiberga, the president of Latvia, waxed most expressively in defense of these commonalities when she told her colleagues that "Man might be a naked ape with the same instincts of destruction and survival found in the lowest animals of the planet. But man is a creature with a brain, which allowed it to write a new program for each new life and new generation. In this regard, humans have the privilege of inheritance."[23]

If the discussions on the Dialogue fixed on such esoteric issues as "what constitutes a civilization," they would have been surprisingly uncharacteristic of the UN. But as one Third World ambassador explained, "In the UN it is difficult to have frank dialogues that don't raise questions of Western superiority. Most of the rest of the world sees the West lecturing to them all the time."[24] The West did in fact do a good bit of lecturing in the consideration of civilizational dialogues, about universalism mostly. Whereas many others used the setting of the Dialogue Among Civilizations to rehearse positions in long-standing political debates and to register familiar complaints tinged in anti-Westernism, Europeans approached the Dialogue from a Western perspective and wanted it to be mostly about human rights and the universal values. The EU's position papers made consistent reference to the Universal Declaration of Human Rights as "a common standard of achievement," recalled the

[22]Statement by Deputy Permanent Representative of Singapore, Ms. Tan Yee Woan on Agenda Item 25: UN Year of Dialogue Among Civilizations, November 8, 2001.
[23]Interview at UN Headquarters, January 10, 2003.
[24]Interview at UN Headquarters, January 9, 2003.

conclusions of the Vienna conference, and repeatedly sought to insert mention of "individuals" and "equal and inalienable rights of all members of the human family."[25] Latin Americans and the Holy See supported the emphasis on human rights, and the former took every opportunity to make reference to universal values that transcended civilizational divides.

As adamantly as the Europeans insisted that human rights must be a central issue in a dialogue among civilizations, non-Westerners had different agendas. These too were familiar. They generally separated the non-West from the West, and they were political. Interestingly, one East European ambassador regretted the whole exercise of the Dialogue because "those opposed to universalism gained some traction with this Dialogue."[26] African delegations appealed to the delegates gathered to consider racism because "the scars of history and individual experiences were too deep and fresh to engage in a dialogue among civilizations without due recognition of racism."[27] Indonesian delegates wanted to link the Dialogue Among Civilizations to issues of protecting national sovereignty. Waving the banner of cultural relativism, President Khatami of Iran spoke of secular and sacred discourses and claimed that the West, although unable to communicate in the latter, at least "should begin to listen to other narratives proposed by other cultural domains."[28] Other countries represented by the OIC pressed to focus the discussions on the issue of cultural security. Several diplomats from the Islamic world emphasized that the purpose of the Dialogue was not simply to promote respect for cultural diversity but to preserve this diversity in a world where modernization was obliterating cultural differences. Muslim representatives argued that for some, "cultural differences can be security threats," and the Dialogue "is the pathway to alleviating such threats."[29] The not-very-veiled implication was that Western cultural hegemony was a threat, as was Western cultural intolerance, and the preferred outcome of the Dialogue Among Civilizations should be to contain such threats. Responding to the European singularity about human rights, Islamic interlocutors argued that for them, the dialogue was not primarily about human rights but about the security implications of cultural diversity among civilizations. "If you change every issue into a question of human rights," one Muslim diplomat noted, "then you will have only one subject. Not only does this sidetrack a dialogue among civilizations, it also erodes the integrity of human rights."[30] In the end, the divide, between those who sought cultural security and those who wanted to focus on universal human rights, was among the most important obstacles to a real dialogue.

---

[25]See various EU Position Papers on Draft Global Agenda for Dialogue Among Civilizations.

[26]Interview at UN Headquarters, January 10, 2003.

[27]Press Release GA/9747: General Assembly Plenary, September 5, 2000.

[28]Ibid.

[29]Interview at UN Headquarters, January 9, 2003.

[30]Interview at UN Headquarters, January 9, 2003.

Although initially embraced to refute of the inevitability of clashing civilizations, the seemingly innocuous concept of intercultural dialogue, when heated in the cauldron of intergovernmental politics at the UN, was largely transformed into a contest between the West and the non-West. Reminiscent of what had occurred at Vienna in 1993, the debates about culture and civilization in 2001 reflected the enduring politics of culture at the UN insofar as it: (1) revealed and highlighted important differences among major cultural communities, (2) respectively attacked and defended Western values and their universality, (3) raised serious issues concerning the political contingency of human rights, and (4) changed no one's mind or political position. From his vantage point of monitor and observer of the Dialogue Among Civilizations, Picco reported that the question is whether the UN "has been able to generate a new mindset among those who have come to work with it, work in it, or benefit from it."[31] If we are to judge the Dialogue on the basis of changing mindsets or even changing the political dynamics of interaction at the UN, it did not get very far beyond signifying a continued cultural discontent that is seriously obstructing cooperation within the world organization.

THE POLITICS OF CULTURE

When the UN takes action, it is often considered to be doing so on behalf of the international community. The notion of the "international community," that is, peoples with much in common, presupposes shared values linking its members together. Nowhere perhaps in UN affairs today does the myth of community strain credulity more than in the discourse surrounding universal values. Affirming human rights is essentially a moral matter that amounts to defining what is appropriate and inappropriate in relations among individuals. But defining what is appropriate and inappropriate in relations between governments and their citizens is a political matter because rights are bestowed by political authorities. By the turn of the twenty-first century, less and less was left of the once broadly accepted conviction that the international community, represented by consensus within the UN, has the political authority to bestow universal human rights. When the ending of the Cold War papered over the world political cleavage between East and West, the coincident rift between the West and the non-West widened. As might be expected, within the UN this rift politicized: universalists, reinforcing Western hegemony, lined up against relativists, who were manifestly antihegemonic. Confrontations about culture marked and marred the World Conference on Human Rights in Vienna in 1993. They continued to affect and obstruct human rights deliberations through the 1990s and then broadened into a politics of culture during the Dialogue Among Civilizations after the turn of the century. Today at

---

[31]Picco et al., *Crossing the Divide*, p. 165.

the UN, the cultural cleavage between the West and the non-West is as wide as ever.

For simplicity's sake, we have been depicting the politics of culture at the UN as a *debate*. Although this rings somewhat truer than the phenomenon's in-house characterization as a dialogue, it is still not the best choice of terms. In Anatol Rapoport's classic distinction among "fights, games, and debates," the politics of culture as played out at the UN are not actually debates because debates have the objective of generating closure by changing minds, that is, convincing the opponent to see things as one sees them.[32] Debates pressed to denouement, clear the table, and clear the air so that collective action can take place. This certainly has not happened regarding cultural issues at the UN. In this sense, moreover, there are really preciously few real debates at the UN. Official minds seem hardly affected by rhetoric, and they do not readily change. Moreover, the politics of culture, at least as played out within the UN (although not necessarily on the outside), are not "fights" because in Rapoport's meaning these are phenomena of pure opposition where opponents try to eliminate or destroy each other. This is hardly possible within the UN. Rather, what we have observed as "debates" between universalists and relativists are best likened to *games*, where opponents plan and execute strategies aimed at gaining advantage or "winning."

Yet it is not clear what one wins by prevailing rhetorically over an ideological opponent at the UN. Some players, who have perhaps been immersed in UN politics for too long, believe that "winning" amounts to having the paragraphs of turgid documents endorse one's own positions and contradict opponents' positions. If these paragraphs are then voted and approved by substantial majorities in the General Assembly or elsewhere, so much more satisfying is the win. No matter in such instances that the results of either drafting or voting in the UN have little consequence in the world beyond the organization. But it could be that the payoffs are actually in playing the games, and playing them well, because they are played before mass media and domestic political and bureaucratic audiences who enjoy good matches, particularly against venerable opponents. This inward orientation of the games of culture at the UN erodes the idea of an international community seeking to address shared problems. In many ways, the politics of culture, with West pitted against non-West, have become yet another game that governments play at the UN. No one yet seems to be decisively winning. But universal values and the UN human rights regime constructed during the second half of the twentieth century appear to be losing, and the notion of an international community with shared values becomes ever more illusory.

---

[32] Anatol Rapoport, *Fights, Games and Debates* (Ann Arbor: University of Michigan Press, 1960), pp. 273–88.

CHAPTER 7

Peacekeeping: Paper, Preparation, and Politics

Peacekeeping and all that it involves and implies has come to be the center-piece of United Nations activity. This was not always the case because during the period of the Cold War most armed conflicts in the world had to do in one way or another with the contest between the United States and the Soviet Union. The superpower contenders were therefore reluctant to allow UN involvement for fear it might affect the course of conflicts in ways that might advantage one or the other. But the ending of the Cold War invited major power cooperation in the Security Council, and this opened the way to dispatching UN peacekeepers to numerous trouble spots in the world. In 2006 there were eighteen UN peacekeeping operations ongoing in Asia, Africa, Europe, and Oceania, involving more than ninety thousand military and civilian peacekeepers and annually budgeted at more than $5 billion (representing 0.5% of global military spending). During the most intense phase of UN involvement in the mid-1990s, there were thirty-eight ongoing operations in the field.

Two important sets of issues surround UN peacekeeping and its future. These may be rather imprecisely categorized as "when to do it" and "how to do it." The "when" issues concern the ongoing controversy over humanitarian intervention. That is, when is it legitimate for the UN acting as an agent of the international community to send armed forces into a sovereign state for the purpose of protecting people? The issue of humanitarian intervention is both very complex and highly charged politically, as discussion elsewhere in this volume makes clear. Because we do deal with this issue elsewhere, we are not going to go into it any length in this chapter.

The "how" question surrounding UN peacekeeping has to do with the capabilities of the United Nations to perform peacekeeping tasks assigned to it. Intervening to make peace or keep peace means at the very least conducting a military expedition. To succeed, everything that goes into such an expedition—planning, procurement, command and control, transport, communications, armaments, and the like—has to be executed in a timely, precise, and professional fashion. These days UN intervention as likely as not involves rebuilding a fractured state and reconstituting a destroyed society. To succeed, extensive knowledge, diverse skills, and suitable and sensitive management must be brought to bear again in a timely, precise, and professional fashion. This chapter focuses mainly on the "how" questions of peacekeeping, and to the extent that UN performance has not been timely, precise, and professional, this chapter also seeks to answer "why."

Let us start with the paper. Since 1999 the UN has generated reams upon reams of paper—scores of documents amounting to thousands of pages of reporting, analysis, commentary, and commitment, all addressing the reform of peacekeeping operations. To set a baseline arbitrarily, let us anchor one end of the paper flow with the *Report of the Secretary-General Pursuant to General Assembly Resolution 53/35*.[1] This November 1999 document was the remarkably candid analysis of UN complicity in the fall of Srebrenica and the massacre that ensued during the Bosnian conflict. The "Srebrenica Report" was followed almost immediately in December 1999 by the *Report of the Independent Inquiry into the Actions of the United Nations During the 1994 Genocide in Rwanda*, another thoroughly unflattering account of a UN peacekeeping mission gone sour and the horrendous loss of human life that resulted.[2] Deeply concerned about the UN's peacekeeping failures during the 1990s, Secretary-General Kofi Annan in March 2000 asked former Algerian foreign minister Lakhdar Brahimi to head a panel of experts and conduct an independent review of all aspects of UN peacekeeping. Ambassador Brahimi's panel was also asked to offer recommendations for improvement. The *Report of the Panel on United Nations Peace Operations* was released in August 2000.[3] In the executive summary to this document, Ambassador Brahimi observed that "over the last decade, the United Nations has repeatedly failed to the meet the challenge" of the Charter to "save succeeding generations from the scourge of war" and "it can do no better today."[4] The so-called Brahimi Report set off flurries of UN-centered and UN-focused activity concerning the reform of

---

[1] A/54/549.

[2] SC/6843, SG/SM/7263/AFR/196, http:www.un.org/News/ossg/rwanda_report.htm.

[3] A/55/305, S/2000/809 (hereafter cited as Brahimi Report). The other members of the independent panel were J. Brian Atwood (United States), Colin Granderson (Trinidad and Tobago), Ann Hercus (New Zealand), Richard Monk (UK), Klaus Naumann (Germany), Hisako Shimura (Japan), Vladimir Shustov (Russian Federation), Philip Sibanda (Zimbabwe), and Cornelio Sommaruga (Switzerland).

[4] Brahimi Report, p. viii.

peacekeeping operations. Discerning the extent to which this activity has enhanced the capacity of the UN to execute peacekeeping assignments is the particular purpose of this chapter. Evaluating UN peacekeeping more generally and anticipating its future are this chapter's broader purposes.

Paper at the UN flowed in great profusion between the autumn of 2000 and the autumn of 2002, that is, between the 55th and the 57th sessions of the General Assembly, and a considerable part of this paper flow had to do with the reform of peacekeeping operations. There were, for example, two major reports by the secretary-general to the General Assembly's Special Committee on Peacekeeping Operations (Committee of 34) that outlined steps that needed to be taken to implement the Brahimi Report's recommendations, a similar report by the secretary-general to the Security Council, several duly recorded and reported debates in the Special Committee, the Fourth Committee, and the Security Council about the secretary-general's proposals, several briefings by the under-secretary-general for peacekeeping operations, and a number of lengthy, periodic reports from both the Special Committee and the Fourth Committee to the General Assembly under a recurrent agenda item titled "Comprehensive Review of the Whole Question of Peacekeeping Operations in All Their Aspects." There were in addition numerous reviews and reports from the Advisory Committee on Administrative and Budgetary Questions (ACABQ) concerning resources required for implementing the Brahimi recommendations, many recorded debates and subsequent reports from the Fifth Committee, also dealing with resources required for peacekeeping reform, and several resolutions emanating from both the General Assembly and the Security Council.[5] UN documents are turgid, tedious, tiresome, redundant, and opaque and as often as not unrevealing concerning the organizational, operational, and political realities with which they purport to deal. Nevertheless, with respect to the reform of UN peacekeeping operations, the documents tell a rather interesting story, and following this paper trail does begin to reveal whether the UN is "doing better" at peacekeeping today than at the time when Ambassador Brahimi released his report.

THE BRAHIMI REPORT

The Brahimi Report's critique of UN peacekeeping operations during the 1990s is familiar. Problematic and failed operations, like those in Somalia and Bosnia, for example, were of a kind that have come to be called "complex." They mix *enforcement* action, where military means are required to separate

---

[5]See especially A/55/305-S/2000/809; A/55/502; A/55/507; A/55/977; A/56/732; A/56/870; A/55/1024; A/56/863; A/56/6 (Sect. 5); A/55/676; A/56/478; A/56/902; A/56/989; A/RES/54/250 A-C; A/RES/56/289; A/RES/56/293; S/RES/1318 (2000); S/RES/1327 (2000); S/RES/1353 (2001).

and pacify warring parties,[6] with *peacekeeping*, where armistices or settlements are monitored and guaranteed, with *peace building*, where the international community assists in the reconstruction of the social order of a failed state or destroyed country. During the transition from peacemaking to peace building, efforts must frequently be made to disarm, demobilize, and reintegrate formerly warring factions—so-called DD&R—and this may constitute yet a fourth distinct cluster of activities. The Brahimi panel found that it is frequently the case that neither the Security Council, which mandates operations, nor the Secretariat, which advises the council prior to its issuing a mandate and later acts in accord with the mandate, are sufficiently knowledgeable concerning crisis situations to discern how much enforcement, peacekeeping, and peace building are involved. Nor has the UN been adequately informed in many instances about difficulties encountered during disarmament, demobilization and reintegration. Such failures of information and understanding have resulted in unrealistic mandates and inappropriately planned and executed operations. Relatedly, the panel observed that mandates and operations following from classic peacekeeping principles of local consent, impartiality and force applied only in self-defense can turn out to be not only inapplicable but hazardous for civilians and peacekeepers. "No failure did more to damage the standing and credibility of UN peacekeeping in the 1990s than its reluctance to distinguish victim from aggressor."[7]

Complex peace operations are likely to be the modes of the future because more intranational conflicts are predictable in the post–Cold War international environment. More weak states will probably fail, and in environments of highly politicized ethnicity and dogmatic religions, more gross violations of human rights will probably occur. These were the Brahimi panel's assumptions, and recommendations following from these emphasized that complex peace operations consist of several distinct kinds of activities: military, police, judicial, institutional/administrative and humanitarian. The Brahimi panel said,

> These operations face challenges and responsibilities that are unique among United Nations field operations. No other operations must set and enforce the law, establish customs services and regulations, set and collect business and personal taxes, attract foreign investment, adjudicate property disputes and liabilities for war damage, reconstruct and operate all public utilities, create a banking system, run schools, pay teachers and collect the garbage—in a war-damaged society, using voluntary contributions, because the assessed mission budget, even for such "transitional administration" missions, does not fund local administration itself. In addition to such tasks, these missions must also try to rebuild civil

[6]The Brahimi Report puts this rather nicely: "United Nations operations thus do not deploy into post-conflict situations so much as they deploy to create such situations. That is, they work to divert the unfinished conflict, and the personal, political or other agendas that drove it, from the military to the political arena, and to make that diversion permanent." See Brahimi Report, p. 4.
[7]Brahimi Report, p. ix.

society and promote respect for human rights, in places where grievance is widespread and grudges run deep.[8]

Effectively preparing for UN interventions into complex conflict situations first requires recognizing the distinctiveness of the different dimensions of missions' complexity, and then planning, training and staffing in appropriate preparation for acting effectively in each dimension. The panel reported that the UN was deficient in planning, training, and staffing in every aspect of complex peacekeeping, and woefully so in the area of postconflict peace building. There is necessarily also a holistic level of activity where the different dimensions of complex operations are integrated into an overall mission, but here too the Brahimi panel found the United Nations less than able.

Rapid response is imperative in crisis situations. In genocidal situations, rapid response is the only kind of response that can possibly make any difference. Yet rapid response has not been one of the hallmarks of UN peacekeeping, which the Brahimi panel emphatically underscored. Moving swiftly requires early intelligence, anticipatory planning, having money on hand, having leaders selected, having personnel on call, having equipment prepositioned, and having transport arranged. Much of this has to do with consultation, cooperation, contracts, and commitments in relations between member states and the UN Secretariat, and the bulk of these arrangements must be concluded before peacekeeping missions are mandated. The Brahimi panel challenged the United Nations to develop the capacity to place a traditional peacekeeping operation—that is, blue-helmeted truce supervision, cease-fire monitoring, or armistice policing—in the field in thirty days and to place a complex operation involving postconflict reconstruction in the field in ninety days. Although such a 30/90 scheme is still something less than what many would consider "rapid response," developing even this capability would amount to an impressive step forward for the UN. It clearly did not exist when the Brahimi Report was released in 2000.

What is now called "peace building" in United Nations terminology amounts to a cluster of activities engaged to reconstruct societies destroyed in civil wars or to otherwise erect political/administrative scaffolding to support failed states. Peace building is a relatively new kind of mission for the UN, and it has been largely undertaken on ad hoc bases as the need for it has occurred. Activities involved in peace building—for example, deploying civilian police officers, installing temporary judiciaries, sometimes writing law codes, administering programs normally tasked to governments, restoring civil society, and all the while preparing for transitions back to local authorities—are wholly different from those involved in traditional peacekeeping. Expertise required is therefore wholly different, as are planning, training, recruitment, and deployment. The Brahimi panel recognized the importance of peace building in projected future missions and also the UN's limited capacity to engage in

---

[8]Ibid., p. 13.

peace building. There was at the time of the Brahimi Report, for example, limited in-house expertise in civilian policing, judicial affairs, or civil administration, limited training available or planned in such areas, and limited knowledge concerning where in the world capable people were to be found who could be rapidly deployed for peace building.

When the Brahimi Report was published in August 2000, the initial reaction among a number of UN watchers was that it said little about the problems of UN peacekeeping that was actually new.[9] This is true, and even more to the point the Brahimi Report said little that was not already known about the managerial malaise and operational inefficiencies of the UN Secretariat more generally, or about the failings of the organization's personnel system, the disconnects between headquarters and field, the confusion that confounds coordination, the surrealism that envelops the General Assembly, and the politics of self-interest that degrade the Security Council. But the Brahimi Report was not addressed to UN watchers; it was rather addressed to UN members. Ambassador Brahimi and his colleagues gathered together the experiences and reflections of a difficult decade and reported on lessons learned and not learned. Then they wrote an indictment and called for rectification. Although many governments saw it differently, and still do, the Brahimi Report's indictment was directed at the UN's member states much more than at the Secretariat. The report's appeals for behavioral change are certainly as much directed at the member states as at the Secretariat.

Nevertheless, reading through the avalanche of UN documents addressed to "implementing the recommendations of the panel on peace operations," particularly those emanating from the intergovernmental committees of the General Assembly, lends the impression that the member states, at least initially, chose to attribute most of the problems with UN peacekeeping to the inefficiencies of the Secretariat. That is, most national delegations have chosen to frame the issue of peacekeeping reform as a question of Secretariat reform. It is the Department of Peacekeeping Operations and related units, they say, that made the messes of the 1990s, and it is therefore their acts that need to be cleaned up. Underlining this interpretation, we read almost ad nauseam in the reports of the Special Committee, the Fourth Committee, and the Fifth Committee, as well as in the debates and discussions, that more efficient use of resources would greatly improve the capacity of the Department of Peacekeeping Operations, that consolidating offices or units within the department would facilitate coordination, that too many small subunits often located in different buildings defy effective management, that subordinates spend too much time writing speeches for their bosses, that communication between the Secretariat and the member states is faulty and improvement is imperative,

---

[9]For example, much of what the Brahimi panel discovered was anticipated by Weiss, Forsythe, and Coate in their 1997 publication, *The Changing United Nations*. See Thomas G. Weiss, David P. Forsythe and Roger A. Coate, *The Changing United Nations*, 2nd ed. (Boulder, Colo.: Westview, 1997), pp. 46–122.

that the international civil servants assigned to the Department of Peacekeeping Operations (DPKO) are not yet a meritocracy, and that headquarters support for field operations leaves much to be desired.

These criticisms of the Secretariat are not entirely unjustified. But, by our reading, and also in the apparent, although deftly expressed, interpretation of Kofi Annan, indicting the Secretariat is not what the Brahimi Report was all about. The report asks for five things: more money; more people; more information, clarification, and specification; more planning and preparation; and more commitment and cooperation on the part of member states. In his own reports concerning the implementation of the Brahimi panel's recommendations, the secretary-general repeatedly asks for the same things. He asks for more money, so that he can recruit more people, who can gather more information and engage in more planning and preparation. He also asks for more money so he can create strategic stocks of equipment, enter into contracts with suppliers and transporters, monitor the preparedness of standby units of peacekeepers, enhance training, produce manuals, and modernize and digitalize communications between headquarters and the field. In the secretary-general's interpretation, and we would say in the Brahimi panel's as well, the UN's peacekeeping capacities were more constrained by limited resources than by bureaucratic maladies, incompetent staff, or most of the other elements in the standard member-state critique of the UN Secretariat.

It must be remembered that the Department of Peacekeeping Operations (DKPO) is a relatively new unit, created only in 1992. During the Cold War, peacekeeping was not a centrally important activity of the UN, and even after the establishment of the DKPO, peacekeeping affairs retained somewhat of an amateurish aura—"gifted amateurism," Annan called it—combined with airs of impermanence.[10] Ambassador Brahimi told the Special Committee in November 2000 that one objective of peacekeeping reform ought to be to retain peacekeeping as a core function of the UN. Yet at the time the Brahimi Report was published, the DPKO had a professional staff of approximately 300 people, who were supporting some 60,000 personnel in engaged in more than a dozen peacekeeping missions. It was allocated about $14 million in UN's regular budget for the 2000–2001 biennium, that is, about $7 million per year.[11] Of the 300 professionals, fewer than 50 were permanent UN employees funded out of the organization's regular budget; most were considered "temporary" and funded out of the Support Account for Peacekeeping Operations that fluctuated from year to year according to the number of peacekeeping missions in the field. There were, at this time, twelve military

---

[10]A/55/977, p. 4.

[11]The actual regular budget allocation to the DPKO for the 2000–2001 biennium was approximately $75 million. Approximately $61 million of this, however, was allocated to financing the United Nations Truce Supervision Organization (UNTSO) in Palestine and the United Nations Military Observer Group in India and Pakistan (UNMOGIP), whose budgets for historical reasons are included in the regular budget for the DPKO. See A/56/6 (Section 5), 6, and 18–20.

officers assigned to DPKO, four civilian police advisers, and no experts in civil affairs or judicial matters. Because the small number of professionals in the DPKO was constantly involved in day-to-day problem solving connected with missions in the field or in servicing the UN's intergovernmental deliberative bodies, there was little time for planning, training, evaluating, monitoring, or preparing for future undertakings; in short, there was little professional time for most of the activities the Brahimi panel identified as central to enhancing peacekeeping capacity.

In the winter of 2001, after being largely rebuffed by the General Assembly the previous autumn in his attempt to gain new resources for enhancing the capacities of the DPKO, the secretary-general enlisted a consulting firm to evaluate the performance of the department. His report to the 56th General Assembly notes that,

> The consultants employed the basic assumption that sound management requires planning on a variety of levels. In the case of peacekeeping, this entails anticipating the demands to be created by future peacekeeping operations and articulating strategic plans for meeting them. It requires the development of policies and capacities to support the strategic plans. And it envisages that such policies and capacities will then be applied effectively, when the time comes, to the operational planning and support of specific peacekeeping operations. In order for all of these things to happen, significant portions of the Department, particularly at senior levels, must be able to find the time to dedicate sufficient attention to them. This requires that there be a strong managerial infrastructure in place so that the majority of the Department is not consumed or overwhelmed by immediate daily demands. . . . The vast majority of the Department's workload, at all levels, is directed towards dealing with short-term issues and day-to-day problems associated with the support of existing peacekeeping operations.[12]

One of the main reasons then why peacekeeping assignments during the 1990s were frequently not handled as well as they could and should have been is that too few people were too often asked to do too much with too little.

At the most fundamental level, the reform of the United Nations' peacekeeping operations as recommended by the Brahimi panel requires a substantial input of new resources, that is, more money. Providing these new resources is the responsibility of the member states. The Brahimi Report therefore emphasized that "changes the Panel recommends will have no lasting impact unless Member States summon the political will to support the UN politically, financially and operationally."[13] Whether reform moves or stalls depends in the first instance on member states' willingness to provide funds. That member states have been unwilling to do this for quite some time is duly noted in the Brahimi Report.

---

[12]A/55/97, p. 11.
[13]Brahimi Report, p. viii.

But the responsibility of the member states does not end with money. "The Secretary-General finds himself in an untenable position," the Brahimi panel explains:

> He is given a Security Council resolution specifying troop levels on paper, but without knowing whether he will be given the troops to put on the ground. The troops that eventually arrive in theatre may still be under-equipped: Some countries have provided soldiers without rifles, or with rifles but no helmets, or with helmets but no flack jackets, or with no organic transport capability (trucks or troops carriers). Troops may be untrained in peacekeeping operations, and in any case the various contingents in an operation are unlikely to have trained or worked together before. Some units may have no personnel who can speak the mission language. Even if language is not a problem, they may lack common operating procedures and have differing interpretations of key elements of command and control and of the mission's rules of engagement, and have differing expectations about mission requirements for the use of force. . . . This must stop.[14]

Member states are responsible for supplying troops and other personnel as they have previously agreed in stand-by arrangements and/or as may be requested by the UN. *All* member states share this responsibility. They are also principally responsible for training their people. To expedite rapid response, national units contributed to UN operations ought to be able to sustain themselves in the field for some time during the startup of missions. National governments are also responsible for contributing to Secretariat efforts to establish and maintain on-call lists of officers, experts, and officials who can be summoned on short notice to serve as UN peacekeepers and peace builders. Most critically perhaps, national governments as members of the Security Council, or in consultation with the Security Council, are responsible for establishing the mandates that become the bases for UN peacekeeping missions. The Brahimi panel recommended that these be "robust and realistic."

Imprecise, ambiguous, erroneous, insensitive, and timid mandates approved by the Security Council directly contributed to flawed UN peacekeeping efforts in Somalia, Bosnia, and Rwanda. Faulty mandates also contributed to the deaths of dozens of UN peacekeepers, to the deaths of many humanitarian assistance workers, and to the deaths of thousands of civilians trapped in war zones and killing fields. Faulty mandates have repeatedly sent UN peacekeepers into dangerous situations armed with too little and arriving too late. Timid rules of engagement have kept peacekeepers standing by while civilians were slaughtered; they have permitted peacekeepers to be humiliated and taken hostage; and they have allowed aggressors free rein while constraining the capabilities of defenders. Mandate writing itself has been hostage to the clashing political interests of members of the Security Council.

---

[14]Ibid., p. 18.

The differing private agendas of Security Council members—some fixed on protecting clients, others reluctant to spend money, still others cautious about intervention—have too often been the reasons for both the "too littles" and the "too lates" haunting UN peacekeeping behavior. Papered-over differences in the Security Council chamber, moreover, become ambiguities in the field, confusion about execution, gaps in coordination, sources of costly mistakes, and reasons for inaction. Mandate writing has as well fallen hostage to the UN's mythologies about impartiality, the nonuse of force, and self-defense. In what the Brahimi panel described as the "less forgiving, more dangerous environments" in which present-day peacekeepers are likely to find themselves, confronting "three or more parties, of varying commitment to peace, with divergent aims, with independent sources of income and arms, and with neighbors who are willing to buy, sell and transit illicit goods," the mandates that box peacekeepers into the confines of traditional UN-isms can invite disaster. Mandates are the responsibility of the UN's member states, members of the Security Council specifically. They are obliged to get these right.

THE REFORM OF UNITED NATIONS PEACEKEEPING OPERATIONS

Interestingly, the Brahimi Report has not gone the way of the countless similar UN documents that have slipped silently into the history's huge dustbin. There has in fact been notable movement toward implementing a number of the Brahimi panel's recommendations, and these initiatives may have improved the UN's capacity to initiate and execute complex peacekeeping missions. The most notable initiative is the creation of the Peacebuilding Commission in 2006 which was perhaps the most uncontested success of the 2005–2006 reform effort. Two caveats, however, are in order: (1) peacekeeping reform is a work in progress and far from complete, and (2) the enhanced capacity that has been created has not been fully tested. Still, the work in progress can claim some progress.

Between 2000 and 2002, the Department of Peacekeeping Operations acquired both additional money and additional people. In two phases, first in December 2000 and then again in December 2001, the DPKO gained 184 new posts, an increase of some 56 percent at the professional level. If increasing the number of posts is tantamount to increasing institutional capacity, then capacity was surely increased. What is rather problematic, however, is that the regular budget of the DPKO did not increase between the 2000–2001 biennium and the 2002–2003 biennium, so that the great majority of the new posts were funded from the Support Account for Peacekeeping Operations, which means that (1) most of the new positions are technically "temporary" appointments, and (2) the greatest number of these new appointments had to be earmarked for the direct support of field operations. One implication of the impermanence of the expanded staff is that in budgetary terms at least the DPKO cannot yet claim the "core" status within the Secretariat that the

Brahimi panel recommended. Assigning the expanded staff mostly to field support, furthermore, does not, at least on the surface, contribute to rectifying the intelligence and planning inadequacies in DPKO that the Brahimi panel underscored. When all is said, however, the member states, wending their way through the UN's Byzantine budgetary processes, did make more resources available for headquarters operations concerning peacekeeping. This is potentially important.

The member states also provided money for enhancing material stocks stored at the UN's logistical base at Brindisi, Italy. The 56th General Assembly allocated approximately $140 million on a onetime only basis to make it possible for the Brindisi base to fully equip one complex peacekeeping mission. Resolution 56/289 also provided for the progressive restocking of the Brindisi base out of the budgets of the field missions using the equipment, thus preparing the UN to have on hand at all times the material wherewithal for a new mission. These steps are important for moving the UN toward its 30/90 day rapid response goals. Financing for the stocking initiative was cobbled together from caches of residual funds left over from completed peacekeeping missions in Croatia and Haiti.[15] That member states were willing to release such funds for the Brindisi stocking rather than asking that they be refunded to original contributors was notable and positive.

Rapid response capacities have also been enhanced by member states agreeing to allow the secretary-general to begin dispensing funds in anticipation of peacekeeping operations, that is, before the issuance of mandates. The Brahimi Report recommended such grants of early startup authority, and Annan asked for this in several representations to the Committee of 34. After two years of talking about premandate spending authority for the secretary-general, and in less than atypical UN fashion, the Advisory Committee on Administrative and Budgetary Questions discovered in 2002 that the secretary-general actually had such authority all along and that there would therefore be "no need to provide additional commitment authority."[16] The result nevertheless was an important opening of bureaucratic space for planning and preparation, which the DPKO moved into immediately by devising a so-called −60/+90 deployment strategy. Ideally, in Secretariat thinking, preparations for a peacekeeping mission should begin 60 days before the finalizing of the Security Council mandate, symbolically represented as "D-day." At D −60 a planning team would be assembled and a warning order concerning possible deployment would be circulated within the Secretariat. By D −30 airlift and sealift services would be contracted, other procurement activities would begin, and standby arrangements with troop contributors would be activated. On D-day the concept of the operation would be finalized and a mission budget would be prepared, although by this time the mission would already have been well prepared. By D +30 a traditional peacekeeping mission

---

[15] A/56/989, p. 7.
[16] A/56/902, p. 4.

would be fully deployed, and by D +90 a complex operation could be up and running.[17] Planning and execution are of course different things, but the importance of the secretary-general's newly acknowledged authority to make financial commitments in anticipation of peacekeeping operations should not be underestimated.

Beyond some bolstering with new resources, the reform of UN peace-keeping operations has also made considerable headway at the conceptual level. There is today a much broader, deeper, and accurate understanding of the nature, requirements, problems, and pitfalls of UN peacekeeping in early twenty-first century environments than there was even a few years ago. An analytical vocabulary has evolved, for example, that distinguishes precisely among "peacekeeping," "peace building" and "enforcement."[18] From all that can be determined from the reports of the secretary-general, the briefings of the under-secretary-general, and the resolutions of both the General Assembly and the Security Council, different kinds of situations that call for different kinds of interventions are today much better understood than was the case earlier. So too are the requirements for success (and reasons for failure) in various situations and environments more clearly comprehended. Much of this institutional learning was acquired from the analysis of "lessons learned." In this regard the secretary-general's extraordinarily candid reports on Srebrenica and Rwanda were remarkable feats of self-critical analysis. Valuable lessons learned are stored today in the filing cabinets and databases of the Department of Peacekeeping Operations and the Department of Political Affairs, as well as in the consciousness of the professionals in these offices and in the field. By looking candidly, critically, and honestly at the UN, the International Peace Academy has also contributed notably to broadening and deepening the UN's understanding of peacekeeping operations.

A fair amount of new insight can also be discerned in the deliberations and pronouncements of the Security Council. "There's been a lot done in the area of mandates," one national delegate recently explained to us. "The formulation of mandates is much more realistic and the rules of engagement are these days much more forceful than earlier on." In fact, one of the Security Council's earliest and firmest commitments in response to the Brahimi Report was to improve all aspects of the process of formulating mandates. According to Security Council Resolution 1327 (2000), these would include (1) giving peacekeeping operations "clear, credible and achievable mandates," (2) beginning "consultations with potential troop contributors well in advance of the establishment of peacekeeping operations" and taking these consultations into consideration in the formulation of new mandates, (3) ensuring that "the mandated tasks of peacekeeping operations are appropriate to the situations on

---

[17]A/56/870, pp. 12–13.
[18]The effort to bring conceptual order to the variety of peacekeeping operations was first attempted by Secretary-General Boutros-Boutros Ghali in *An Agenda for Peace 1995*, 2nd ed. (New York: UN Department of Public Information, 1997).

the ground," (4) taking account of "the potential need to protect civilians and the possibility that some parties may seek to undermine peace through violence," and (5) requiring member states to ensure "the capability of their peacekeepers to fulfill mandates assigned to them."[19] The same resolution also took up rules of engagement and affirmed that Security Council resolutions must "clearly set out the circumstances in which force may be used to protect all mission components and personnel, military or civilian," and "the rules of engagement should support the accomplishment of the mission's mandate."[20]

Considerable evidence suggests that lessons learned from the failures of the 1990s are influencing change. Observers have pointed out that UN operations in the Congo, Liberia, Sierra Leone, Burundi, and the Ivory Coast are governed by much more realistic and robust mandates than were earlier undertakings in Africa. "They all have their own rules of engagement," Marc Lacey of the *New York Times* reported in the spring of 2005, "but they have also moved well beyond the notion of peacekeeping in which blue helmets occupy a neutral zone."[21] Regarding the UN operation in the Congo (MONUC), Lacey went on to point out that "for years, they were criticized for huddling in their camps as atrocities recurred in the countryside. Now critics condemn them for being too aggressive." In contrast to the early 1990s, in more recent operations UN peacekeepers are clearly mandated—and appropriately armed—to return fire, and they do. David Harland of the UN's Department of Peacekeeping operations explained that "the ghost of Rwanda lies very heavily over how the UN and the Security Council have chosen to deal with [the Congo]."

The issue of access to Security Council decision making while peacekeeping mandates are being formulated (or reformulated) is politically charged. But it too is being confronted. Countries contributing troops to UN peacekeeping missions, these days mostly Third World countries, have pressed for access to decision making regarding mandates, as well as other matters concerning the conduct of missions. Their main concerns stem from the fact that while their nationals are being placed in harm's way, they have been allowed little say in the formulation of mandates or the designing of the operations to which their people are committed. Those contributing troops to peacekeeping operations, many governments insist, ought to have a say in what their troops are going to be asked to do, how well their safety is going to be looked after, and under what rules of engagement they would be acting. Security Council members have resisted pressures for broader consultation with troop-contributing countries because they interpret such overtures as moves to usurp the decision-making prerogatives of the council. Tensions

---

[19]S/RES/1327 (2000).
[20]S/RES/1327 (2000).
[21]Marc Lacey, "After Failures, UN Peacekeepers Get Tough," *International Herald Tribune*, May 24, 2005, p. 2 (reprinted from *New York Times*, May 23, 2005).

over these issues continue, but they were attenuated to some extent by the Security Council's adoption of Resolution 1353 in June 2001.[22] This rather far-reaching resolution opens the way to both direct and indirect consultations between troop contributors and the Security Council. It endorses exchanges of information on all aspects of peacekeeping operations and it allows as well for three-way discussions among the Security Council, the Secretariat, and the contributing countries. Resolution 1353 does not open access to Security Council decision making, which disappoints some governments. But it does potentially enrich the informational contexts within which the decisions of the Security Council are made, and this may well prove very important when mandates are being formulated. These disappointments may find some relief if the new Peacebuilding Commission functions as a effective catalyst for collaboration among the major stakeholders in peace operations and provides a model for better collaboration within the Security Council. The Peacebuilding Commission is comprised of 31 members including: seven members of the Security Council (including all P-5); seven members of ECOSOC with experience in post-conflict reconstruction; five of the top ten financial contributors to the UN budget; five of the top ten troop contributing countries; and seven additional members from the General Assembly to round out the remaining geographical imbalances and ensure representation by those countries with post-conflict rebuilding experience.

The Brahimi Report and the reform process that it provoked have also led to a considerable amount of bureaucratic restructuring in the Secretariat. For one thing, the division of labor between the Department of Peacekeeping Operations and the Department of Political Affairs (DPA) has been clarified, with DPKO tasked mainly with initial "peacekeeping" in both its military and civilian police aspects, and DPA, on handoff from DPKO, would be tasked with executing everything concerning "peace building." There has also been a good deal of conceptual work done on how the handoffs, or transitions, among phases of complex operations ought to take place, along with a fair amount of sub rosa grumbling over the fact that the transitions did not go particularly well in East Timor.[23] Operations in East Timor and later in Sierra Leone did testify, however, to the considerable institutional learning about peacekeeping that was taking place both within the UN Secretariat and within the foreign ministries of key member states. Within the DPKO, military operations have been more clearly separated from civilian police operations, thus acknowledging and institutionalizing the different kinds of expertise required for success in each area.

Equally importantly, the Secretariat has adopted a planning and coordination system based on the concept of Integrated Mission Task Forces (IMTF). Envisaged in the Brahimi Report, these units are composed of officials from all

---

[22]S/RES/1353 (2001).
[23]See Simon Chesterman, *East Timor in Transition: From Conflict Prevention to State-Building* (New York: International Peace Academy, 2001), pp. 18–21.

of the UN departments and agencies, including the specialized agencies and the Bretton Woods organizations, that are called on to contribute to particular peacekeeping missions. Task forces are mission specific, variously composed for each field undertaking. They can be virtual, with members linked via communications devices rather than face to face, thus making cooptation from the headquarters of far-flung agencies feasible. Still, for the duration of activities of each task force, and with regard to task force assignment, members work under the authority of task force leaders instead of their agency directors. The main purpose of the IMTF is planning in anticipation of field operations aimed toward defining headquarters and field assignments and minimizing problems of interagency coordination during operations. The first test of IMTF came in the context of preparing for the postwar rehabilitation of Afghanistan beginning in the late autumn of 2001. "The experience gained in Afghanistan, the first real case of implementation of the task force strategy," the under-secretary-general for peacekeeping operations told the Fourth Committee in December 2001, "would contribute to further improvement in the Organization's ability to coordinate the management of crises."[24] How useful either this task force in particular or the IMTF concept more generally prove to be is not yet clear.

In an atmosphere of buoyed morale within the DPKO under then Under-Secretary-General Jean-Marie Guehenno, and with the benefit of an expanded staff, the Secretariat in 2001–2002 restarted a number of projects aimed at improving peacekeeping capacity. A number of on-call lists, for example, were created, revised, or extended. Such lists constitute inventories of experts in military and civil affairs, recommended by national governments or otherwise identified, who can be summoned on short notice to participate in UN peacekeeping operations. Other on-call lists identify individuals suited to serve as special representatives of the secretary-general, as force commanders, or as candidates for other leadership assignments. Recently, steps have also been taken to enhance training procedures, to reach out in this regard to Africa and African peacekeepers, to write new training manuals, particularly pertaining to peace-building procedures, to include training components within field operations, and to sponsor a number of regional seminars on peacekeeping. The cumulative effects of such activities could contribute importantly to improving the UN's peacekeeping capacities.

THE COMMITMENT GAP

Whether, in the final analysis, the reform of peacekeeping amounts to anything more than writing reports and moving desks around depends on a nebulous but quite perceptible quality called *political will*. Nothing happens at the UN without it, and all of the players in the UN political game recognize this. The Brahimi panel, for example, admonished the member states to "summon the

[24]A/C.4/56/SR.20, p. 3.

political will to support the United Nations" and indicated that efforts to reform peacekeeping would have little lasting effect otherwise.[25] The secretary-general, appealing to the General Assembly for support in implementing the Brahimi panel's recommendations, looked for the "political will of Member States to match the mandates with human, financial and political support required to enable their full implementation."[26] Elsewhere, he spoke of a "commitment gap" and "the lack of political will to contribute to peacekeeping in Africa."[27] And, speaking before the Fourth Committee in November 2000, Croatia's Jelena Grcic Polic, summarized most eloquently: "The fact that the process to reform the United Nations was geared toward improving much-needed capacity to carry out peacekeeping operations did not reduce it to being just about capacity, or just about resources. . . . It was as much about political will."[28]

It is true that member states acting in both the General Assembly and the Security Council have involved themselves in implementing important parts of the Brahimi Report. Still, how much real commitment to enhancing the UN's peacekeeping capacity there is among member states is difficult to determine. UN observers reckon that there is a good deal less commitment than the supportive rhetoric might suggest, with some even concluding that "the whole idea of reform has already been abandoned."[29] Our findings, however, do not suggest that the peacekeeping reform is over, although they do underline that few *new* resources have actually been allocated to UN peace-keeping and that much that has apparently changed remains untested. What is clear, in addition, is that an enormous amount of political contention sur-rounds both peacekeeping issues and reform issues. And what is also clear is that within the political melee, improving the UN's capacities is not very high on almost anyone's agenda. Like almost everything else at the UN, reforming peacekeeping is a political process, and political outcomes, not bureaucratic adjustments, will determine peacekeeping's future.

The flavor of the politics of peacekeeping reform was nicely captured in an intervention at a Berlin conference by Ambassador Michel Duval, Canada's deputy permanent representative to the UN. In June 2001 Duval had just arrived in Berlin to attend an international workshop on "The Brahimi Report" sponsored by the Stiftung Wissenschaft und Politik. Upon mounting the podium, Ambassador Duval was in a rather exasperated frame of mind because, as he explained, "yesterday . . . I was in New York chairing the Working Group of the Special Committee on Peacekeeping" . . . who were "reviewing the Report of the Secretary-General . . . containing the findings of the first in-depth and comprehensive review of the Department of Peacekeeping Operations."

[25]A/55/305-S/2000/809, p. 1.

[26]A/55/977, p. 4.

[27]SG/SM/7639 (November 2000), p. 2.

[28]GA/SPD/199 (November 8, 2000), p. 3.

[29]Interview, International Peace Academy, January 2003.

Saying things to his Berlin audience that he probably could not say in the Special Committee, Ambassador Duval went on to explain:

> [It] seems paradoxical to me that the reinforcement of UN peacekeeping capabilities recommended by the Panel on United Nations Peace Operations, the Brahimi Report, seems to be slowed down mostly by the "demandeurs" of peace operations. They are:
> - countries demanding more and more aggressive peacekeeping, condemning the North for not intervening forcefully in Rwanda and in the DRC, but, by the same token, fearing for their sovereignty and rejecting the concept of intervention;
> - countries demanding more planning, organization, support, financing, training, logistics from the UN, but blocking Brahimi recommendations to strengthen the Secretariat;
> - countries claiming that peacekeeping is diverting money from development and refusing to accept the organic link between peacekeeping and development, in a full continuum from prevention to reconstruction after conflicts;
> - countries demanding more engagement from the North in Sub-Saharan Africa, but endorsing the lack of support of host countries and parties to the conflict and porting the UN as an intruder of the sacrosanct sovereignty and at the expense of responsibilities of the hosts and the parties;
> - countries complaining that decision-making in the Security Council is held hostage to the Permanents' veto, yet in return demanding to be granted the same privileges for the sake of balance, but at what cost to efficiency?
> - finally, countries hesitating to engage their troops with the UN and refusing the financing needed to support and realize the reform they request.
> What are the reasons for this paradox? Or could it be, more simply, a reciprocal lack of confidence between the partners in peacekeeping and the symptoms of a general lack of faith in the United Nations as a peacekeeper?[30]

The agendas of most member states being played out in the politics surrounding peacekeeping reform are largely obstructionist. They mainly have to do with things that member states do not want to happen during the overhaul of UN peacekeeping. The Group of 77, for example, does not want peacekeeping capacities to be enhanced at the expense of development, which sets in motion a rather interesting political dynamic because the major donor countries do not want peacekeeping capacities to be enhanced by increasing the UN's regular budget. Where "within existing resources," therefore, is peacekeeping money to be found except perhaps in accounts earmarked for development? As Ambassador Duval explained, many countries, mostly in the Third World, do not want enhanced peacekeeping capacities to mean expanded prerogatives for interventions ordered by the Security Council. These are interpreted as assaults on sovereignty and deemed unwelcome. Relatedly, many countries, again particularly member states from the Third

[30]Stiftung Wissenschaft und Politik, *The Brahimi Report: Overcoming the North–South Divide*, 6th International Workshop, Berlin, June 29–30, 2001, pp. 145–146 (hereafter cited as Stiftung).

World, do not wish to grant the UN any enhanced capacity for information gathering or analysis because such capacities are also viewed as threatening sovereignty. Improving the UN's intelligence capacities was one of the major recommendations of the Brahimi panel, and Annan's first proposal for implementing Brahimi included a plan for an Information and Strategic Analysis Secretariat (ISAS). But as William Durch, one of the authors of the "Rwanda Report," later explained,

> While the idea was to enable the UN Secretariat to anticipate problems on the basis of abundant, open source information, some states seemed to view this staff as a potential conduit for member state intelligence sharing and as a means by which states could be put in the international cross-hairs for potential military intervention.[31]

Better to keep the UN blind and deaf than to give the organization capacity to look in on "domestic affairs." Better also to preserve political patronage and guarantee jobs for nationals than to recruit the most highly qualified people for critical assignments. Judging by the number of times that the euphemisms "equitable geographic distribution" and "gender balance" are repeated during Fourth Committee and Special Committee debates, one might conclude that inequitable geographic distribution and gender imbalance in staff appointments were the most serious problems confronting UN peacekeeping. Of course they are not, but for many governments they are issues of high priority because they have to do with (1) opening channels for political patronage, and (2) rectifying the overrepresentation of Westerners and men in the international civil service. Affording opportunities for political patronage should be not a legitimate concern, although recruiting to rectify regional and gender imbalances is not unreasonable. But neither ought to trump competence, efficiency, and effectiveness. Yet they do, as illustrated in Simon Chesterman's review of the United Nations Transitional Administration in East Timor:

> Clearly UNTAET faced extraordinary difficulties in the early stages of its implementation. Nevertheless, a recurring criticism has been the introduction of large numbers of under-trained and often disinterested staff. The recruiting processes of the UN, with the emphasis on diversity and inter-agency bickering, appear to have taken precedence over merit, local knowledge, and language skills.[32]

What Chesterman could have gone on to say is that pressures to hire unqualified people, because such people are the political favorites of particular national governments, are not failings of the Secretariat's personnel

---

[31]Stiftung, p. 154.
[32]Chesterman, "East Timor," p. 18.

system. They and their results are rather an outcome of petty politics among member states. Taking issue over allocating the meager resources of a resource-starved organization, displaying prickliness about sovereignty, and posturing for Secretariat positions are seemingly perennial parts of the petty politics of the UN. They are not without consequence inasmuch as they obstruct reform, nurture cynicism, and sap political will. Petty politicking has affected the reform of peacekeeping operations by changing resource issues into matters of irreconcilable North–South debate, by hampering the building of information gathering and research and analysis capability within the Secretariat and by interfering with the rational recruiting of competent personnel.

There is, however, also a *high politics* surrounding the question of peacekeeping capacity that raises issues not only about the quality of UN operations but about the future of UN peacekeeping as such. Western countries are increasingly unwilling to commit troops to UN peacekeeping missions and particularly unwilling to commit troops to operations in Africa. In November 2000 the Malaysian representative told the Fourth Committee that "presently more than 75 percent of UN peacekeepers came from developing countries and, in most cases, were serving in high-risk mission areas." He said, "The absence of troops from developed countries, particularly in Africa, under United Nations auspices was particularly noticeable." This situation, he went on to say, "had raised questions about the commitment to United Nations peacekeeping," as he expected that "given their resources, developed countries should be among the top troop contributors."[33] Concurring with this assessment, in the spring of 2005, Marc Lacey, reporting for the *New York Times*, observed that "After the failed missions of the 1990s, Western countries began contributing significantly fewer troops overseas. In 1998, about 45 percent of peacekeepers came from Western armies. The figure is now less than 10 percent; most now come from the developing world."[34] True enough: most of the blue-helmeted personnel in the field these days are not from the industrialized countries. The concurrent unwillingness of several traditional supporters of peacekeeping among the developed countries to continue to contribute troops seems not to be coincidence. Many factors are contributing to the reluctance: the peacekeeping disasters of the 1990s; lack of confidence in UN command and control procedures or, in the American case, a refusal to place troops under UN command; disbelief concerning UN intentions to rethink mandates and rules of engagement; dread of taking casualties in distant theaters of little national concern; Africa weariness; and the increasing attractiveness of alternatives to UN peacekeeping using outside instrumentalities. Reluctance on the part of the developed countries physically to support

---

[33]GA/SPD/199, p. 3.
[34]Marc Lacey, "After Failures, UN Peacekeepers Get Tough," *International Herald Tribune*, May 24, 2005, p. 2.

peacekeeping has complicated a host of related issues, such as the question of troop contributors' access to Security Council decision making, the question of the selection of leadership in the field, even the question of priority in appointments within the Department of Peacekeeping Operations. NAM countries are insisting with some vehemence, and also with some justification, that their disproportionate commitments of soldiers ought to be matched by disproportionate influence over the operations that involve them. That developed countries on the Security Council do not necessarily see things this way not only turns the whole domain of peacekeeping into an arena of North–South contest, but it also fuels the underlying and deeply contentious issue of Security Council reform.

Many UN members, and not only Third World governments, see the problem of peacekeeping reform as more fundamentally an issue of the legitimacy of the Security Council. This is not the place to rehearse the debate over the representativeness of the Security Council, the question of the veto or proposals for change. But all of this is related to the future of UN peacekeeping. Let it suffice to say there is a great deal of suspicion today about the standards and the procedures of the Security Council with respect to mandating, enforcement, peacekeeping, and peace building. Where the UN intervenes, how it intervenes, and, even more revealingly, where it does not intervene and why, all lead to questioning the actions and the authority of the Security Council. The Peacebuilding Commission, an advisory body reporting to both the General Assembly and the Security Council, is unlikely to alter the deep misgivings in some quarters about the legitimacy of Security Council actions and authority. There is today some particularly harsh questioning regarding the actions of the Permanent Five and harsher questioning still about the whims of the Permanent One. In the background, of course, is the UN Charter, which says in Article 24 that the organization's "members confer on the Security Council primary responsibility for the maintenance of international peace and security, and agree that in carrying out this responsibility the Security Council acts on their behalf." At present, there is some room for asking on whose behalf the Security Council acts in the realm of peacekeeping. Member states are in fact asking this question, but this inquiry in itself divides the membership and further saps the political will of those who are otherwise predisposed to support the UN.

Conversely, there are some today who do not really care whether the Security Council represents everyone, anyone, or no one at all. Nor do they particularly care whether the UN improves its peacekeeping procedures, whether the Security Council consults more meaningfully with troop contributors, whether the council writes more realistic mandates, whether the DPKO achieves its 30/90-day rapid response objectives, or whether the Brindisi Logistics Base can support one, two, or three missions at the same time. The most critical political question looming over UN peacekeeping is whether the UN will actually be doing very much of it in the future. Out of frustration and exasperation over the endless, and usually meaningless, politics that envelop and suffocate all aspects of UN affairs, will not national governments increasingly seek to move peacekeeping outside the UN?

David Malone, a former director of the International Peace Academy who has said many wise and prophetic things about the UN, was most likely again on target in June 2001 when he discussed the Brahimi Report with colleagues at an international seminar. He was concerned that the Brahimi Report had sharply divided North and South when it was debated at the UN in the autumn of 2000. He therefore addressed the question: "What went wrong?"

> Clearly, the Report itself, while containing some debatable, indeed optional, rec-
> ommendations, was not the basic problem. I will argue that the intergovern-
> mental process at the UN, especially stuck in the dynamics of the immediate
> post-Colonial period, is probably the greatest challenge facing the organization,
> poisoning most substantive debates and reducing virtually all issues to questions
> of process and tactical advantage. Success is not measured by action in the field
> but rather by negotiating triumphs recorded in turgid communiqués and decla-
> rations of interest to nobody in the real world. Thus, many UN debates appear
> hopelessly arcane to most non-initiates. They are not seen to address real needs
> of actual people anywhere.[35]

Malone's concern and that of many governments who must address "the real needs of actual people" is that decisions about future peacekeeping missions, like several in the recent past, will drown in the senselessness of North–South sparring over what Michel Duval calls the excruciating debate on "how should it be done in full respect of the principles of the Charter, as we interpret them? Or 'within existing resources?'"[36]

It is already the case that the world goes outside the UN when enforce-ment action is perceived to be necessary, urgent, and in the interests of those who harbor such perceptions. When rapid deployment is absolutely essential and military force must be applied, the UN is a blunt instrument. And the UN becomes even less useful when it takes weeks or months to decide on intervention and then more weeks or months to find financing. "Rapid response is not really that much of a problem," a military officer associated with the UN explained during an interview. "A well-equipped modern army can move in a matter of hours." The Australians demonstrated this in East Timor, as did NATO in Kosovo and the Americans in Afghanistan. The UN can-not respond rapidly to bring decisive military force to bear, but some individual member states can, and "coalitions of the willing" most certainly can—and do. Beyond rapid deployment for enforcement purposes, the temptation today, which some see as the increasing tendency for the future, is to go outside the UN when peacekeeping becomes necessary (and perhaps even when

---

[35]Stiftung, p. 159.
[36]Ibid., p. 147.

peace building becomes necessary as well). Ambassador Duval makes the case emphatically:

> We are still far away from a cooperative formula, and while the debate is raging at the United Nations, pragmatic responses have emerged outside the UN and they offer more rapid and flexible modes of response to crises and their management, involving the partners in the decision-making process. Coalitions of the willing, regional and sub-regional organizations have acted as they saw the need for it. They have done so swiftly [and] forcefully. . . . [A]s the debate over intervention in Kosovo demonstrated, the Security Council has "primary" responsibility for the maintenance of international peace and security; it does not have "exclusive" responsibility. Thus, if we cannot get it right within the UN context, we will not hesitate to go elsewhere, if our cause is just.[37]

And then later in the same presentation: "The real lesson of Rwanda and Srebrenica is to be found in Bosnia, Kosovo, East Timor, Sierra Leone, Afghanistan and Iraq: 'if you need to do it, do it outside the UN.'"[38] It is not the shortcomings of the DPKO that jeopardize the future of UN peacekeeping but the dilatory gamesmanship and obstructionist effects of North–South politics that have already rendered the General Assembly largely irrelevant to the world outside the UN and that today are penetrating even the Security Council.

Let us bear in mind as we observe these goings on that peacekeeping outside the UN is no longer activity on behalf of the international community in accord with the UN Charter but rather action engaged in the national interest of members of self-appointed coalitions of the willing. Presently, such coalitions ritualistically seek post hoc legitimation from the UN. In the future such rituals may be forsaken, thereby completely marginalizing the UN and transporting the world back to something like the Concert system of the nineteenth century.

[37]Ibid., pp. 147–48.
[38]Ibid., p. 151.

CHAPTER 8

Development and Its Discontents

As the international community moves into the twenty-first century, two things remain clear: first, if the economic development of the poorer countries of the world is to occur at all, it must happen in the context of the capitalist world economy, and second, if the UN system is to play a constructive role in support of development, the major powers, including most notably the United States, will need to act in concert. Otherwise, the institutions of the UN system cannot be made to function adequately for the huge task at hand. Yet in reality, the international politics of development as played out within the UN during the 1960s and 1970s were not about the adequate functioning of institutions and programs but instead about maintaining versus transforming the liberal capitalist status quo. Those in the North who favored this status quo insisted that development could and should flourish in accord with workings of the global market. Northern governments continue to this day to affirm this position. Those in the South who rejected the status quo insisted that Third World development could never happen in the context of the capitalist world order either because the market is biased against them or because they would never be granted full access to the market. Later, around the turn of the twenty-first century and after the end of the Cold War, issues in the UN surrounding development focused less on changing the capitalist world order and more on northern obligations and southern responsibilities within that order. The South wanted economic commitments from the North, and the North wanted responsible governance from the South. This chapter examines the political dynamics that have driven for more than fifty years the continuing debate about development within the UN.

STRUCTURAL CONTEXTS OF UN DEVELOPMENT POLITICS

Since the end of the Cold War, the UN system has become increasingly free to function in the political-economic realm the way it was designed to function, that is, in the service of promoting a liberal capitalist order. But the international norms and institutional forms that underpin this global system have been the almost constant source of frustration, contestation, and profound misunderstanding among many of those who have sought to transform it. The transformers, who have endeavored to use the United Nations as a mechanism for redressing global imbalances in wealth and material well-being by promoting economic development, have failed at almost every turn. Development strategies have come and gone—"takeoff," "import substitution," "trade not aid," "basic human needs," "the New International Economic Order," "sustainable development," "sustainable human development"—but expected leaps forward in economic growth among the poorer countries have mostly failed to follow from policies and projects informed by the different strategies. With every failure at promoting development, North–South politics at the UN have been further fired with acrimony, and the North–South divide over economic issues has widened and deepened.

The Bretton Woods institutions, as noted earlier in this volume, preceded the United Nations organization in their founding and constituted central components of the new liberal world order being constructed. In important ways, they served as the new order's main foundation. This is especially true when it comes to development issues. The UN organization in New York was deliberately limited in economic areas, with the main economic work being assigned either to the UN system's specialized agencies or most importantly to the Bretton Woods institutions. The World Bank and the International Monetary Fund (IMF) were endowed with capacities that enabled them to penetrate the national sovereignties of those states that they assisted, often to the extent that the national macroeconomic policies of Third World clients were devised and prescribed at the headquarters of the World Bank and the IMF.

At the same time, the allocation of influence among members of the World Bank and the IMF in accordance with the size of their financial contributions constrained both of these organizations to avoid policies that collided significantly with Western views and interests and American ones in particular. Thus, as with the UN Security Council, the UN system's seemingly one government-one vote principle was contradicted by the prerogatives of special majorities. Like questions of military security, economic questions within the UN system are ultimately decided by a concert of major powers. But in this case, it is a concert of "economic" not military powers, and the roster of participants is slightly but not altogether different. In theory, of course, states could avoid the long arm of the Bretton Woods institutions by refusing to become involved with them. However, in practice, the embrace was difficult, if not impossible, to avoid. From where else was urgently needed economic assistance to come? To such assistance there were always conditions attached, however, and these conditions were dictated by the major Western economic powers, and again most especially the United States.

Laissez-faire and free trade have been the World Bank and the IMF's international policy prescriptions for almost all political-economic ailments. These, Western elites have insisted, are the keys both to prosperity and peace and security. From the beginning, this fundamental belief in connections among freely operating markets, prosperity, and peace was made explicit. "Unhampered trade dovetailed with peace; high tariffs, trade barriers, and unfair economic competition, with war . . . if we could get a freer flow of trade—freer in the sense of fewer discriminations and obstructions . . . thereby eliminating the economic dissatisfaction that breeds war, we might have a reasonable chance of a lasting peace."[1] As originally envisioned by postwar planners, the stillborn International Trade Organization (ITO) was to serve as the institutional anchor of this aspect of the new world order. However, as if to portend later events, the 1948 Havana Charter establishing the ITO was doomed in the U.S. Senate. The charter endeavored to accommodate at least some of the interests of the developing countries, but the organization it established was viewed by many in the United States as a threat to American economic interests and sovereignty. Consequently, the functions that were to be performed by the ITO were later relegated via executive agreement to the General Agreements on Tariffs and Trade (GATT). This agreement created a negotiating forum, which by and large became a club of the rich industrial states wherein they sorted *their* trade-related concerns.

CONVOLUTED NORMS AND RESTRAINED INSTITUTIONAL FORMS

In the early postwar years, the continuation of European imperialism constrained the liberalization of the capitalist world economy. European governments, except for those within the Soviet bloc that remained isolated outside the system, were quite willing to entertain laissez-faire norms and the international organizations that promoted these as long as the norms and organizations did not interfere with their domestic political-economic structures and policies. "Domestic" naturally also meant "intraimperial" because what went on within empires was the exclusive business of the metropolis. Negotiations in GATT focused almost exclusively on manufactured goods, so that liberalizing trade among the Western countries could and did progress because all could expect benefits from eliminating barriers to industrial trade. Conversely, colonial restrictions removed from GATT consideration of the commodities—often agricultural—produced in the poorer regions of the world, so that most of the

---

[1]Quoted in Richard N. Gardner, *Sterling-Dollar Diplomacy in Current Perspective: The Origins and Prospects of Our International Economic Order* (New York: Columbia University Press, 1980), p. 9.

story about trade liberalization in the post–World War II era had little to do with anything in which the poorer countries might be interested. In any event, most of what was to become the Third World initially had no voice at all in international economic affairs because the peoples and their territories were invariably parts of one European empire or another and economic liberalization that did occur often reflected metropolitan interests.

Yet even as early as 1943, an agenda was being set for what was later to erupt as a classic confrontation between North and South. At the Bretton Woods conference, delegations from the few, mostly Latin American, developing countries that were then politically independent complained about being relegated to the status of serving as mere providers of raw materials.[2] Industrialization, they asserted, was the pathway to enhancing national wealth, but this pathway for them was obstructed by an international division of labor that obliged the poorer countries to remain exporters of plantation, forest, and mineral products. The governments of the wealthier countries neither looked at the world this way nor exhibited, in any event, any predilection for altering the global division of labor. Again, at the Inter-American Conference in Mexico City and afterward at the San Francisco Conference in 1945, representatives from some of the poorer countries accepted that peace and prosperity were connected, but, they insisted, so were conflict and human misery. Conditions that perpetuated misery therefore could not be conducive to peace. The poorer countries therefore called for the creation of "equitable foundations" in international economic relations.[3]

Given that the imbalance of political influence in the United Nations greatly favored the United States and the West during the formative years of the organization, little could emanate from the UN that took issue with the premise that what was good for Western capitalism was good for the world. Transformation, however, was in the offing, as the waves of decolonization were soon to sweep across the globe. This transformation occurred with such rapidity and dynamism that international institutions were caught quite off guard. The newly independent states were eager to participate as sovereign equals in international organizations, including economic ones, and the logics of collective security and universality implored their inclusion. The political weight of the developing world in the United Nations progressively increased. This altered the politics of the UN General Assembly, removing at once the automatic majority for American initiatives and removing perhaps forever any majority for northern initiatives on economic issues. Injected into

[2]*Proceedings and Documents of the United Nations Monetary and Financial Conference. Bretton Woods, New Hampshire, July 1–22, 1944*. Volume II. Department of State Publication 2866. International Organization and Conference Series I, 3 (Washington D.C.: U.S. Government Printing Office, 1948.), pp. 429–32, 484, 1167–68, 1175–77, 1205–6.

[3]*Inter-American Conference on Problems of War and Peace, Mexico City, February 21–March 8, 1945. Report Submitted to the Governing Board of the Pan American Union by the Director General* Congress and Conference Series, No. 47 (Washington, D.C.: Pan American Union, 1945).

the discourse of the General Assembly were new conceptions of needs, values, interests, and political stakes that soon took the form of demands from the Third World for a better deal from the world economy. Practically speaking, centering the affairs of the General Assembly on Third World economic demands was also the end of the assembly as an authoritative institution, but few in the newly assembled poor-country majority perceived this at the time.

INSTITUTIONAL INCAPACITY

The UN itself had a rather narrowly constrained institutional capacity to deal with economic development. Drafters of the Charter, preoccupied with peace, security, and not having to fight another world war, did not give much thought to fitting out the UN organization in New York as an economic development agency. Other UN-system agencies were to play the central role in global economic affairs. The world organization's primary organ, the General Assembly, had original jurisdiction over all issues, including development, but in practice it was endowed with almost no capacity—not even its own staff—to carry out such work. One of its main committees was designated to deal with financial and economic issues but, again, primarily in the form of a debating arena.

The Economic and Social Council (ECOSOC) was more specifically mandated to deal with development concerns. Over the years, the ECOSOC has built up a series of functional and regional commissions to assess needs and promote strategies for development. ECOSOC is also charged to coordinate the UN system where a disparate array of commissions, committees, and agencies has been given mandates to deal with economic and social problems. But like the General Assembly, the ECOSOC must rely on the Secretariat for staffing, which because of resource limitations and extraordinary demands always turns out to be understaffing. In the context of a decentralized institutional system of autonomous and semiautonomous agencies that do not desire to be centrally coordinated, ECOSOC's coordination has tended to be rather haphazard and on the whole unsuccessful. At one point, for example, eighty-three UN bodies were dealing with matters pertaining to food and hunger. Many of these were working redundantly and many were also working at cross purposes, although no one knew this because little coordination came from the ECOSOC or, for that matter, from anywhere else. To complicate the situation, large member states, most notably the United States, had an equally poor, if not worse, record of coordinating effectively their representation in and across the numerous international agencies dealing with development concerns. The result was support for overlapping, redundant, and sometimes contradictory mandates and programs in the various governing bodies. UN agencies became easy scapegoats for the diplomatic failings of the member states themselves.

The UN moved into the development arena slowly, and it did so in considerable measure because the U.S. government, in Cold War mode, concluded that economic betterment and social stability in Third World countries were important deterrents to the spread of communism. Here the UN was conceived not so much as a development agency but as an instrument of U.S. foreign policy useful for containing the Soviet Union. Whatever the purpose for upping the development-promoting capacity of the UN, the move was conditionally welcomed by the poorer countries. But, as was to be recurrently the case, they expected much more than they received. Following on President Truman's Point IV initiative and the U.S. Act for International Development of 1949, the General Assembly established the Expanded Program of Technical Assistance (EPTA), which provided development assistance in the form of advice, equipment, and training. The United Nations and its five specialized agencies at the time were the program's original participating parties. Over the next decade and a half, this group was joined by another half-dozen agencies.

But technical assistance proved hardly sufficient for launching development. Finance capital and investments in infrastructure were identified as the key ingredients necessary for starting and sustaining economic growth. Developing countries therefore applied strong pressures during the 1950s for creating a Special United Nations Fund for Economic Development (SUNFED) whose activities would augment technical assistance with long-term low-interest loans aimed at building infrastructure. This move to create such a fund was opposed by major donors, especially the United States, although, in spite of this, the General Assembly agreed in 1958 to create a special fund to provide "preinvestment" capital to be used to stimulate private as well as public investment that would complement technical assistance. These early skirmishes over financing for technical assistance prefaced the much larger battle to come over development financing because they placed the blatant question of "how much?" on the North–South political agenda. How much money was going to be transferred from the North to the South by way of the UN and its development programs? The South's consistent answer to this question has been "more," and the North's answer has been "less." Later, development debaters at the UN added the question, "To do what?" as many in the South sought assistance to underwrite their state-run economies while most in the North, and in the United States most emphatically, insisted that international assistance was to be used for freeing markets and encouraging private enterprises and private entrepreneurs. At this early point, however, the United States and other donors were able to dictate the terms under which the funding they supplied would be given and used.

Despite early Western dominance of the development dialogue, challenges to the purely liberal, market-driven development model were emerging. Statist strategies, including the public ownership of leading enterprises, the governmental direction of major investment, central planning, and trade and capital controls in international dealings, were naturally encouraged by the Soviet Union and its allies. Indeed, statist approaches to development—within a broader system of international capitalism—were also championed by some Western governments whose social welfare systems involved significant state intervention. Such strategies were congenial to the governments of postcolonial societies, where private economic sectors were in some places nearly nonexistent, where centrally managed economic development was seen as a necessary aspect of nation building, where economic centralization complemented one-party governance, and where anticapitalism meshed with anti-imperialism.

Early credence was also given to statist development strategies, particularly with regard to the administrative management of foreign trade and capital movements. This orientation was prominent in studies produced by the Economic Commission for Latin America (ECLA), inspired by the work of Argentine economist Raúl Prebisch, who directed the organization during the 1950s. ECLA studies documented the existence of a long-term process of deterioration in the terms of trade of Latin American countries. That is, as time moved on, these countries were obliged to pay relatively more for imports from industrialized countries while they received relatively less for exports to these countries. ECLA reports therefore called for regulatory regimes in international trade and finance that would, by intervening in the market, lessen tendencies toward unequal exchange. The ECLA studies influenced a large number of other economists working in the UN Secretariat at the time, and they generated further ideas about the structural factors that influence the development process.

The ECLA theses, and related statist development strategies that emerged from the intellectual gestations of the 1950s and 1960s, later blossomed into the *dependencia* school of economic thought and analysis, which set down as a first principle that economic development in the Third World is incompatible with the flourishing of unbridled liberal capitalism. The reasoning behind this assumption is less important than the fact that it was widely accepted in the South, and in some quarters still is, and it offered a seemingly credible alternative to the tenets of liberal political economy championed by the United States and others in the industrialized North.[4] This new thinking that assigned the state a central internal and external role in economic development soon became conventional wisdom in development economics, at least as widely theorized in the Third World and among the economists of the UN Secretariat. The new economic thinking also served as the foundation for a wide range of demands by developing countries in the UN. It led to a widening gulf between the UN organization and the Bretton Woods institutions. Calls emerged for transforming international institutions in ways that would obviate the inequities in international economic relations stemming from capitalist pursuits.

---

[4]For an early useful overview, see Sidney Dell, "Contributions of the United Nations to Economic Thinking and Action," *Journal of Development Planning* 17 (1987): 113–23. For a more recent treatment that still draws on Dell's insights, see Louis Emmerij, Richard Jolly, and Thomas G. Weiss, *Ahead of the Curve? UN Ideas and Global Challenges* (Bloomington: Indiana University Press, 2001).

By the 1960s the process of decolonization had transformed the demographics of the United Nations. The year 1964 stands as a benchmark in the evolution of political dynamics within the world organization. By this time, membership in the UN organization stood at 115, and all but 10 of the countries that joined the UN between 1945 and 1964 were former European colonies. Although economic growth in the decolonized Third World advanced at a relatively robust pace during the 1950s and early 1960s, the gaps in wealth and well-being between the industrialized North and the developing South were not disappearing. They were in fact growing larger, and the UN Secretariat's statistical agencies drove this message home with gusto. Southern frustrations were also mounting, not only over the prevailing inequality among states and peoples, but also over the restrained response by the northern-dominated multilateral institutions to the South's development needs. Tensions between the poor and the affluent crystallized in Geneva in 1964 at first meeting of the United Nations Conference on Trade and Development (UNCTAD). At this conference, representatives of the developing countries formally united to form the Group of 77, the Third World caucusing group that would shape the intense North–South debate for the next decade and a half. Raúl Prebisch's thinking and ECLA doctrines provided a good deal of the intellectual cement that initially bound the G-77, and reports critical of the world capitalist order issued by the newly created UNCTAD Secretariat fanned the flames of southern discontent. Perceiving power in their numbers, at UNCTAD I the G-77 majority pushed through an agenda for promoting national economic development and redressing imbalances and inequalities in the capitalist world economy. Still perceiving power in their numbers, over the following decade, the developing countries rather doggedly pushed to create what came to be called the New International Economic Order, or NIEO. This bold program aimed to change the rules and the structure of the international political economy in ways that would channel greater benefits to developing countries.

After a number of preliminary meetings of the Third World in various institutional settings such as UNCTAD, the Group of 77, and the NAM, the main thrust in the southern campaign to transform the way the international economy functioned came during the Sixth Special Session of the UN General Assembly in the late spring of 1974. Here UN members adopted the *Declaration and Program of Action on the Establishment of a New International Economic Order*. The demands written into this declaration were wide ranging. Except for G-77 calls for greater access to northern markets and increased aid, a good part of the NIEO had to do with canceling, circumventing, or otherwise diminishing the functioning of international markets. Developing countries, for example, wanted price supports for their commodity exports, an indexing of their export prices to the prices they paid for manufactured imports, substantial increases in concessional food transfers, technology transfers without royalty obligations, and capital transfers without considerations of returns to investment. Otherwise, they sought the relocating of a number of manufacturing industries from the North to the South, considerable increases in official development assistance, and further increases in financial assistance that would follow from creating additional special drawing rights (SDRs) at the IMF. Most significant in a political sense was the Third World call for greater influence, commensurate with numbers rather than capital contributions, in decision making within the Bretton Woods institutions.[5] These issues were to be raised time and again in various ways and in various settings during the remainder of the decade, and they have not been altogether abandoned even today.

The venues of choice for the G-77 were the UN General Assembly, the UN-sponsored global conferences focusing on specific issues, such as population and food, and the more comprehensive Conference on International Economic Cooperation, which met in December 1975 and June 1977. Again, the expectation on the part of the South was that majorities counted, that voting power amounted to political power, and that the demands of the developing countries would ultimately yield a new international economic order. Third World leaders at the UN also believed that they could prevail politically because they were engaged in a process with northern interlocutors that resembled collective bargaining. Each side in search of a mutually acceptable outcome would trade concessions until such an outcome emerged. Otherwise, many Third World leaders were confident that the brief for greater equality written into the Declaration would prevail because it was the morally superior position. And if moral rectitude were not enough, in the political background in the early 1970s was the demonstrated clout of the Organization of Petroleum Exporting Countries (OPEC). Petroleum power was real, and it was certainly intimidating.

The northern countries, led by the United States, meanwhile insisted that the proper forums for discussions about the structure and functioning of the international economy were the Bretton Woods institutions. Throughout the process of North–South engagement over the NIEO, northern countries settled into a discourse consisting of pious statements of good intentions mixed with detailed criticisms of the South's proposals. Washington especially was steadfastly against revising the liberal international economic order by curtailing the market because American representatives proposed again and again that trade liberalization was the pathway to development. Some concessions to the NIEO in the form of price stabilization schemes for commodities were offered, food aid was increased, and ideas for the transfer of technology were entertained. But as far as the North was concerned, alterations in the structure of international economic power, either within international institutions or without, were not negotiable. From the northern perspective, the process of engagement with the South was not collective bargaining but

---

[5]See Robert S. Jordan, "Why an NIEO? The View from the Third World," in *The Emerging International Economic Order: Dynamic Processes, Constraints and Opportunities*, Harold K. Jacobson and Dusam Aidjanski, eds. (Beverly Hills, Calif.: Sage, 1982).

rather a zero-sum game with no mutually acceptable outcome possible. Nor did the moral rectitude of the southern position appeal to the North nearly as much as the theoretical rectitude of liberal economics. As for OPEC and its clout, history showed the oil-producing countries to be less interested in the well-being of the Third World broadly construed than in their own well-being much more narrowly construed.

By the end of the 1970s, it was reasonably clear, even to many of the NIEO enthusiasts, that the great North–South debate about the New International Economic Order had reached stalemate. For the South this was tantamount to failure because stalemate meant little change in economic relations between the rich countries and the poor, and it meant even less with regard to political influence either in the United Nations or the world. Passing resolutions in the UN General Assembly, no matter how impressive the majorities, did not amount to changes in the world because outside the context of UN delegate bodies, material power still counted. The fizzling of the NIEO project left the developing countries frustrated and embittered on the one hand, but wizened on the other. Some Third World governments accepted that a frontal assault by the weak against the strong was a questionable strategy. Others recognized that the UN General Assembly was not, and probably never could be, an agent of political-economic change, and for many this recognition was the beginning of progressive Third World disenchantment with the United Nations. Nevertheless, the critical analysis of the world capitalist system that underpinned the NIEO was never entirely abandoned, and those most ideologically wedded to it never fully retreated from their advocacy.

By the early1980s, there were clear signs that the pendulum was swinging back to earlier conceptions of development more congruent with liberal views and market mechanisms. With a new administration in Washington bent on reassessing all U.S. multilateral commitments and a like-minded conservative prime minister in charge in Britain, the stage was set for a new phase in the global development debate, which was over time to become much more complex and multifaceted. As far as substance goes, the Reagan administration's advocacy of free market and liberal democratic principles was hardly a novel U.S. position.

What was new was the pugnacity of the tone and the determination either to restore American control over UN processes and policies or decimate the world organization if that failed. In the eyes of many in Washington who were still smarting from the NIEO confrontations and suffering from myopic vision, the United Nations had become a seedbed of anti-Americanism, a hothouse for anticapitalist economic doctrines, and a virtual garden of statist philosophies. The administration's decisions to suspend U.S. participation in the negotiations over the Law of the Sea, to withdraw from UNESCO, and to stir Congress into applying financial pressures on the UN with the avowed aim of "reforming" it were unambiguous moves designed either to reassert American power in the organization or damage it.

Within a few years, this objective was by and large achieved. Confused by the failure of the NIEO initiative, intimidated by the American backlash, and crushed by the weight of the global debt crisis that locked poor countries into a debilitating "lost decade of development," the Third World coalition weakened considerably as a coherent, organized political force at the UN. Neither the G-77 nor the NAM ever fully recovered from the political setbacks to the Third World, and its leadership suffered in the 1970s and 1980s. In addition, several countries, mainly in Asia and around the Pacific Rim, that had been members of the coalition of the poor, chose to adopt development strategies that were almost diametrically opposite from those being promoted during the period of the NIEO. They experienced rapid and impressive growth, and therefore found it difficult to identify with the positions that the G-77 and the NAM were taking in the General Assembly and other UN delegate bodies. For example, one Asian representative to whom we spoke about Third World solidarity was quick to underline that "Thailand is not Africa." Already divided politically because of varying Cold War allegiances that were only superficially camouflaged by the symbolism of nonalignment, the Third World was also beginning to fragment economically.

For the UN, the results in the early 1980s were a distinct toning down of North–South "politicization" related mainly to lessened, although not altogether abandoned, propensities for southern delegates to harangue the North. There was also a manifest retreat from "statist" theories of development as the discourse of *dependencia* both fell out of intellectual fashion and began to encounter empirical anomalies. Later, the collapse of the Soviet Union amounted to a profound delegitimizing of the state as authoritative actor in the economic realm, which led to a further discrediting of economic thinking that found fundamental fault with capitalism. The 1980s at the UN were also years that saw the reining in of the excessive administrative and budgetary growth that had been spurred by the Third World majority's effort to build an institutional home for the NIEO. Novel streaks of pragmatism even began to creep into UN public debates as the search for policies that might have material impact replaced grandiose schemes for global economic transformation.

As disputes over a new international economic order faded, the focus of attention concerning matters of development decidedly shifted from redistributive schemes to export promotion and the search for ways and means to create an atmosphere favorable to direct foreign investment in the poorer countries. With U.S. prodding and fueled by the winding down of the Cold War, a new development paradigm, built from elements of the so-called Washington Consensus, was beginning to take hold of the UN agenda. "Marketization and privatization" emerged as a development slogan. Private sector activities were the new keys to economic growth. Competitiveness in national and on international markets was the key to success in the private sector. Competitiveness followed from productivity, and productivity followed from combining factors of production in ways that maximized output while minimizing input. Growth followed from directing investments toward the most productive combinations of factors and away from the least productive. The new strategy discouraged governmental intervention into markets. It eschewed exchange manipulations, fiscal deficits, government-owned enterprises, bloated public bureaucracies, and the unnecessary accumulation of capital in government hands.

The Washington Consensus was hardly a consensus inasmuch as any number of Third World governments and influential economists and diplomats in the North as well as the South criticized it harshly. They argued, with some reason, that the short-run impacts of marketization and privatization would amount to removing social safety nets in Third World countries, as limited as they already were, while concurrently heightening levels of unemployment. Critics also anticipated that the laissez-faire assumptions underlying marketization and privatization would be taken by northern governments as an invitation to reduce official development assistance (ODA) and turn even farther away from the needs of the poorer countries. This certainly proved to be the case.

By the mid-1980s, the voice of the South at the UN was divided and muted. Action in the UN on development issues, moreover, was no longer centered in the General Assembly, where the Third World could at least speak, even if it was not seriously listened to. It had become apparent that changes in the structure and functioning of the world economy could not be legislated because the General Assembly was not a legislature. To the extent that any real change could be fostered through intergovernmental institutional means, the Bretton Woods institutions had to play a large role in the process. These bodies remained the institutional core of the liberal world order. Yet they were still very much controlled by the major industrial states, especially by the United States. Accordingly, the Bretton Woods institutions championed marketization and privatization. Those governments in the industrialized North that might have moderated the Washington Consensus were unable to act concertedly within the Bretton Woods institutions.[6]

A more pragmatic, less accusatory approach by Third World diplomats was clearly noticeable at the General Assembly Special Session on Africa in 1987. Attacking the North had gotten them little. Economic conditions affecting the poorest countries had changed dramatically for the worst, and in this context of urgency the abstract issues of global equity and social and economic justice that had sustained North–South acrimony during the NIEO years lost their immediacy. One Latin American ambassador said to us, "What's the use of talking about charters, rights and duties when people are literally dying in large numbers?" During most of the 1980s, the full attention

---

[6]Lorenzo Smaghi analyzes the failure of the European Union to act in concert within the IMF even as the collective contribution of the EU member states greatly exceeds the U.S. contribution. See Lorenzo Bini Smaghi, "A Single EU Seat in the IMF?" *Journal of Common Market Studies* 42:2 (2004) 229–248.

of many Third World countries had to be focused on their debts and the deteriorating social conditions that debt-inflicted austerity was causing. Others, particularly the governments and peoples of Africa, had to deal with the combined effects of civil war, economic collapse, the HIV/AIDS pandemic, and ecological disaster.

In all of this, the United Nations organization came to be looked on more as a conduit for immediate aid and less as a legitimizer of new principles of global economic order. The organization became, as one developing country representative told us, "no longer a forum for defining together what is wrong, [because] the only thing people are interested in is how to get assistance in the midst of a deteriorating situation." By virtue of their situation, developing countries still made familiar demands for debt relief, development capital, technical assistance, access to markets, stabilized commodity prices, food aid, and the wherewithal to satisfy other basic human needs. Economic and social cooperation continued in the UN system. But much of this was in the form of emergency relief or other stopgap measures designed to stem deterioration rather than to promote systematic long-term economic development. The eruption of civil wars in such places as Somalia meant that scarce UN resources had to be allocated to military and humanitarian operations rather than to investment to promote economic growth. Consequently, by the early 1990s many on the social and economic side of the organization had resigned themselves to the reality that the UN was to be much more an *aid* organization providing emergency relief and technical assistance and much less a *development* organization that would conceive, design, and execute grand strategies for uplifting humankind. This relegation was congenial to many in the North, and again to the United States in particular, but disappointing to many in the South, who, in any event, had little capacity to alter the situation.

The end of the Cold War, the collapse of communist control in central Europe, and the breakup of the former Soviet Union also attracted attention in the North away from Third World development concerns. This was especially true in Washington, where the South had suddenly become strategically much less important. But it was also true more generally throughout the West. Development assistance monies, in real terms and as a percentage of GDP, were decreasing.[7] Those in the South, as well as those on the staffs of the marginalized UN development agencies, sought a way to elevate development concerns on the international agenda and to recapture the attention of northern donors. *Sustainable development* offered a potential means for redirecting some of the lost focus and garnering new support for Third World development.

---

[7]Oran Young, "The Politics of International Regime Formation: Managing Natural Resources and the Environment," *International Organization* 43: 3 (Summer 1989): 349–75.

THE POLITICS OF DEVELOPMENT IN A NEW PERSPECTIVE

The best way to characterize the 1990s with regard to development questions at the United Nations is to label the decade an era of new thinking. The liberal vision of privatization and marketization was summarized, advocated, and applauded, mostly by the North, as *globalization*. This was the privileged discourse in international economic affairs because alternatives were assumedly discredited. But amid the anomalies, and between the theoretical and empirical cracks of neoliberalism, there grew during the 1980s and 1990s, an evolving collection of development visions, respectively called "sustainable development," "human security," and "sustainable human development."

Sustainable development added to the conventional model of development, via industrialization and structural transformation, the caution that growth in earlier generations could lead to collapse in later ones if the natural environment was sacrificed to market imperatives. Accepting this wisdom, *sustainable* development implied making a commitment to protecting and preserving the earth's ecosystem. It implied a commitment on the part of developing countries to take the environmental results of industrialization into account. But this was linked to the expectation that developed countries would supply the additional technical and capital assistance necessary to make sustainable development real. Sustainable development gained the favor of the South because it was after all a doctrine of development; it brought the promise of additional development resources and it put the UN back into the business of promoting development. It also disarmed those in the North who dreaded the environmental implications of more peoples becoming affluent consumers. It was greeted by those European and various other Western governments who generally endorsed the development efforts of the international community. Sustainable development found the Americans largely indifferent, and possibly relieved, inasmuch as it was not another call for the restructuring of the international economy.

"Human security" surfaced as a development doctrine with the publication of the United Nations Development Programme's *Human Development Report* in 1993, and it was the central theme of the UNDP's annual report in 1994 where the authors urged that "it is time to make a transition from the narrow concept of national security to the all-encompassing concept of human security."[8] Elaborating the concept, the UNDP stressed that in the twenty-first century there ought to be less emphasis on "national security" and more on "human security," implying that the thrust in development, and therefore the attentions of the international community, ought to be on freeing individuals from threats to their physical and psychological well-being. The notion of promoting "human security" consequently embodied attending

---

[8]United Nations Development Programme, *Human Development Report 1993* (New York: Oxford University Press, 1993); United Nations Development Programme, *Human Development Report 1994* (New York: Oxford University Press, 1994).

to basic human needs, such as food, water, shelter, health, education, and income, and also protecting individuals from violence, injustice, castigation, and oppression. Although it was promoted with some enthusiasm by the UNDP and welcomed by some northern governments, human security did not go down well with a number of Third World governments, who saw in it an invitation to the international community—meaning the West—to scrutinize and intervene in their domestic affairs. The very idea of individuals and not governments as the subjects of international organizational action was very difficult to accept, and it remains so for many to the present day.

Nevertheless, the genius of the UNDP in the early 1990s, strongly supported by Secretaries-General Boutrous Boutrous-Ghali and Kofi Annan, was in combining "sustainable development" and "human security" to arrive at "sustainable human development." The primary emphasis on *development* satisfied the South; the prerequisites of *sustainability* and *human security* found support in the North. These development doctrines that originated within the UN during the 1990s were not rebuttals to economic liberalism but rather programs offered to civilize or humanize it by focusing critical attention on the collateral damage that marketization and privatization were inflicting on the earth's ecosystem and on human beings. Sustainable development, human security, and sustainable human development are in effect counterpoint, not contradiction, to the main theme of development via the free play of market forces.

Development affairs at the UN during the decade of the 1990s involved not only new doctrines but also new players in both the intellectual and the political arenas. Needless to say, some of the old players in the politics of development were still there, pretty much where they always were both institutionally and politically, that is, in the General Assembly and on the issue of the causes and injustice of economic inequity in the world. This debate, however, had become a monologue, conducted largely by the radicalized leadership of the G-77, who spoke more for themselves than for other members of their Third World associations. They continued to command a certain amount of deference, however, although they were hardly leading the development dialogue within the UN. Instead, the UNDP, or better said, the leadership of the UNDP, moved into the intellectual vacuum left by the collapsing, fragmenting G-77.

Throughout the 1990s, and continuing today, the UNDP has used its annual *Human Development* reports as well as all manner of subsidiary documentation to present exhaustive, statistical, economic, analytical, political, moral, and philosophical arguments in defense of human values ridden over roughshod by economic globalization. Although UNDP positions largely support Third World appeals for the alleviation of poverty and economic justice in world affairs, much of what the UNDP has called for under rubrics such as "good governance," "democracy," "human rights," and "human security" smacks, as noted, of intervention into domestic affairs. These have not exactly been pleasant pills to administer to the sovereignty-sensitive Third World. Into all of this stepped Annan, acting more political than a secretary-general per-haps should, but nevertheless intelligently trying to bridge differences among the North, the South, the UNDP, and the Bretton Woods institutions, and within the North and South, respectively, and also trying to take account of the interests and agitations of international civil society that largely approves of UNDP thinking.

What was most noteworthy, and in the UN context perhaps extraordi-nary, about the development debates of the 1990s is that they appeared to be moving in constructive directions. Economic growth driven by market forces was not deemed to be incompatible with broad-based increases in human well-being or with preserving the natural resources of the planet for future generations. To many it appeared that a convergence in thinking about what it would really take to alleviate poverty in the poorer countries might possibly lead to collective action through the UN. Development advocates within the Secretariat almost forgot for a historical moment during the 1990s that the UN was still a club of self-interested governments and that few of these were prepared to let the UNDP or any other branch of the international civil service make policy for the international community. But even among the member governments an aura of seeming acquiescence prevailed, and the House therefore continued to inject substance into the new slogan "sustain-able human development" that almost immediately became the acronym SHD.

During the 1990s and the opening years of the new century, a series of global conferences helped develop and highlight the SHD agenda. Beginning with the World Summit for Children in 1990 and concluding with World Sum-mit on Sustainable Development in 2002, some twenty-two UN-sponsored world gatherings concerned with food, population, human rights, women, children, HIV/AIDS, trade and finance, environmental degradation, and dozens of other issues established the agenda for the international commu-nity's efforts at sustainable human development. One of the most striking out-comes to emerge from these conferences was an apparent convergence of views concerning a global development agenda. The development debate took on a new character as the concepts of human development and sustain-able development became fused in the concept sustainable human develop-ment. This concept began to take more concrete form in the mid-1990s as the UNDP moved to promoting "sustainable human development" as its primary mission. Like other development concepts before it, sustainable human devel-opment was viewed as a key requisite for creating and maintaining a secure and peaceful world order. The conferences also informed public opinion, mobilized NGOs, and energized some governments to press for international action. This convergence over SHD led many member states of the United Nations to expect the organization to play some meaningful role in pursuing development goals. At least temporarily, Washington backed away from its customary skepticism concerning the UN and development, and although "team player" would be too strong a description, U.S. officials seemed more willing to at least try to be somewhat accommodating with regard to dealing with issues of extreme poverty and degradation in the Third World.

Participation and empowerment were two of the priority themes stressed by the UN's central operational development arm, the UNDP, throughout the 1990s in its annual reviews on human development. The associated discourse has given shape and meaning to the concept of participation. The way to eradicate poverty, UNDP reports have argued, is to empower the poor and marginalized elements of society to provide for the satisfaction of their own basic needs and values. It sought to promote "the empowerment of people through measures to build their coping and adapting capacities, to increase their productivity and income; and to participate more fully in decision-making."[9]

The UNDP adopted a multipronged strategy in its war on poverty. One cornerstone of that strategy was good governance. Creating sustainable livelihoods was another dimension of the agency's strategy. This entailed supporting local cooperatives and micro enterprises, providing assistance and extending credit to disadvantaged and previously marginalized groups in society, increasing employment opportunities for displaced persons and refugees, and making technology available and spawning local productive enterprises. An important element of this strategy was to redefine economic growth so as to link it to family income not solely to national account statistics.

By decade's end, the political distance separating the UN agencies like the UNDP from the Bretton Woods institutions had been substantially narrowed. While remaining cognizant, and critical, of the destructive efforts of free-wheeling free markets, UNDP officials accepted that if human development is to take place at all, it must occur in the context of the capitalist world economy. This, after all, was the only world economy immediately available, and certainly the only one that the powers behind the Bretton Woods institutions would condone. During this period, the World Bank had moved closer to the new UNDP orientation.

Secretariat officials argued that promoting sustainable human development required new forms of cooperation and partnerships among states, markets, the private sector, voluntary and civic organizations, and local communities. "We live today in a world of stakeholders, not simply a world of sovereign states." one senior UN official declared. All stakeholders ought to have some say in how the economy is supposed to work, or, better still, all stakeholders ought to cooperate to make the economy work to their mutual benefit. "[W]e must learn from past mistakes," former UNDP administrator Gus Speth argued, "and ensure that development cooperation supports the polity and not just the economy. . . . The challenges of growing poverty and widening inequity will not be met without democratization and good

---

[9]United Nations Development Programme, *UNDP Today: Reform in Action* (New York: United Nations, 1999).

governance."[10] Good governance as a foundation for development was similarly endorsed by the Bretton Woods institutions, which through the efforts of Secretary-General Annan were, seemingly willingly, and as the Charter originally intended, moving toward closer coordination with the Economic and Social Council, the UNDP, and other development bodies of the UN organization. The World Bank's development report for 1997 was titled *The State in a Changing World*. In an apparent meandering away from the Washington Consensus, the bank refocused on the role of state mechanisms in producing welfare outcomes.[11] Building democracy and promoting human rights, rule of law, and protecting fundamental freedoms all became components of development.

DEAD END OR NEW BEGINNING?

The stage was well set and the time was right, or so it seemed to the secretary general, for launching a bold initiative aimed at eradicating extreme poverty and associated ills. He called the UN member states to action in his Millennium Report to the 55th General Assembly, *We the Peoples: The Role of the United Nations in the 21st Century*, and further challenged them to make good on their commitments in his report to the Preparatory Committee for the High-Level Intergovernmental Event on Financing for Development.[12] A new development framework was endorsed by UN member states in the United Nations Millennium Declaration adopted at the 2000 New York Millennium Summit. This document enumerated specific goals and associated targets and indicators, the so-called millennium development goals (MDGs), to be achieved by 2015. It pledged to eradicate extreme poverty, create enabling environments conducive to development, promote good governance, mobilize financial resources for development, address the special needs of the least developed and heavily indebted developing countries, promote gender equality and the empowerment of women, develop and implement strategies to increase employment opportunities, make essential medicines more widely available in developing countries, develop strong partnerships with civil society, and ensure that the benefits of new technologies, especially information and communication technologies, are available to all.[13]

An elaborate strategy was put in place to facilitate the attainment and monitoring of progress on the MDGs. The centerpiece was the Millennium

---

[10]"Non-Benign Neglect: America and the Developing World in the Era of Globalization;" National Press Club, Washington, D.C., October 14, 1998.
[11]World Bank, *World Development Report 1997: The State in a Changing World* (New York: Oxford University Press, 1997).
[12]UN Document A/AC.257/12, December 18, 2000.
[13]UN Document A/AC.257/12, December 18, 2000.

Project, headed by Columbia University professor Jeffrey Sachs. This project's main task was to identify the operational priorities, organizational means of implementation, and financing structures necessary to achieve the MDGs and to assess implementation. The project's interim report (hereafter referred to as the Sachs Report) was published in January 2005 and served as the basic background document for the 2005 World Summit.[14]

The Sachs Report, although finding some positive things to report especially at the global level, was overall quite pessimistic in regard to the world being on track to attain the MDGs. Tremendous differences persisted both across and within regions and countries. In many parts of the developing world, conditions remained stagnant or were getting worse. Many of the positive trends were in eastern and southern Asia and were largely accounted for by strides made in China and India. Sub-Saharan Africa was found not on track with regard to achieving any of the goals; the poverty rate actually rose slightly over the period, and the spread and impacts of HIV/AIDS were out of control. The Sachs Report identified four reasons why the world is not on track for attaining the MDGs to date: governance failures, poverty traps, pockets of poverty, and policy neglect. The report went to great lengths to identify a detailed strategy for putting the MDG process back on track. Based on the Sachs Report and its recommendations, the secretary-general in March 2005 issued his report entitled *In Larger Freedom: Towards Development, Security and Human Rights.* He challenged the heads of state and government, who were to meet in a special World Summit in September 2005 to review progress made over the past five years toward achieving the MDGs, to take the bold initiatives necessary to turn things around.[15]

During preparations for the World Summit, the looming question was whether the member states of the UN possessed sufficient will to make and carry out the kinds of major commitments needed to get the job done of enhancing human security worldwide. But illusion was beginning to meet reality. From the beginning of the 1990s and up to the very eve of the World Summit in 2005, the program to promote sustainable human development was steered by the UN Secretariat, including the Office of the Secretary-General. The process had produced more than twenty world conferences, numerous high-level commissions, scores of reports, dozens of action plans, many memorable speeches, and tens of thousands of pages of paper. Most notably, a consensus had emerged over the basic framework of a global development agenda. Also, an unprecedented level of UN system cooperation in the development sphere had been forged. What it had not materialized was very much meaningful collective action on the part of the member states of the UN, very much development assistance, very many partnerships with the

[14]United Nations. *Investing in Development: A Practical Plan to Achieve the Millennium Development Goals* (Report of the Millennium Project to the Secretary-General), January 17, 2005.
[15]UN Document A/59/2005, March 21, 2005.

private sector, very much progress in environmental preservation, very much human security in the face of oppression, or very much new accomplishment in "good governance."

Hailed agreements were mostly reached by papering over differences about almost all meanings and aspects of "sustainable," "human," and "development." North and South never agreed about financing Third World development. Neither did they agree about who was responsible for preserving the earth's resources, who exactly owned the earth's resources, or who was to pay for protecting the environment. The United States consistently remained out of step with most of the rest of the UN membership, but it was never clear which national stances reflected commitment, which were taken for convenience, and which represented confusion concerning the issues at hand. Disagreement was in evidence within the North. North and South never agreed on the material conditions that constituted "human security," and the West and non-West never agreed about the societal and political conditions. Also at issue were questions regarding the prerogatives of the international community in promoting human security and even the more fundamental questions of who constituted "the international community" and how its will was to be expressed.

Careful review of the proceedings and outcomes of the many world conferences held between 1990 and 2002 reveals that sharp North–South or West–non-West divisions arose at all of them. Most of the conferences also displayed a world that was frequently divided between the United States and almost everyone else, and these divisions tended to turn proceedings into cavalcades of antihegemonism. During the preparations for the World Summit in September 2005, the United States did not even have a confirmed permanent representative to the UN, and the ambassador designate, John Bolton, had a long history of being dismissive toward the world body. When Washington's new chief delegate finally entered the preparatory negotiations for the World Summit, he brought with him scores of proposed amendments to previously agreed sections of the draft outcome statement. It was therefore quite clear that the leadership needed to make the summit into something tangible was not to come from the United States.

The summit's focus also had become clouded by the introduction of a variety of other issues, including nuclear proliferation, WMDs, UN reform, human rights, peace building, and fighting terrorism. Although most of the speeches by the 154 heads of state and government focused on dealing with poverty, the actual negotiations of the text of the draft outcome statement was conducted on a closed-door consensus basis and had to be carefully scripted to avoid the embarrassing potential of no agreed upon statement. While the leaders from the developing world exhorted rich countries to do more to fight poverty and help the world's poorest people, rich country leaders tended to focus on other issues that were of concern to them. U.S. President Bush won praise for speaking positively about the UN and declaring that "poverty breeds terrorism," but he went on to suggest that the way to promote prosperity and deal with poverty was through free trade.[16]

Although the World Summit had to do with many matters besides development, diplomats and activists, literally from Bongo to Bono, were nevertheless anxious to move the global development agenda forward, and they expected to accomplish this in New York.[17] However, in the end and despite much self-aggrandizement combined with attempts to paint a positive picture of the outcome, the summit largely flopped. At the very least, it fell far short of the expectations and desires of those who conceived of the summit as a springboard into consequential action on development. Bickering, battling, self-interested intransigence, and blatant arrogance proved to be the flavor of the day. The South lined up against a noncohesive North, the North and the South, respectively, lined up against themselves, and almost everyone lined up against the United States. This largest gathering ever of heads of state and government demonstrated once again how an unbridled politics of national and factional advantage seeking can thwart even the most carefully planned and hopeful organizational design.

What Secretary-General Kofi Annan had heralded as a once-in-a-generation opportunity for the international community to seize the day and move forward toward eradicating poverty ended in a mediocre thirty-five-page outcome statement. In it, matters in the realm of human security, such as agreement that it is the collective responsibility of the international community to protect populations from genocide, war crimes, and ethnic cleansing, drew firmer commitments than matters of development. Little immediate relief for impoverished peoples was written into the outcome statement. The declaration avoided targets and firm commitments. It relegated real action to the future, and as one Pakistani columnist reported, "the draft declaration got acceptance only when some concrete plans were turned into vague ideas and pledges were scaled down."[18]

Little came from the World Summit that could give much encouragement to those who hoped from advances in promoting Third World development. Annan admitted that the outcome of the World Summit was "disappointing" and the declaration was "watered down." Less generously, President Ali Rodriguez Araque of Venezuela dubbed the declaration a document "conceived in darkness" that was the product of "grotesque procedures."[19] Zambia's president, Levy Mwanawasa, summed up the feelings of many

[16]ABC News, "World Leaders OK Document at U.N. Summit," http://abcnews.go.com/US/wirestory?id=1134475&CMP=OTC-RSSFeeds0312.
[17]Reference is to President Omar Bongo of Gabon, cochair of the summit, and Bono, the leader singer of U2 and cofounder of DATA.
[18]*Pakistan Times*, September 18, 2005, p. 3.
[19]UN Document A/60/L.1, September 20, 2005; "Adoption of 2005 World Summit Outcome Hailed as Historic Step Towards UN reform," UN News Centre, September 27, 2005.

developing country leaders: "We hope that the commitments we have undertaken will not remain mere empty words."[20] On the northern side, Tony Blair provided a slightly different framing:

> Stalking this summit, like a spectre, are the Millennium Development goals. The struggle against global poverty will define our moral standing in the eyes of the future. . . . I have heard people describe the outcomes of this Summit as modest. No summit requiring unanimity from 190 nations can be more than modest. But if we did what we have agreed on doubling aid, on opening up trade, on debt relief, on HIV/AIDS and malaria, on conflict prevention . . . our modesty would surprise. . . . The effect would be measured in the lives of millions of people who will never hear these speeches or read our statements.[21]

A week or so following the Summit, President Mwanawasa and others were provided at least a little ray of hope when the World Bank and IMF agreed to cancel up to $55 billion in debts owed by his government and seventeen others. This action was made possible when richer countries agreed to provide extra funds for the bank. In the context of the beleaguered World Summit, this action indicates that in the development realm in the UN, the Bretton Woods institutions still call the shots and remain the foundation of the UN system's development capacity. In this regard, it is noteworthy that almost simultaneously with the vote on debt relief came the publication of the World Bank's *2006 World Development Report: Equity and Development.*[22] Breaking with past tradition, the report acknowledges that reducing inequality is a key to eliminating poverty. Perhaps a commitment by the Bretton Woods institutions to the dual challenges of widespread poverty and deep inequality might mean the politics of development is moving in more productive directions.

After more than a half century of United Nations involvement in Third World development, the verdict is still clearly out on whether the international community acting through the UN system can muster the commitment and follow through needed to make genuine progress toward eliminating poverty and thereby actually enhancing human security. If the history of UN development cooperation is any guide, the prospects appear rather grim. Yet the need for effective economic and social cooperation is more acute than ever.

---

[20]ABC News, "UN Assembly Focuses on World's Poor," http://abcnews.go.com/US/wirestory?id=138788.

[21]H.E. The Right Honourable Tony Blair, Prime Minister, Speech to the General Assembly at the 2005 UN World Summit, United Kingdom of Great Britain and Northern Ireland, September 14, 2005.

[22]World Bank, *World Development Report 2006: Equity and Poverty* (Washington, D.C.: Author, September 2005).

CHAPTER 9

Reconsidering the United Nations

When scholars expert in United Nations affairs gathered in New York to evaluate the world organization and make recommendations for reform, two contributions were particularly noteworthy. Commenting in his paper on the UN's main organs and subsidiary bodies, Gene M. Lyons, the founder of the Academic Council on the United Nations System, told his colleagues,

> in the eyes of many developing countries, the world has not changed. The unanimity of the permanent members of the Security Council is perceived not necessarily as a return to the principles of the Charter but rather as evidence that the great powers are determined to dominate the international system and use the United Nations as an instrument of their own national interests. By the same token, the annual session of the General Assembly—where developing countries carry a majority under the formula of one nation-one vote—has been reduced to meaningless and repetitive debate as the industrialized countries concentrate on economic growth and stability in the World Bank and the International Monetary Fund where they retain effective control. . . . If East-West tensions have abated, North-South relations in the United Nations have become more complex and tendentious.[1]

Then Edward C. Luck, past president of the United Nations Association of the United States, reflected that "the sad history of reform efforts at the UN underlines how difficult it is to achieve deep and durable reform in a highly decentralized system. . . . The political, humanitarian and structural

---

[1] Gene M. Lyons, "Competing Visions: Proposals for UN Reform" (unpublished manuscript, March 1993).

obstacles are immense and a combination of vision and persistence will be needed. This is, nevertheless, the most propitious time in memory to push hard, deep and fast."[2]

As it turns out, this particular academic conference on reforming the United Nations was held more than a dozen years ago in March 1993. That time may have been propitious for reforming the UN, as Dr. Luck encouraged, but no hard, deep, or fast effort to reform the organization ensued. By its agenda—great power dominance via the Security Council, the growing irrelevance of the General Assembly, unproductive North–South relations, double standards in human rights, and other familiar themes—this conference could have been held yesterday. The political maladies that obstructed the effectiveness of the United Nations in 1993 remain. These same roadblocks combined with bureaucratic inertia, insufficient resources, and other familiar factors that render large organizations allergic to change have set the UN adrift. By reverse token, our book, *United Nations Politics*, could have been written in 1993 because neither politics at the United Nations nor indeed the United Nations itself have changed much during the last decade. This is a sad commentary because efforts to reform the UN have been continually in train for at least the last decade, and because the agenda for reform has little changed, real progress is difficult to discern. Some in fact would say that UN reform has by now become more of a myth than a project.

THE NEW REFORM AGENDA

The rancorous debate in early 2003 over how to deal with Iraqi noncompliance with resolutions of the Security Council pitted the United States and the United Kingdom standing virtually alone against much of the rest of the world. It coincided with emerging concerns about the role of the UN in providing collective security in the post–Cold War environment. Even this was in the context of broader questions of whether multilateral responses to global problems could be cobbled from the combative factions and less than compatible interests of a politically fragmented world. Although the UN has seemingly always been in crisis, even the UN's most ardent supporters insist that the "crisis of multilateralism" in the early twenty-first century "is different" and that today the continuing relevance of the entire institution is genuinely at stake.[3]

In November 2003 UN secretary-general Kofi Annan declared that the organization was at a "fork in the road." Either the UN would move toward meaningfully addressing the challenges to national and human security that were intensifying as the twenty-first century dawned or it would descend further

---

[2]Edward C. Luck, *Steps Toward UN Reform* (New York: United Nations Association of the United States, March 19, 1993), p. 1.

[3]John G. Ruggie, "This Crisis of Multilateralism Is Different," speech delivered to the UNA-USA National Forum on the United Nations, June 26, 2003.

into irrelevance. The secretary-general was convinced that the UN could and would be revitalized through internal reform, and he therefore moved ahead to solicit the support of member governments for the reform effort. Annan proceeded to establish a high-level panel on "Threats, Challenges, and Change" and asked this expert group to examine the challenges of collective security. The panel, composed of eminent diplomats and political leaders, evaluated the UN system of collective security, issued a report titled *A More Secure World*, and recommended that the UN had to take greater account of the intrastate origins of contemporary threats to international peace, which was also the a conclusion of an earlier report prepared by the International Commission on Intervention and State Sovereignty titled *The Responsibility to Protect.*[4]

The high-level panels acknowledged that internal conflicts are difficult for the UN to address because the Charter mandates respect for sovereignty, but the groups nevertheless concluded that the UN Charter still provides the multilateral tools necessary for effective collective security. Article 51, for example, allows member states the right to self-defense and, more importantly, Chapter VII provides for a full range of responses—from preventive to reactive measures—so long as the use of force is a product of consensus by members of the Security Council. Should the Security Council reach consensus concerning a threat to international peace and security, including the potential for terrorists to acquire weapons of mass destruction, it has carte blanche to take any action, even preventive intervention in disregard of national sovereignty, to address that threat. The experts concluded that the instruments at the UN's disposal are adequate. In effect, the obstacles to timely and appropriate collective action were not legal or constitutional constraints under the Charter. They were instead political. What really needed to be addressed were processes of decision making and consensus building. And, the experts observed, if the Security Council could be reformed to have greater legitimacy and efficacy, then the instruments available to it could be put to more effective use.

In March 2005 Annan produced a comprehensive report titled *In Larger Freedom.*[5] This document, the secretary-general anticipated, would frame the discussion of UN reform scheduled to take place among heads of state during the 60th session of the General Assembly in 2005. The secretary-general's report integrated the findings of a number of commissions and panels established since the late 1990s—the Brahimi Report, the Millennium Development Report, *The Responsibility to Protect*, and *A More Secure World*—into a comprehensive program for UN reform. His emphasis on the interdependence of

[4]Gareth Evans et al., *The Responsibility to Protect: Report of the International Commission on Intervention and Sovereignty: December 2001* (Ottawa, Ont.: International Development Research Center, 2001); "A More Secure World: Our Shared Responsibility," *Report of the Secretary-General's High-Level Panel on Threat, Challenges and Change* (New York: United Nations, 2003), http://www.un.org/secureworld/report.pdf.
[5]Kofi Annan, *In Larger Freedom: Towards Development, Security and Human Rights for All*, Report of the Secretary General, General Assembly A/59/2005, March 21, 2005.

collective security, development, and human rights was intended as an effort to foster commitment to reforming the UN by member states with widely divergent interests and assumptions about the priorities of the world organization. Annan acknowledged that perceptions of insecurity vary according to the wealth, regional location, and power of countries. But, the secretary-general underlined, collective security in the twenty-first century requires an appreciation for how threats are linked. "The rich are vulnerable to the threats that attack the poor and the strong are vulnerable to the weak." A nuclear attack on the United States or a European country by a terrorist organization would have devastating effects on the whole world by causing a global economic downturn that would plunge millions worldwide into deeper poverty. An inadequate health care system on one side of the world can incubate a communicable disease that would invariably debilitate rich as well as poor societies. In this kind of interconnected world, it is in every country's self-interest that all sources of insecurity are addressed effectively. In his report, the secretary-general implored member states to recognize that collective security is only truly collective if common actions respond to the different insecurities sensed by different members of the international community.

In Larger Freedom called for major reforms of the UN in the areas of peace and security, economic and social cooperation, human rights, and administration. With regard to economic and social cooperation, the agenda for reform suggested national strategies for meeting the Millennium Development Goals established in 2000. These included a halving of hunger and poverty by 2015, attaining universal primary education, reducing child and maternal mortality, promoting gender equality, improving environmental sustainability, reversing the spread of deadly diseases, increasing development assistance, and improving the world trading system. The secretary-general's report called for significantly increased financing for development, emphasized broadened market access for developing countries and completion of the Doha Round of trade negotiations, and asked for new approaches to managing as well as writing off Third World debt. Annan's proposals for enhancing peace and security called for a clear and agreed-upon definition of terrorism and the drafting, signing, and ratification of a comprehensive convention against terrorism. The secretary-general wanted definite progress toward stemming the proliferation of nuclear, biological, and chemical weapons; he recommended establishing a peace-building commission to better help countries making the transition from war to peace.

In the area of democracy and human rights, which the secretary-general associated with freedom to live in dignity, proposals contained in *In Larger Freedom* called for the creation of a democracy fund to help countries establish or strengthen democratic institutions. The report also recommended replacing the fractious and politicized Human Rights Commission with a smaller Human Rights Council that would be endowed with enforcement capability somewhat comparable to the Security Council. Recommended administrative reforms included streamlining the agenda of the General Assembly to make deliberations more meaningful, restructuring the Security Council to make it more representative of power, influence, and interests in the contemporary world, empowering the Economic and Social Council to serve as a high-level development cooperation forum, and enabling the secretary-general to exercise greater control over the Secretariat so as to make the international civil service more like a centralized organization and less like a system of bureaucratic fiefdoms.

The loud and clear message of *In Larger Freedom* was that the member states of the United Nations must change their behavior so their organization can operate more effectively in the world political environment of the early twenty-first century. Reforming the UN requires agreement among member states to change structures and processes so that international cooperation and collective action might more readily ensue. During the months leading up to the September 2005 summit meeting in New York, the secretary-general's ambitious agenda for reform was received with surprising seriousness by the member states, who sought to negotiate a package of changes that would take into account the principal concerns of all factions and interests. There was some expectation therefore that structural and procedural reform in the UN might actually result from the World Summit and the General Assembly's 60th session. Some such reform was actually accomplished. The summit agreed to establish a Human Rights Council to strengthen UN capabilities for promoting human rights, and a Peace Building Commission was created to guide UN efforts at reconstructing failed states and reintegrating shattered societies. Most importantly, perhaps, the outcome statement of the World Summit endorsed the principle of humanitarian intervention, specifically with regard to preventing genocide where the international community agreed that "governments can no longer use sovereignty and non-intervention norms as excuses to avoid having to act to protect civilians from mass killings."[6] That the UN officially lined up in support of intervention and in contravention of sovereignty was definitely a victory for the secretary-general, who was a strong advocate of international community action against genocide. It was also a victory for the West inasmuch as most of the opposition to circumventing sovereignty came from the non-West.

In fact, if one had kept political score, the results of the World Summit would have heavily favored the West and the North over the non-West and the South. Not only did most of what happened at the summit reflect First World preferences, but so too did most of what did not happen. As reported earlier in this volume, the overall results of the World Summit in 2005 were disappointing for the Third World. About the summit's lukewarm commitments to promoting development and alleviating poverty we have already spoken. Oxfam, a leading NGO involved in combating hunger, also spoke out: "World leaders appeared nonchalant about the lack of real progress on more aid, fairer trade and debt relief. If current trends continue it will take 100 years instead of 10 to

---

[6]United Nations, 2005 *World Summit Outcome,* A/60/L/1, September 15, 2005.

meet the internationally agreed poverty reduction targets, the Millennium Development Goals."[7] Meanwhile, neoliberal economic orthodoxy was reinforced at the summit, and "free trade" was still understood to allow for First World restrictions on imports from the Third World. Some debt relief was offered, but targets for increased development assistance were eluded. Regarding other issues prominent on the preconference agenda, the restructuring of the Security Council was abandoned, stemming nuclear proliferation and promoting nuclear disarmament were not included in the outcome statement, terrorism was left undefined, the International Criminal Court was not mentioned, and the secretary-general was denied enhanced authority over the Secretariat.

Despite its shortcomings, Annan described the World Summit of 2005 as a step in the right direction for the UN. Perhaps so: but neither the changes apparently accomplished, like the Human Rights Council, the Peace Building Commission, and the commitment to the responsibility to protect, nor the failed reforms like restructuring the Security Council and increasing the authority of the secretary-general effectively address the contentious, fragmented, and insecure world that is intruding into UN affairs and undermining the organization's cooperative purposes. The central message of much of the analysis presented in this book is that this is not "the most propitious time in memory to push hard, deep, and fast" for a more effective UN. Even if everything that *In Larger Freedom* recommends were realized in UN practice, the polarized political structure of the membership will persist—North versus South, West versus Non-West, weak versus powerful, the United States versus almost everyone else. Reformed structures and streamlined processes are promising only if member states are able to use them to build consensus and launch collective action, and today there is very little in the world politics surrounding and greatly affecting the UN that points to consensus.

REASSESSING THE UNITED NATIONS

The reality concerning the effectiveness of the UN, and also the consistent message conveyed in this book, is that intergovernmental politics and national and factional pursuits of narrowly defined self- interests obstruct meaningful multilateral responses at the United Nations. Although the UN is nowadays a reasonably effective peacekeeper, it is still a poor promoter of peace and security because the governments of the world cannot agree on political, economic, and social conditions that must be preserved or on conditions that have to be changed to ensure peace. Today's status quo is certainly not to everyone's liking, but all alternatives are equally contentious. The UN is similarly a poor advocate for human rights because the governments of the world cannot agree on what rights people and peoples are to be granted or on who

---

[7]Oxfam Press Release, September 16, 2005; http://www.oxfam.org.uk/press/releases/.

should grant them. Governments are also predisposed to attribute virtue to their own respect for human rights and to indict their ideological enemies as abusers. Nor is the UN especially adept at promoting development because among member governments there are deep-seated economic-philosophical differences over what development actually means and especially over how best to foster and nurture it.

Still, the UN remains useful, even in the politically cacophonous world of today. For one thing, the peacekeeping missions of the UN, over the many decades of the organization's operation, have likely saved millions of lives. There have been notable failures, to be sure, but there have also been arguable successes like Namibia, Cambodia, East Timor (at least until the recent backsliding into conflict), and the operations in the Congo and in Kosovo ongoing at present. There has been in addition considerable learning from past mistakes so that the peacekeeping and peace-building capacities of the UN are certainly better today than a decade ago. It needs also to be noted that the UN has dispatched to difficult assignments some of the most talented negotiators, mediators, and conciliators of the last half century. With few exceptions, the special representatives of the secretary-general have time and again risen to immense challenges and exercised exemplary—yet quiet— statesmanship on behalf of the UN and in the interest of peace. Men like Alvaro de Soto, who negotiated the settlement in El Salvador; Diego Cordovez, who paved the diplomatic pathway out of Afghanistan for the Russians; Marti Ahtissari, who kept peace among contending parties while Nambia gained independence; Olaf Palme, who helped end the decade-long war between Iran and Iraq; and Giandomenico Picco, who calmed tensions in Lebanon; and many, many more like them made few headlines. But they did great service, and in its upper echelons the United Nations continues to be able to recruit this kind of talent.[8]

The UN is probably also the only vehicle available for getting the world to pay attention to issues of truly global concern. Prevailing poverty, over-population, environmental deterioration, pandemic diseases, transnational crime, oppressed women, mass human migration, and international terrorism are global issues. They concern, affect, and involve all nations, even though some, from narrow national perspectives, are reluctant to look at the world this way. Although the UN has not been able to bring about very much collective action on the part of member states to greatly ameliorate the damaging effects of these conditions, it has at least been able to drive home the message that the problems are indeed global and that collective action is required. Politicizing global issues, as so often happens at the UN, ostensibly contributes little toward productively confronting them, yet it does enhance their prominence and again compels governments and their constituents to pay

---

[8]Donald J. Puchala, "The Secretary-General and His Special Representatives," in *The Challenging Role of the UN Secretary-General: Making "The Most Impossible Job in the World" Possible*, Benjamin Rivilin and Leon Gordenker, eds. (Westport, Conn.: Praeger, 1993), pp. 81–97.

attention. In a similar sense, were it not for the United Nations, the poor, the weak, and the politically voiceless would likely receive very little attention in the grander games of world politics. During our interviews with Secretariat officials, we frequently asked them why the UN was useful. One of the most memorable responses was offered by an assistant to the secretary-general who returned our question with one of his own: "If it weren't for the UN, who would look out for the little guys?" Just so: the UN gives smallness, weakness, and poverty a voice in world politics that the "little guys" might otherwise never have, and to some extent membership in the UN protects their interests, which would probably otherwise be ignored.

The UN is also a forum of intellectual ferment, and, as reported elsewhere in this volume, a font of ideas. Most importantly, ideas emanating from the UN, from Secretariat branches, special agencies, or intergovernmental committees, councils, and commissions, tend frequently to be unorthodox. They challenge conventional outlooks, and often usefully so, because in a world of hegemonic domination, unorthodox ideas are easily ignored or repressed. Alternatives to orthodox thinking are crucially important because conventional wisdom, particularly when validated by power, is typically slow to adjust to changing times and conditions. In addition, conventional wisdom usually privileges those who propagate it because in the context of world politics there is very little politically neutral information. Through many decades, the United Nations via many of its agents and agencies outside the Bretton Woods cluster has consistently questioned the assumptions and projections connected with classical liberal and neoliberal economics, contending always that such thinking and the policies that follow buttress a status quo that rewards the rich and penalizes the poor. Reactions to UN thinking about doctrines such as import substitution, the new international economic order, basic human needs, and sustainable human development typically have ranged from dismissive to celebratory, depending on affinities for or rejections of prevailing orthodoxy. UN critiques have never won out over intellectual orthodoxy backed by power. But this is less important than the fact that the UN has been able to inject alternatives into international economic discourse, and very often to present Third World perspectives in sufficiently sophisticated ways that they had to be taken seriously. Without the UN, these intellectual offerings would be mostly ignored because the North does not as rule give very much credence to southern thinking. Much the same sort of interpretation regarding orthodoxy and alternatives can be offered regarding the prerogatives of sovereignty, where preserving, protecting, and invoking sovereignty represents the conventional wisdom of traditional international relations, which is being confronted today by new thinking emanating in considerable measure from the office of the secretary-general of the UN.

Some would argue, as we ultimately do, that the further usefulness of the UN is in the organization's progressive opening of political space to international civil society. The UN remains a club of governments, but NGOs are seeking changes in the qualifications for membership. They are actually seeking influence more than membership per se because, as reported earlier in this volume, many NGOs through their leaders believe they have something useful to offer concerning international public policy. Many NGOs, moreover, are legitimate and effective *political* players within various countries and especially within democratic countries where linkages among civil society, politics, and government are close. They are not yet legitimate and effective political players at the international level, however, because there are very few legitimate or institutionalized linkages among international civil society, world politics, and global governance. Willy-nilly these linkages are developing in the United Nations system, which is the only logical institutional setting in which they could develop. This is likely happening to the dismay of many governments, but probably, as some within and without the UN contend, it is in the better interest of international public policy.

Despite all of the criticisms, including our own, of the UN as merely a "talk shop," something remains to be said about the value of having a global forum for intergovernmental dialogue. In point of fact, the UN is really the only place in the world where the issues of greatest importance for the future of international relations are actually discussed, and they are most exhaustively discussed in the much maligned General Assembly. These include; first, how should the world deal with United States, the "only remaining superpower," and more generally with the hegemonic structure of the present-day international system? It is fair to say this is a concern of the highest priority in the foreign policy of every country of the world, and it affects stances on nearly all issues on the UN agenda. Second, how solid should the wall of national sovereignty be? Because the principles of intervention and nonintervention are in flux, UN efforts in numerous issue areas are obstructed. But the governments of the world need to know what sovereignty is going to mean ten to twenty years hence, and their interactions in the UN—and with the UN—may well inform them. Third, are there universal values or behavioral norms that ought to set standards for all of humanity, or is humanity a cluster of different cultural communities with different values and varying standards? This question has cast the international human rights regime into turmoil and by implication has affected relations between citizens and their governments the world over. Answering it one way or the other continues to challenge the United Nations, but answering it is nevertheless crucial for the peoples of the world. Fourth, whose responsibility is global poverty? Much of the world's response to Third World development has taken the form of a flight from responsibility regarding poverty, and disagreement about causes has been a continuing excuse for lack of remedial action. The reasonable position of the international civil service is that combating global poverty is everyone's responsibility. Because this gains much lip service but sparks little action, the question of poverty continues to dominate the UN agenda. Allowing this question to go unanswered may well be the difference between peace and war in later decades of our new century. Fifth, should the UN remain a club of governments, or would the world benefit from a new kind of international organization that offers effective access to international civil society? Until history ultimately answers this question, UN member governments will surely continue to debate it.

ADAPTING TO THE TWENTY-FIRST CENTURY

It is admittedly inconsistent to argue that the world is not ready for the rather modest reforms of the UN proposed by Kofi Annan at the turn of the present century, and then to say that only much more sweeping reforms will keep the UN relevant. But so it is: reforms of the UN proposed to date, and even those that member states dared not to approve, do not go far enough. New committees, councils, and commissions may create work for diplomats, and they certainly enhance the volume of UN paper produced. But there is little guarantee such new structures would be any more effective in mobilizing collective action or bettering the human condition than the countless committees, councils, and commissions that resulted from previous efforts at reforming the UN. Similarly, restructuring the UN Secretariat one more time would probably increase the efficiency of the organization about as much as did restructuring the Secretariat one time ago or the time before that. Besides, the UN Secretariat is not nearly as inefficient or as profligate as critics make out, so that redrawing tables of organization is not really a very high priority. Rendering the UN more central to the international relations of the early twenty-first century will require fundamental changes in the organization that are much more radical than the secretary-general perhaps dared to propose in 2005. Reforming the UN to make it more effective will require equally radical changes in the attitudes of member states regarding both the organization and what they seek to accomplish by participating in its affairs. If the UN is to move toward accomplishing the aims of its Charter, it must be a place where governments go to cooperate, not conflict. To contribute to peace in the twenty-first century, the UN is going to have to assist in enhancing both national security and human security, and contributing in either of these spheres will require major changes in the ways that member governments *decide on the policies that guide their collective actions*. Absent this, the UN will remain more a part of the problem than a part of the solution in the dawning Age of Increasing Insecurity.

The UN and most other international organizations of our time are products of the system of international law and the philosophy of international relations paramount from the late eighteenth century onward. As such, they are based on the contradictory tenets of the sovereign equality of states on the one hand and the prerogatives of power on the other. Sovereign equality accords to every recognized state the privilege to participate in the diplomacy of world affairs, to don and display all of the symbols and ceremonies of diplomatic decorum, to "strut and fret" on the diplomatic stage, as it were, and to be admitted to membership in international intergovernmental organizations.

The principle of sovereignty also limits membership in such organizations to sovereign states per se while it shields their domestic doings from outside intervention.

Conversely, the prerogatives of power allocate influence in international affairs and in international organizations as well to the wealthy and powerful, and this frequently renders any practical meaning of sovereign equality moot. Traditionally, this interweaving of international law and organization yielded a diplomacy of nicety and decorum, which determined very little, and a politics of power, which determined nearly everything. Such was the environment within which the UN was founded, and the structure and functioning of the organization continue to reflect this originating environment. If by "governance" we mean "maintaining or managing a social order," the United Nations today approximates a system of *global governance*, albeit not a very authoritative, effective, or efficient one. More importantly, perhaps, the United Nations is not a very *democratic* system of global governance. With regard to decision making, the system is in fact rather oligarchic and authoritarian, and it probably cannot become very much more authoritative, effective, or efficient until it becomes more democratic. This means at the very least that democratization, not only of the members but of the world organization itself, must be a principal goal of meaningful UN reform. It also may well mean that in the twenty-first century the UN is going to have to move beyond its eighteenth-century legal and philosophic origins and its identity as a club of governments.

As underlined repeatedly in this book, the world today, and with it the UN, is polarized along political fault lines separating North from South in social and economic issue-areas and West from Non-West regarding cultural questions. Here we surrender some accuracy and nuance and summarize this political polarization as First World versus Third World. The low esteem accorded to the UN by the government of the United States follows in considerable measure from the myth that the UN is a "Third World institution" because of the numerical majority of developing states in the organization. Those who nurture this myth imagine that during the 1970s, after decolonization, the Group of 77, the NAM, and other agents of the new majority acting in the various UN forums succeeded in "capturing the organization" and refashioning it into an instrument of anticolonial retribution and economic redistribution. Of course the factual history of the United Nations is quite different: the organization consistently has been, and still remains, an instrument of the First World and a source of great frustration for the Third World. This is because the large industrialized countries control not only the resources that allow the UN to act, they also control decision making in crucial forums like the Security Council and the powerful specialized agencies such as the IMF and the World Bank. Throughout the UN's existence, the First World has allowed little to happen that contradicted its preferences. In fact, if we accept that bluster and rhetoric are readily discountable in world affairs, and even if we acknowledge that the bias of the international civil service somewhat favors the Third World, it remains a fact that little of substance or consequence has happened in UN policy making that has contradicted First World preferences. As one Secretariat official was quick to point out, the UN is a "northern" institution. The frustration and ultimate fate of the UN's former secretary-general Boutros Boutros-Ghali revealingly illustrate what happens when the First World's domination of the organization is challenged.[9] Regarding the Bretton Woods institutions, there has been no need for mythology about who controls policy making. The IMF and the World Bank have always been, and remain, First World institutions. The General Agreement on Tariffs and Trade was also a First World institution, and the World Trade Organization that superseded it most certainly is one also.

It is important to understand the First World dominance of the UN system for two reasons. First, this dominance breeds resentment, or it at least fosters frustration, and it therefore exacerbates the North–South cleavage in international relations, which, as we explained earlier, is a principal axis of twenty-first-century world politics. Here, regarding insecurity, the international institutions of the UN system become part of the problem, rather than elements or instruments for the solution because they become arenas for conflict between the rich and poor countries rather than instruments for cooperation. Second, and equally significant, if the international institutional system is not reformed, First World dominance will continue into the twenty-first century and international organizations will probably be used by the First World to maintain the present international political and economic status quo. This too is likely to aggravate rather than alleviate conditions of both national and human insecurity.

Unlike the Third World, the industrialized countries of the First World are not plagued with insecurities, except perhaps for their presently pervasive anxiety about transnational terrorism. Otherwise, they have established a zone of peace among themselves that is likely to endure, and they collectively constitute a zone of prosperity that has produced unprecedented material qualities of life. Their interest is to keep things as they are, and their understandable interest in international institutions, which they largely control, is to use these as instruments to assist in keeping things the way they are, that is, as they are in the First World. The First World attitude toward the Third World is neither malevolent nor exploitative; nor is there any perceptible First World conspiracy aimed toward keeping the Third World poor and weak. Rather, the governments of the industrialized countries look on the Third World with relative indifference, and this translates into international institutional policies of political-military quarantine and economic tutelage.

The First World would rather not be involved in the political-military disorders of the Third World, and, if they must be, they seek to enter as mediators, moderators, or monitors, or, in desperate situations as police officers or

---

[9]Thomas G. Weiss, David P. Forsythe, and Roger A. Coate, *The United Nations and Changing World Politics.* 4th ed. (Boulder, Colo.: Westview, 2004), p. 169.

peacekeepers. These kinds of involvements are facilitated by international organizations, which the major governments of the First World find useful for such tasks. Referring to international policing, an American official once explained to us, "That's what the UN is supposed to do." Whether such interventions succeed in restoring order or not (and they often do not), they at least keep the political-military distresses of the Third World at arm's length, and this is the First World's preference. It also appears to be the case that there are some instances of disorder out there "at the ends of the earth" that First World governments reckon to be insufficiently consequential, or potentially too expensive, to warrant international policing, and in such instances they press to keep the international organizations they control inactive.

Economically, what the First World appears most willing to give to the Third World is advice, which tends to change as one set of development slogans gives way to the next. The advice today is to "structurally adjust" by privatizing enterprises, reducing public sector spending and social services, eliminating economic frontiers, integrating into the global economy, and devaluing national currencies as needed. And, while all of this adjusting is happening, every caution must be exercised to protect the natural environment so development can be "sustained." The international economic institutions controlled by the First World, the World Bank and IMF in particular, are used by the First World to proffer the advice of the day. These institutions also allocate money, particularly when international economic crises threaten the environments or returns for First World investors.

The First World is also advising that every effort must be made to nurture democracy within countries, which is not only the political complement to a market economy, but also the political-institutional manifestation of accomplished modernity. And the political-philosophical complement to both market and democracy is the philosophical liberalism that flowed originally out of the eighteenth-century Enlightenment in France, England, and British North America. Liberalism, the First World advises, is surely preferable to the archaic ideologies of the Third World, which tend to justify all manner of "oriental despotism." Much of this advice channeled by the First World through the international organizational system may be sound. Still, many in the Third World find it grating. Many also suspect that it is offered more in the interest of those who give it than in the interest of those to whom it is given.

The point here in underlining the extent to which the international institutional system is controlled by the First World is not to castigate this group of countries, which acts understandably in its own interests. What needs to be understood, however, is that in the absence of institutional reforms that would render international organizations less "First World" and more global by allowing Third World governments and interests greater influence over policies and policy making, the future impacts of the UN and the world financial institutions will be little different from the present impacts. First World governments and interests will continue to use the international institutions to push the current political and economic status quo into the twenty-first century. Although this may contribute to enhancing both national and human security *in the First World*, it will probably not be the case in the Third World, if for no better reason than that the present status quo obviously is not contributing to security there. Extending it into the future promises little change. Pushing the present status quo into the future will also likely polarize world politics further along First World–Third World lines, thus rendering international organizations like the UN even less authoritative and effective in alleviating national and human insecurities than they are today.

DEMOCRATIZING INTERNATIONAL INSTITUTIONS

If international organizations are to become less "First World" in policy bias and perform differently in the future, *democratization* is the principle that must undergird reform. What "democratization" means is equitable access to international policy making for all of the legitimate interests represented in debates about international public policy. Democracy is a method, a means to the end of representation, which itself is a means to the end of arriving at policies that the community (here the international community) can accept as legitimate. Democratic decision making may assume various forms—majoritarian, weighted majoritarian, consociational, pluralist, populist, and others—all of them more equitable than the hegemony of the wealthy and powerful that is today the policy-making mode of most international institutions.

The First World's, and especially the American, model for reforming the United Nations, mainly concerns making the organization more efficient in the use of its resources, that is, "leaner and meaner" and overall less costly to operate.[10] There is no marked First World interest in altering decision-making structures or processes either in the UN or in the Bretton Woods institutions. Here, the reluctance to allow any altering of policy processes stems in considerable measure from the dread of majority tyranny. That is, if representation is allocated according to the principle of "one state-one vote" and "majority rule" is the decision-making norm, then majorities will have opportunity to ride roughshod over minorities, and in polarized political environments, where the composition of majorities and minorities remain relatively constant across issues and over time, majoritarianism readily deteriorates into populist tyranny. Needless to say, international organizations are today, and into the foreseeable future will remain, politically polarized along a First World–Third World axis, and the member states from the Third World will hold commanding majorities. One state-one vote in international organizations is therefore as unacceptable to the First World as hegemony is to the Third World.

---

[10]Richard Thornburgh, *Report to the Secretary-General of the United Nations* (New York: The United Nations, 1993), passim. This American approach to UN reform has been remarkably consistent from the 1980s extending to the 2005 reform effort.

But there are alternatives, and they all tend to follow from the principle of *concurrent majorities*, which stipulates that democratic representation tends to be more equitable, and democracy therefore becomes more workable when decision making is based on a *concurrence of interests rather than a preponderance of numbers.* Simply put, democratic decisions should embody a concurrence of relevant interests present in a given community, not only the preferences of a numerical majority, and decision making should be structured and proceed in such a way as to make such a concurrence possible. Moving in such directions internationally is not altogether out of the question. Weighted voting, for example, well serves the European Union: here, the accepted formula protects the interests of both large and small member states. A consociational mode, which is also a variety of concurrence, characterizes the decision-making procedures of the International Labor Organization, where it is more important that interests—of workers, employers, and governments—should be represented than member states as such. Within countries, bicameralism is used as a way to provide representation for both populist interests and constituent governments. Many states today also operate democratically via modes of consociation.

Why not attempt some such system of democratic concurrence at the international level as well? Surely our constitutional imaginations are sufficient to fashion international institutions more appropriate for the political environments of the twenty-first century. If such a new set of rules for decision making by concurrence of interests can be arrived at for the international community, they should be adopted and enforced in every forum where international public policy is made. This includes the UN Security Council, where the real issue today is not who the members will be, or how many there will be, but how the council's decisions are made. Decisions by numerical majority will not do, nor of course will decisions by the hegemony of the Permanent Five or the obstinacy of the Permanent One. Policy-making procedures in the UN Economic and Social Council also need to be redesigned in such a way that serious questions of human security will actually be debated and decided. Otherwise only trivial policies or no policies at all can actually result. The one state-one vote procedure that guarantees the Third World a permanent majority in the ECOSOC and its committees and commissions also invites First World countries to discount all of these institutions. So too will the UN General Assembly become a more useful institution of international governance only when its resolutions reflect the convergent interests of the international community instead of the whims of one combative, partisan coalition or another, or the extremism of factional leaders. The one state-one vote procedure is unlikely ever to produce responsible policy making in the UN General Assembly. Needless to say, the oligarchic decision-making procedures of the IMF and the World Bank mock democracy in the international community and lead understandably to questions about whose interests the policies of the IMF and World Bank actually serve.

Most of these reformed decision-making procedures would have the effect of giving the small, the weak, and the poor greater influence over the policies of international organizations. If sensibly formulated, such decision-making reforms would not turn the organizations over to the Third World because First World interests could, and would, be protected. One result would be that the First World would no longer be able to use international organizations as instruments for protecting and projecting a status quo deemed unsatisfactory by much of the Third World. Similarly, Third World suspicions concerning the dominating and exploitative aspirations of the First World might also be alleviated and political polarization may diminish while national security in the Third World increases. Conversely, imperatives for incorporating First World as well as Third World interests into the concurrences that yield international public policies could well lead to more reasonable and responsible, and less polemical, initiatives on the part of the Third World and possibly to greater and more meaningful attention to problems of human insecurity.

Equipping international organizations to deal more effectively with problems of national and human security in the early twenty-first century requires constitutional reform as a first step. Global governance needs to be democratized, and until meaningful moves are made in this direction, no genuine policy changes can be expected. Yet surely these are utopian recommendations, to which even the sympathetic must respond with great skepticism. A system of states founded on, jealous of, and zealous in protecting the principle of sovereign equality cannot transform itself into a structure of democratic global governance. The weak especially cannot abandon the corollary principle of one state-one vote because their single votes are among the only bargaining chips they possess. Nor will the wealthy and powerful voluntarily abandon their prerogatives. Why should they? Admittedly, no compelling logic renders the democratization of international institutions likely, and therefore there is no good reason to expect that international organizations will deal with problems of national or human security in the decades ahead any differently, or more effectively, than they have thus far.

Nevertheless, if the United Nations as well as other multilateral institutions are to be reformed, the initiative and the impetus must come from the Third World because the governments of the poorer and weaker states have a good deal more to gain from institutional democratization than the governments of the industrialized countries. Because the First World is being asked to surrender advantages that accrue from wealth and power, the greatest political concessions along the way to democratizing international institutions therefore have to come from the Third World. This shifts the responsibility for shaping the future of international institutions onto the Third World, and, frankly, little evidence in recent experience suggests that Third World governments and leaders are seriously seeking or accepting this responsibility. Complaining, indicting, condemning, and haranguing the North and West in international organizational forums, dwelling on a colonial past that is less and less relevant to new problems, and transforming all global issues into questions about transferring resources from the wealthy to the poor is not tantamount to opening the way for a serious discussion about improving the effectiveness of international institutions via democratization. Whether Third World diplomats will rise to the challenge of international institutional reform in the early twenty-first century remains to be seen. Yet a good deal in early twenty-first international relations will depend on whether they do accept this challenge.

INCORPORATING INTERNATIONAL CIVIL SOCIETY

Yet even if international institutions are reformed in such ways that the governments of the Third World gain greater access to decision making, this may not be sufficient to effectively focus international public policy on problems of human insecurity. It may also not push international institutions as far as they need to be pushed toward democratization in the next century. Although states with national governments as their agents will remain the most prominent international actors in the decades ahead, NGOs of various sorts are likely to gain both prominence and influence. The world in fact is already beginning to look like an extensive society, that is, a *transnational civil society*, where all manner of organizations and associations, promoting all manner of interests and pursuing all manner of goals, assemble and function across state boundaries very much in the way that societal groups within countries assemble and function across provincial or regional boundaries. The composition of transnational civil society today is massive: business corporations, financial institutions, labor unions, humanitarian organizations, professional associations, environmental groups, ethnic communities, police forces, political parties, drug cartels, terrorist groups, and many, many more. In a holistic sense, even national governments may be considered to be organizations functioning as constituent groups in transnational civil society. There is much to suggest that the extensiveness and complexity of transnational civil society will increase, perhaps quite dramatically, in the years ahead.

Politically, what many of these transnational organizations are seeking is influence over the policies and the policy-making processes of international organizations. Practically speaking, the transnational civil society even today manages more than a modicum of influence in some spheres. Environmental policies at the global level, for example, are influenced by coalitions of scientific research organizations, activist conservation groups, eco-industries, international bureaucracies, and proactive governments that mobilize, communicate, conspire, and collectively lobby to affect the wording of international treaties and allocations of international organizational attentions and resources to better protect the earth's environment. Global-level undertakings to further the protection of human rights, to heighten the well-being of women and children worldwide, or to speed the removal of land mines from former war zones have similarly mobilized transnational civil society and brought pressures to bear on international organizations. Again, there is much to suggest that similar and greater pressures from transnational civil society will be parts of the politics of international policy making in the future.

It might be surmised that if the international community is actually going to take steps toward alleviating human insecurity in the early twenty-first century, these moves are much more likely to be prompted by pressures on international organizations from transnational civil society than from initiatives taken by national governments. This is the reason perhaps why the democratization of international institutions only to the point of enhancing the influence of Third World governments does not go far enough. Although there are some outstanding exceptions, the record to date of Third World governments actually doing very much to alleviate human insecurity is not especially impressive. In fact, the activities of several Third World governments surely have contributed to increased human insecurity in their own and often in neighboring countries as well.

A most dramatic, but at the same time a most promising, reform of the international institutional system would be a constitutional change that admitted legitimate and responsible elements of transnational society into formal roles in global governance.[11] This would extend democracy in the international community to the grassroots level and also alter the form of democracy from concurrence to pluralism. Here, global governance would begin to resemble national government in modern pluralist democracies. It would begin to approximate giving people a voice in the making of international public policy, allowing them perhaps to deal with their own insecurities according to their own perceptions, preferences, and prescriptions. The institutional structures and procedural rules that could accommodate admitting transnational society into global governance are not easily imagined, although they would most likely involve some form of bicameralism. At this point it is difficult to even wonder whether such a transformation in international institutions is possible even as far into the twenty-first century as it is practicable to gaze. Resistance from national governments, both First World and Third World, would be immense and intense because their authority would be

---

[11]Secretary General Kofi Annan appointed a Panel of Eminent Persons on United Nations—Civil Society Relations to review the relationship between civil society and the UN. The report of this panel, chaired by Fernando Henrique Cardoso, acknowledged that the substance of politics is globalizing while the process of politics is stuck at national or local levels. Although the report advanced the position that engaging civil society is critical to the UN's future, the Cardoso Report also conceded that "The unique role of the UN as an intergovernmental forum is vitally important and must be protected at all costs. But today's challenges require that the United Nations be more than just an intergovernmental forum: it must engage others too. To do so risks putting more pressure on the Organization's crowded meeting rooms and agendas, which are becoming ever more crowded; this calls for selective and not just increased engagement." *We the Peoples: Civil Society, the United Nations and Global Governance—Report of Eminent Persons on United Nations—Civil Society Relations* (A/58/817, June 7, 2004), p. 8.

greatly diminished, and for the foreseeable future at least, their resistance is likely to be decisive.

However, let us not forget how modern states themselves first emerged. In Europe, during the sixteenth and seventeenth centuries, political entities congealed that increasingly looked, and behaved, like modern states, both with regard to their internal governance and their external relations. In 1648 the Treaty of Westphalia formally recognized these new entities as sovereign states. What is noteworthy is that the Treaty of Westphalia did not in itself *create* or *establish* these states. They were already there when the treaty was signed. They signed it! Westphalia merely recognized and accepted a reality already in being. It may very well be that the twenty-first century will be the turning point in global governance that the seventeenth century was regarding the modern state. Global governance founded on the immanence of, and emerged from, the politics of transnational society may be taking shape in our time. It may also be speaking increasingly meaningfully and innovatively to problems of human insecurity. At some point near midcentury, let us say possibly by 2048 or some four hundred years after Westphalia, such a structure of global governance may have only to be recognized, accepted, and formalized. It will not have to be established because it will already be there.

Granted, none of this, neither equalizing decision-making prerogatives nor opening international organizations to international civil society, will ever eliminate world politics. Nor should it: the play of politics is the source of public policy. Democratic institutions, however, contain, constrain, and channel politics toward serving community interests. In this perhaps lies the slim, but not unreal, possibility that a more democratic UN might actually serve the peoples of the world.

APPENDIX A

The United Nations System

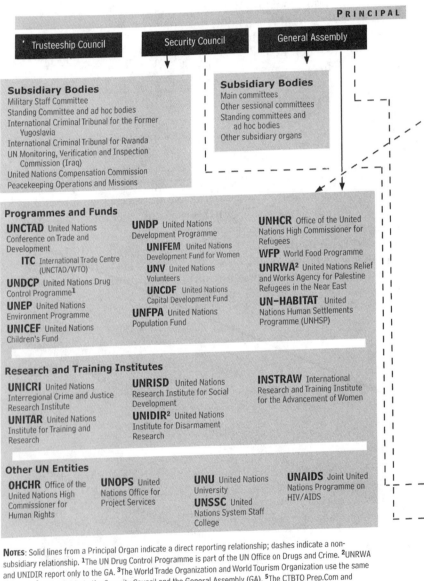

PRINCIPAL

Trusteeship Council **Security Council** **General Assembly**

Subsidiary Bodies
Military Staff Committee
Standing Committee and ad hoc bodies
International Criminal Tribunal for the Former
    Yugoslavia
International Criminal Tribunal for Rwanda
UN Monitoring, Verification and Inspection
    Commission (Iraq)
United Nations Compensation Commission
Peacekeeping Operations and Missions

Subsidiary Bodies
Main committees
Other sessional committees
Standing committees and
    ad hoc bodies
Other subsidiary organs

Programmes and Funds

UNCTAD United Nations
Conference on Trade and
Development
    ITC International Trade Centre
    (UNCTAD/WTO)
UNDCP United Nations Drug
Control Programme[1]
UNEP United Nations
Environment Programme
UNICEF United Nations
Children's Fund

UNDP United Nations
Development Programme
    UNIFEM United Nations
    Development Fund for Women
    UNV United Nations
    Volunteers
    UNCDF United Nations
    Capital Development Fund
UNFPA United Nations
Population Fund

UNHCR Office of the United
Nations High Commissioner for
Refugees
WFP World Food Programme
UNRWA[2] United Nations Relief
and Works Agency for Palestine
Refugees in the Near East
UN-HABITAT United
Nations Human Settlements
Programme (UNHSP)

Research and Training Institutes

UNICRI United Nations
Interregional Crime and Justice
Research Institute
UNITAR United Nations
Institute for Training and
Research

UNRISD United Nations
Research Institute for Social
Development
UNIDIR[2] United Nations
Institute for Disarmament
Research

INSTRAW International
Research and Training Institute
for the Advancement of Women

Other UN Entities

OHCHR Office of the
United Nations High
Commissioner for
Human Rights

UNOPS United
Nations Office for
Project Services

UNU United Nations
University
UNSSC United
Nations System Staff
College

UNAIDS Joint United
Nations Programme on
HIV/AIDS

NOTES: Solid lines from a Principal Organ indicate a direct reporting relationship; dashes indicate a non-subsidiary relationship. [1]The UN Drug Control Programme is part of the UN Office on Drugs and Crime. [2]UNRWA and UNIDIR report only to the GA. [3]The World Trade Organization and World Tourism Organization use the same acronym. [4]IAEA reports to the Security Council and the General Assembly (GA). [5]The CTBTO Prep.Com and OPCW report to the GA. [6]Specialized agencies are autonomous organizations working with the UN and each other through the coordinating machinery of the ECOSOC at the intergovernmental level, and through the Chief Executives Board for coordination (CEB) at the inter-secretariat level.

| Economic and Social Council | International Court of Justice | Secretariat |

Functional Commissions

Commissions on:
- Human Rights
- Narcotic Drugs
- Crime Prevention and Criminal Justice
- Science and Technology for Development
- Sustainable Development
- Status of Women
- Population and Development

Commission for Social Development

Statistical Commission

Regional Commissions

Economic Commission for Africa (ECA)

Economic Commission for Europe (ECE)

Economic Commission for Latin America and the Caribbean (ECLAC)

Economic and Social Commission for Asia and the Pacific (ESCAP)

Economic and Social Commission for Western Asia (ESCWA)

Other Bodies

Permanent Forum on Indigenous Issues (PFII)

United Nations Forum on Forests

Sessional and standing committees

Expert, ad hoc and related bodies

Related Organizations

WTO[3] World Trade Organization

IAEA[4] International Atomic Energy Agency

CTBTO PREP.COM[5] PrepCom for the Nuclear-Test-Ban-Treaty Organization

OPCW[5] Organization for the Prohibition of Chemical Weapons

Specialized Agencies[6]

ILO International Labour Organization

FAO Food and Agriculture Organization of the United Nations

UNESCO United Nations Educational, Scientific and Cultural Organization

WHO World Health Organization

WORLD BANK GROUP

IBRD International Bank for Reconstruction and Development

IDA International Development Association

IFC International Finance Corporation

MIGA Multilateral Investment Guarantee Agency

ICSID International Centre for Settlement of Investment Disputes

IMF International Monetary Fund

ICAO International Civil Aviation Organization

IMO International Maritime Organization

ITU International Telecommunication Union

UPU Universal Postal Union

WMO World Meterological Organization

WIPO World Intellectual Property Organization

IFAD International Fund for Agricultural Development

UNIDO United Nations Industrial Development Organization

WTO[3] World Tourism Organization

Departments and Offices

OSG Office of the Secretary-General

OIOS Office of Internal Oversight Services

OLA Office of Legal Affairs

DPA Department of Political Affairs

DDA Department for Disarmament Affairs

DPKO Department of Peace-keeping Operations

OCHA Office for the Coordination of Humanitarian Affairs

DESA Department of Economic and Social Affairs

DGACM Department for General Assembly and Conference Management

DPI Department of Public Information

DM Department of Management

OHRLLS Office of the High Representative for the Least Developed Countries, Landlocked Developing Countries and Small Island Developing States

UNSECOORD Office of the United Nations Security Coordinator

UNODC United Nations Office on Drugs and Crime

UNOG UN Office at Geneva

UNOV UN Office at Vienna

UNON UN Office at Nairobi

Published by the UN Department of Public Information
DPI/2342—March 2004

APPENDIX B:

Charter of the United Nations

Preamble

PREAMBLE TO THE CHARTER OF THE UNITED NATIONS

WE THE PEOPLES OF THE UNITED NATIONS DETERMINED
to save succeeding generations from the scourge of war, which twice in our
lifetime has brought untold sorrow to mankind, and to reaffirm faith in fundamental human rights, in the dignity and worth of the human person, in
the equal rights of men and women and of nations large and small, and to
establish conditions under which justice and respect for the obligations arising from treaties and other sources of international law can be maintained,
and to promote social progress and better standards of life in larger freedom,
AND FOR THESE ENDS
to practice tolerance and live together in peace with one another as good
neighbours, and to unite our strength to maintain international peace and
security, and to ensure, by the acceptance of principles and the institution of
methods, that armed force shall not be used, save in the common interest,
and to employ international machinery for the promotion of the economic
and social advancement of all peoples,
HAVE RESOLVED TO COMBINE OUR EFFORTS TO ACCOMPLISH
THESE AIMS
Accordingly, our respective Governments, through representatives assembled
in the city of San Francisco, who have exhibited their full powers found to be
in good and due form, have agreed to the present Charter of the United
Nations and do hereby establish an international organization to be known as
the United Nations.

CHAPTER I: PURPOSES AND PRINCIPLES

Article 1

The Purposes of the United Nations are:

1. To maintain international peace and security, and to that end: to take
   effective collective measures for the prevention and removal of threats
   to the peace, and for the suppression of acts of aggression or other
   breaches of the peace, and to bring about by peaceful means, and in
   conformity with the principles of justice and international law, adjustment or settlement of international disputes or situations which
   might lead to a breach of the peace;
2. To develop friendly relations among nations based on respect for the
   principle of equal rights and self-determination of peoples, and to
   take other appropriate measures to strengthen universal peace;
3. To achieve international co-operation in solving international problems
   of an economic, social, cultural, or humanitarian character, and in

promoting and encouraging respect for human rights and for fundamental freedoms for all without distinction as to race, sex, language, or religion; and

4. To be a centre for harmonizing the actions of nations in the attainment of these common ends.

Article 2

The Organization and its Members, in pursuit of the Purposes stated in Article 1, shall act in accordance with the following Principles.

1. The Organization is based on the principle of the sovereign equality of all its Members.
2. All Members, in order to ensure to all of them the rights and benefits resulting from membership, shall fulfill in good faith the obligations assumed by them in accordance with the present Charter.
3. All Members shall settle their international disputes by peaceful means in such a manner that international peace and security, and justice, are not endangered.
4. All Members shall refrain in their international relations from the threat or use of force against the territorial integrity or political independence of any state, or in any other manner inconsistent with the Purposes of the United Nations.
5. All Members shall give the United Nations every assistance in any action it takes in accordance with the present Charter, and shall refrain from giving assistance to any state against which the United Nations is taking preventive or enforcement action.
6. The Organization shall ensure that states which are not Members of the United Nations act in accordance with these Principles so far as may be necessary for the maintenance of international peace and security.
7. Nothing contained in the present Charter shall authorize the United Nations to intervene in matters which are essentially within the domestic jurisdiction of any state or shall require the Members to submit such matters to settlement under the present Charter; but this principle shall not prejudice the application of enforcement measures under Chapter VII.

CHAPTER II: MEMBERSHIP

Article 3

The original Members of the United Nations shall be the states which, having participated in the United Nations Conference on International Organization at San Francisco, or having previously signed the Declaration by United

Nations of 1 January 1942, sign the present Charter and ratify it in accordance with Article 110.

Article 4

1. Membership in the United Nations is open to all other peace-loving states which accept the obligations contained in the present Charter and, in the judgment of the Organization, are able and willing to carry out these obligations.
2. The admission of any such state to membership in the United Nations will be effected by a decision of the General Assembly upon the recommendation of the Security Council.

Article 5

A Member of the United Nations against which preventive or enforcement action has been taken by the Security Council may be suspended from the exercise of the rights and privileges of membership by the General Assembly upon the recommendation of the Security Council. The exercise of these rights and privileges may be restored by the Security Council.

Article 6

A Member of the United Nations which has persistently violated the Principles contained in the present Charter may be expelled from the Organization by the General Assembly upon the recommendation of the Security Council.

CHAPTER III: ORGANS

Article 7

1. There are established as the principal organs of the United Nations: a General Assembly, a Security Council, an Economic and Social Council, a Trusteeship Council, an International Court of Justice, and a Secretariat.
2. Such subsidiary organs as may be found necessary may be established in accordance with the present Charter.

Article 8

The United Nations shall place no restrictions on the eligibility of men and women to participate in any capacity and under conditions of equality in its principal and subsidiary organs.

CHAPTER IV: THE GENERAL ASSEMBLY

COMPOSITION

Article 9

1. The General Assembly shall consist of all the Members of the United Nations.
2. Each Member shall have not more than five representatives in the General Assembly.

FUNCTIONS AND POWERS

Article 10

The General Assembly may discuss any questions or any matters within the scope of the present Charter or relating to the powers and functions of any organs provided for in the present Charter, and, except as provided in Article 12, may make recommendations to the Members of the United Nations or to the Security Council or to both on any such questions or matters.

Article 11

1. The General Assembly may consider the general principles of co-operation in the maintenance of international peace and security, including the principles governing disarmament and the regulation of armaments, and may make recommendations with regard to such principles to the Members or to the Security Council or to both.
2. The General Assembly may discuss any questions relating to the maintenance of international peace and security brought before it by any Member of the United Nations, or by the Security Council, or by a state which is not a Member of the United Nations in accordance with Article 35, paragraph 2, and, except as provided in Article 12, may make recommendations with regard to any such questions to the state or states concerned or to the Security Council or to both. Any such question on which action is necessary shall be referred to the Security Council by the General Assembly either before or after discussion.
3. The General Assembly may call the attention of the Security Council to situations which are likely to endanger international peace and security.
4. The powers of the General Assembly set forth in this Article shall not limit the general scope of Article 10.

Article 12

1. While the Security Council is exercising in respect of any dispute or situation the functions assigned to it in the present Charter, the General Assembly shall not make any recommendation with regard to that dispute or situation unless the Security Council so requests.
2. The Secretary-General, with the consent of the Security Council, shall notify the General Assembly at each session of any matters relative to the maintenance of international peace and security which are being dealt with by the Security Council and shall similarly notify the General Assembly, or the Members of the United Nations if the General Assembly is not in session, immediately the Security Council ceases to deal with such matters.

Article 13

1. The General Assembly shall initiate studies and make recommendations for the purpose of:
   a. promoting international co-operation in the political field and encouraging the progressive development of international law and its codification;
   b. promoting international co-operation in the economic, social, cultural, educational, and health fields, and assisting in the realization of human rights and fundamental freedoms for all without distinction as to race, sex, language, or religion.
2. The further responsibilities, functions and powers of the General Assembly with respect to matters mentioned in paragraph 1 (b) above are set forth in Chapters IX and X.

Article 14

Subject to the provisions of Article 12, the General Assembly may recommend measures for the peaceful adjustment of any situation, regardless of origin, which it deems likely to impair the general welfare or friendly relations among nations, including situations resulting from a violation of the provisions of the present Charter setting forth the Purposes and Principles of the United Nations.

Article 15

1. The General Assembly shall receive and consider annual and special reports from the Security Council; these reports shall include an account of the measures that the Security Council has decided upon or taken to maintain international peace and security.
2. The General Assembly shall receive and consider reports from the other organs of the United Nations.

Article 16

The General Assembly shall perform such functions with respect to the international trusteeship system as are assigned to it under Chapters XII and XIII, including the approval of the trusteeship agreements for areas not designated as strategic.

Article 17

1. The General Assembly shall consider and approve the budget of the Organization.
2. The expenses of the Organization shall be borne by the Members as apportioned by the General Assembly.
3. The General Assembly shall consider and approve any financial and budgetary arrangements with specialized agencies referred to in Article 57 and shall examine the administrative budgets of such specialized agencies with a view to making recommendations to the agencies concerned.

VOTING

Article 18

1. Each member of the General Assembly shall have one vote.
2. Decisions of the General Assembly on important questions shall be made by a two-thirds majority of the members present and voting. These questions shall include: recommendations with respect to the maintenance of international peace and security, the election of the non-permanent members of the Security Council, the election of the members of the Economic and Social Council, the election of members of the Trusteeship Council in accordance with paragraph 1(c) of Article 86, the admission of new Members to the United Nations, the suspension of the rights and privileges of membership, the expulsion of Members, questions relating to the operation of the trusteeship system, and budgetary questions.
3. Decisions on other questions, including the determination of additional categories of questions to be decided by a two-thirds majority, shall be made by a majority of the members present and voting.

Article 19

A Member of the United Nations which is in arrears in the payment of its financial contributions to the Organization shall have no vote in the General Assembly if the amount of its arrears equals or exceeds the amount of the contributions due from it for the preceding two full years. The General Assembly may, nevertheless, permit such a Member to vote if it is satisfied that the failure to pay is due to conditions beyond the control of the Member.

PROCEDURE

Article 20

The General Assembly shall meet in regular annual sessions and in such special sessions as occasion may require. Special sessions shall be convoked by the Secretary-General at the request of the Security Council or of a majority of the Members of the United Nations.

Article 21

The General Assembly shall adopt its own rules of procedure. It shall elect its President for each session.

Article 22

The General Assembly may establish such subsidiary organs as it deems necessary for the performance of its functions.

CHAPTER V: THE SECURITY COUNCIL

COMPOSITION

Article 23

1. The Security Council shall consist of fifteen Members of the United Nations. The Republic of China, France, the Union of Soviet Socialist Republics, the United Kingdom of Great Britain and Northern Ireland, and the United States of America shall be permanent members of the Security Council. The General Assembly shall elect ten other Members of the United Nations to be Non-permanent members of the Security Council, due regard being specially paid, in the first instance to the contribution of Members of the United Nations to the maintenance of international peace and security and to the other purposes of the Organization, and also to equitable geographical distribution.
2. The non-permanent members of the Security Council shall be elected for a term of two years. In the first election of the non-permanent members after the increase of the membership of the Security Council from eleven to fifteen, two of the four additional

members shall be chosen for a term of one year. A retiring member shall not be eligible for immediate re-election.

3. Each member of the Security Council shall have one representative.

FUNCTIONS AND POWERS

Article 24

1. In order to ensure prompt and effective action by the United Nations, its Members confer on the Security Council primary responsibility for the maintenance of international peace and security, and agree that in carrying out its duties under this responsibility the Security Council acts on their behalf.
2. In discharging these duties the Security Council shall act in accordance with the Purposes and Principles of the United Nations. The specific powers granted to the Security Council for the discharge of these duties are laid down in Chapters VI, VII, VIII, and XII.
3. The Security Council shall submit annual and, when necessary, special reports to the General Assembly for its consideration.

Article 25

The Members of the United Nations agree to accept and carry out the decisions of the Security Council in accordance with the present Charter.

Article 26

In order to promote the establishment and maintenance of international peace and security with the least diversion for armaments of the world's human and economic resources, the Security Council shall be responsible for formulating, with the assistance of the Military Staff Committee referred to in Article 47, plans to be submitted to the Members of the United Nations for the establishment of a system for the regulation of armaments.

VOTING

Article 27

1. Each member of the Security Council shall have one vote.
2. Decisions of the Security Council on procedural matters shall be made by an affirmative vote of nine members.
3. Decisions of the Security Council on all other matters shall be made by an affirmative vote of nine members including the concurring votes of the permanent members; provided that, in decisions under Chapter VI, and under paragraph 3 of Article 52, a party to a dispute shall abstain from voting.

PROCEDURE

Article 28

1. The Security Council shall be so organized as to be able to function continuously. Each member of the Security Council shall for this purpose be represented at all times at the seat of the Organization.
2. The Security Council shall hold periodic meetings at which each of its members may, if it so desires, be represented by a member of the government or by some other specially designated representative.
3. The Security Council may hold meetings at such places other than the seat of the Organization as in its judgment will best facilitate its work.

Article 29

The Security Council may establish such subsidiary organs as it deems necessary for the performance of its functions.

Article 30

The Security Council shall adopt its own rules of procedure, including the method of selecting its President.

Article 31

Any Member of the United Nations which is not a member of the Security Council may participate, without vote, in the discussion of any question brought before the Security Council whenever the latter considers that the interests of that Member are specially affected.

Article 32

Any Member of the United Nations which is not a member of the Security Council or any state which is not a Member of the United Nations, if it is a party to a dispute under consideration by the Security Council, shall be invited to participate, without vote, in the discussion relating to the dispute. The Security Council shall lay down such conditions as it deems just for the participation of a state which is not a Member of the United Nations.

CHAPTER VI: PACIFIC SETTLEMENT OF DISPUTES

Article 33

1. The parties to any dispute, the continuance of which is likely to endanger the maintenance of international peace and security, shall, first of all, seek a solution by negotiation, enquiry, mediation, conciliatio

arbitration, judicial settlement, resort to regional agencies or arrangements, or other peaceful means of their own choice.

2. The Security Council shall, when it deems necessary, call upon the parties to settle their dispute by such means.

Article 34

The Security Council may investigate any dispute, or any situation which might lead to international friction or give rise to a dispute, in order to determine whether the continuance of the dispute or situation is likely to endanger the maintenance of international peace and security.

Article 35

1. Any Member of the United Nations may bring any dispute, or any situation of the nature referred to in Article 34, to the attention of the Security Council or of the General Assembly.
2. A state which is not a Member of the United Nations may bring to the attention of the Security Council or of the General Assembly any dispute to which it is a party if it accepts in advance, for the purposes of the dispute, the obligations of pacific settlement provided in the present Charter.
3. The proceedings of the General Assembly in respect of matters brought to its attention under this Article will be subject to the provisions of Articles 11 and 12.

Article 36

1. The Security Council may, at any stage of a dispute of the nature referred to in Article 33 or of a situation of like nature, recommend appropriate procedures or methods of adjustment.
2. The Security Council should take into consideration any procedures for the settlement of the dispute which have already been adopted by the parties.
3. In making recommendations under this Article the Security Council should also take into consideration that legal disputes should as a general rule be referred by the parties to the International Court of Justice in accordance with the provisions of the Statute of the Court.

Article 37

1. Should the parties to a dispute of the nature referred to in Article 33 fail to settle it by the means indicated in that Article, they shall refer it to the Security Council.

2. If the Security Council deems that the continuance of the dispute is in fact likely to endanger the maintenance of international peace and security, it shall decide whether to take action under Article 36 or to recommend such terms of settlement as it may consider appropriate.

Article 38

Without prejudice to the provisions of Articles 33 to 37, the Security Council may, if all the parties to any dispute so request, make recommendations to the parties with a view to a pacific settlement of the dispute.

CHAPTER VII: ACTION WITH RESPECT TO THREATS TO THE PEACE, BREACHES OF THE PEACE, AND ACTS OF AGGRESSION

Article 39

The Security Council shall determine the existence of any threat to the peace, breach of the peace, or act of aggression and shall make recommendations, or decide what measures shall be taken in accordance with Articles 41 and 42, to maintain or restore international peace and security.

Article 40

In order to prevent an aggravation of the situation, the Security Council may, before making the recommendations or deciding upon the measures provided for in Article 39, call upon the parties concerned to comply with such provisional measures as it deems necessary or desirable. Such provisional measures shall be without prejudice to the rights, claims, or position of the parties concerned. The Security Council shall duly take account of failure to comply with such provisional measures.

Article 41

The Security Council may decide what measures not involving the use of armed force are to be employed to give effect to its decisions, and it may call upon the Members of the United Nations to apply such measures. These may include complete or partial interruption of economic relations and of rail, sea, air, postal, telegraphic, radio, and other means of communication, and the severance of diplomatic relations.

Article 42

Should the Security Council consider that measures provided for in Article 41 would be inadequate or have proved to be inadequate, it may take such action by air, sea, or land forces as may be necessary to maintain or restore international peace and security. Such action may include demonstrations, blockade, and other operations by air, sea, or land forces of Members of the United Nations.

Article 43

1. All Members of the United Nations, in order to contribute to the maintenance of international peace and security, undertake to make available to the Security Council, on its call and in accordance with a special agreement or agreements, armed forces, assistance, and facilities, including rights of passage, necessary for the purpose of maintaining international peace and security.
2. Such agreement or agreements shall govern the numbers and types of forces, their degree of readiness and general location, and the nature of the facilities and assistance to be provided.
3. The agreement or agreements shall be negotiated as soon as possible on the initiative of the Security Council. They shall be concluded between the Security Council and Members or between the Security Council and groups of Members and shall be subject to ratification by the signatory states in accordance with their respective constitutional processes.

Article 44

When the Security Council has decided to use force it shall, before calling upon a Member not represented on it to provide armed forces in fulfillment of the obligations assumed under Article 43, invite that Member, if the Member so desires, to participate in the decisions of the Security Council concerning the employment of contingents of that Member's armed forces.

Article 45

In order to enable the United Nations to take urgent military measures, Members shall hold immediately available national air-force contingents for combined international enforcement action. The strength and degree of readiness of these contingents and plans for their combined action shall be determined within the limits laid down in the special agreement or agreements referred to in Article 43, by the Security Council with the assistance of the Military Staff Committee.

Article 46

Plans for the application of armed force shall be made by the Security Council with the assistance of the Military Staff Committee.

Article 47

1. There shall be established a Military Staff Committee to advise and assist the Security Council on all questions relating to the Security Council's military requirements for the maintenance of international peace and security, the employment and command of forces placed at its disposal, the regulation of armaments, and possible disarmament.
2. The Military Staff Committee shall consist of the Chiefs of Staff of the permanent members of the Security Council or their representatives. Any Member of the United Nations not permanently represented on the Committee shall be invited by the Committee to be associated with it when the efficient discharge of the Committee's responsibilities requires the participation of that Member in its work.
3. The Military Staff Committee shall be responsible under the Security Council for the strategic direction of any armed forces placed at the disposal of the Security Council. Questions relating to the command of such forces shall be worked out subsequently.
4. The Military Staff Committee, with the authorization of the Security Council and after consultation with appropriate regional agencies, may establish regional sub-committees.

Article 48

1. The action required to carry out the decisions of the Security Council for the maintenance of international peace and security shall be taken by all the Members of the United Nations or by some of them, as the Security Council may determine.
2. Such decisions shall be carried out by the Members of the United Nations directly and through their action in the appropriate international agencies of which they are members.

Article 49

The Members of the United Nations shall join in affording mutual assistance in carrying out the measures decided upon by the Security Council.

Article 50

If preventive or enforcement measures against any state are taken by the Security Council, any other state, whether a Member of the United Nations or not, which finds itself confronted with special economic problems arising from the carrying out of those measures shall have the right to consult the Security Council with regard to a solution of those problems.

Article 51

Nothing in the present Charter shall impair the inherent right of individual or collective self-defence if an armed attack occurs against a Member of the United Nations, until the Security Council has taken measures necessary to maintain international peace and security. Measures taken by Members in the exercise of this right of self-defence shall be immediately reported to the Security Council and shall not in any way affect the authority and responsibility of the Security Council under the present Charter to take at any time such action as it deems necessary in order to maintain or restore international peace and security.

CHAPTER VIII: REGIONAL ARRANGEMENTS

Article 52

1. Nothing in the present Charter precludes the existence of regional arrangements or agencies for dealing with such matters relating to the maintenance of international peace and security as are appropriate for regional action provided that such arrangements or agencies and their activities are consistent with the Purposes and Principles of the United Nations.
2. The Members of the United Nations entering into such arrangements or constituting such agencies shall make every effort to achieve pacific settlement of local disputes through such regional arrangements or by such regional agencies before referring them to the Security Council.
3. The Security Council shall encourage the development of pacific settlement of local disputes through such regional arrangements or by such regional agencies either on the initiative of the states concerned or by reference from the Security Council.
4. This Article in no way impairs the application of Articles 34 and 35.

Article 53

1. The Security Council shall, where appropriate, utilize such regional arrangements or agencies for enforcement action under its authority. But no enforcement action shall be taken under regional arrangements or by regional agencies without the authorization of the Security Council, with the exception of measures against any enemy state, as defined in paragraph 2 of this Article, provided for pursuant to Article 107 or in regional arrangements directed against renewal of aggressive policy on the part of any such state, until such time as the Organization may, on request of the Governments concerned, be

charged with the responsibility for preventing further aggression by such a state.

2. The term enemy state as used in paragraph 1 of this Article applies to any state which during the Second World War has been an enemy of any signatory of the present Charter.

Article 54

The Security Council shall at all times be kept fully informed of activities undertaken or in contemplation under regional arrangements or by regional agencies for the maintenance of international peace and security.

CHAPTER IX: INTERNATIONAL ECONOMIC AND SOCIAL CO-OPERATION

Article 55

With a view to the creation of conditions of stability and well-being which are necessary for peaceful and friendly relations among nations based on respect for the principle of equal rights and self-determination of peoples, the United Nations shall promote:

a. higher standards of living, full employment, and conditions of economic and social progress and development;
b. solutions of international economic, social, health, and related problems; and international cultural and educational cooperation; and
c. universal respect for, and observance of, human rights and fundamental freedoms for all without distinction as to race, sex, language, or religion.

Article 56

All Members pledge themselves to take joint and separate action in co-operation with the Organization for the achievement of the purposes set forth in Article 55.

Article 57

1. The various specialized agencies, established by intergovernmental agreement and having wide international responsibilities, as defined in their basic instruments, in economic, social, cultural, educational, health, and related fields, shall be brought into relationship with the United Nations in accordance with the provisions of Article 63.
2. Such agencies thus brought into relationship with the United Nations are hereinafter referred to as specialized agencies.

Article 58

The Organization shall make recommendations for the co-ordination of the policies and activities of the specialized agencies.

Article 59

The Organization shall, where appropriate, initiate negotiations among the states concerned for the creation of any new specialized agencies required for the accomplishment of the purposes set forth in Article 55.

Article 60

Responsibility for the discharge of the functions of the Organization set forth in this Chapter shall be vested in the General Assembly and, under the authority of the General Assembly, in the Economic and Social Council, which shall have for this purpose the powers set forth in Chapter X.

CHAPTER X: THE ECONOMIC AND SOCIAL COUNCIL

COMPOSITION

Article 61

1. The Economic and Social Council shall consist of fifty-four Members of the United Nations elected by the General Assembly.
2. Subject to the provisions of paragraph 3, eighteen members of the Economic and Social Council shall be elected each year for a term of three years. A retiring member shall be eligible for immediate re-election.
3. At the first election after the increase in the membership of the Economic and Social Council from twenty-seven to fifty-four members, in addition to the members elected in place of the nine members whose term of office expires at the end of that year, twenty-seven additional members shall be elected. Of these twenty-seven additional members, the term of office of nine members so elected shall expire at the end of one year, and of nine other members at the end of two years, in accordance with arrangements made by the General Assembly.
4. Each member of the Economic and Social Council shall have one representative.

FUNCTIONS AND POWERS

Article 62

1. The Economic and Social Council may make or initiate studies and reports with respect to international economic, social, cultural, educational, health, and related matters and may make recommendations with respect to any such matters to the General Assembly to the Members of the United Nations, and to the specialized agencies concerned.
2. It may make recommendations for the purpose of promoting respect for, and observance of, human rights and fundamental freedoms for all.
3. It may prepare draft conventions for submission to the General Assembly, with respect to matters falling within its competence.
4. It may call, in accordance with the rules prescribed by the United Nations, international conferences on matters falling within its competence.

Article 63

1. The Economic and Social Council may enter into agreements with any of the agencies referred to in Article 57, defining the terms on which the agency concerned shall be brought into relationship with the United Nations. Such agreements shall be subject to approval by the General Assembly.
2. It may co-ordinate the activities of the specialized agencies through consultation with and recommendations to such agencies and through recommendations to the General Assembly and to the Members of the United Nations.

Article 64

1. The Economic and Social Council may take appropriate steps to obtain regular reports from the specialized agencies. It may make arrangements with the Members of the United Nations and with the specialized agencies to obtain reports on the steps taken to give effect to its own recommendations and to recommendations on matters falling within its competence made by the General Assembly.
2. It may communicate its observations on these reports to the General Assembly.

Article 65

The Economic and Social Council may furnish information to the Security Council and shall assist the Security Council upon its request.

Article 66

1. The Economic and Social Council shall perform such functions as fall within its competence in connexion with the carrying out of the recommendations of the General Assembly.
2. It may, with the approval of the General Assembly, perform services at the request of Members of the United Nations and at the request of specialized agencies.
3. It shall perform such other functions as are specified elsewhere in the present Charter or as may be assigned to it by the General Assembly.

VOTING

Article 67

1. Each member of the Economic and Social Council shall have one vote.
2. Decisions of the Economic and Social Council shall be made by a majority of the members present and voting.

PROCEDURE

Article 68

The Economic and Social Council shall set up commissions in economic and social fields and for the promotion of human rights, and such other commissions as may be required for the performance of its functions.

Article 69

The Economic and Social Council shall invite any Member of the United Nations to participate, without vote, in its deliberations on any matter of particular concern to that Member.

Article 70

The Economic and Social Council may make arrangements for representatives of the specialized agencies to participate, without vote, in its deliberations and in those of the commissions established by it, and for its representatives to participate in the deliberations of the specialized agencies.

Article 71

The Economic and Social Council may make suitable arrangements for consultation with non-governmental organizations which are concerned with matters within its competence. Such arrangements may be made with international organizations and, where appropriate, with national organizations after consultation with the Member of the United Nations concerned.

Article 72

1. The Economic and Social Council shall adopt its own rules of procedure, including the method of selecting its President.
2. The Economic and Social Council shall meet as required in accordance with its rules, which shall include provision for the convening of meetings on the request of a majority of its members.

CHAPTER XI: DECLARATION REGARDING NON–SELF-GOVERNING TERRITORIES

Article 73

Members of the United Nations which have or assume responsibilities for the administration of territories whose peoples have not yet attained a full measure of self-government recognize the principle that the interests of the inhabitants of these territories are paramount, and accept as a sacred trust the obligation to promote to the utmost, within the system of international peace and security established by the present Charter, the well-being of the inhabitants of these territories, and, to this end:

a. to ensure, with due respect for the culture of the peoples concerned, their political, economic, social, and educational advancement, their just treatment, and their protection against abuses;
b. to develop self-government, to take due account of the political aspirations of the peoples, and to assist them in the progressive development of their free political institutions, according to the particular circumstances of each territory and its peoples and their varying stages of advancement;
c. to further international peace and security;
d. to promote constructive measures of development, to encourage research, and to co-operate with one another and, when and where appropriate, with specialized international bodies with a view to the practical achievement of the social, economic, and scientific purposes set forth in this Article; and
e. to transmit regularly to the Secretary-General for information purposes, subject to such limitation as security and constitutional considerations may require, statistical and other information of a technical nature relating to economic, social, and educational conditions in

the territories for which they are respectively responsible other than those territories to which Chapters XII and XIII apply.

Article 74

Members of the United Nations also agree that their policy in respect of the territories to which this Chapter applies, no less than in respect of their metropolitan areas, must be based on the general principle of good-neighbourliness, due account being taken of the interests and well-being of the rest of the world, in social, economic, and commercial matters.

CHAPTER XII: INTERNATIONAL TRUSTEESHIP SYSTEM

Article 75

The United Nations shall establish under its authority an international trusteeship system for the administration and supervision of such territories as may be placed thereunder by subsequent individual agreements. These territories are hereinafter referred to as trust territories.

Article 76

The basic objectives of the trusteeship system, in accordance with the Purposes of the United Nations laid down in Article 1 of the present Charter, shall be:

a. to further international peace and security;
b. to promote the political, economic, social, and educational advancement of the inhabitants of the trust territories, and their progressive development towards self-government or independence as may be appropriate to the particular circumstances of each territory and its peoples and the freely expressed wishes of the peoples concerned, and as may be provided by the terms of each trusteeship agreement;
c. to encourage respect for human rights and for fundamental freedoms for all without distinction as to race, sex, language, or religion, and to encourage recognition of the interdependence of the peoples of the world; and
d. to ensure equal treatment in social, economic, and commercial matters for all Members of the United Nations and their nationals, and also equal treatment for the latter in the administration of justice, without prejudice to the attainment of the foregoing objectives and subject to the provisions of Article 80.

Article 77

1. The trusteeship system shall apply to such territories in the following categories as may be placed thereunder by means of trusteeship agreements:
   a. territories now held under mandate;
   b. territories which may be detached from enemy states as a result of the Second World War; and
   c. territories voluntarily placed under the system by states responsible for their administration.
2. It will be a matter for subsequent agreement as to which territories in the foregoing categories will be brought under the trusteeship system and upon what terms.

Article 78

The trusteeship system shall not apply to territories which have become Members of the United Nations, relationship among which shall be based on respect for the principle of sovereign equality.

Article 79

The terms of trusteeship for each territory to be placed under the trusteeship system, including any alteration or amendment, shall be agreed upon by the states directly concerned, including the mandatory power in the case of territories held under mandate by a Member of the United Nations, and shall be approved as provided for in Articles 83 and 85.

Article 80

1. Except as may be agreed upon in individual trusteeship agreements, made under Articles 77, 79, and 81, placing each territory under the trusteeship system, and until such agreements have been concluded, nothing in this Chapter shall be construed in or of itself to alter in any manner the rights whatsoever of any states or any peoples or the terms of existing international instruments to which Members of the United Nations may respectively be parties.
2. Paragraph 1 of this Article shall not be interpreted as giving grounds for delay or postponement of the negotiation and conclusion of agreements for placing mandated and other territories under the trusteeship system as provided for in Article 77.

Article 81

The trusteeship agreement shall in each case include the terms under which the trust territory will be administered and designate the authority which will exercise the administration of the trust territory. Such authority, hereinafter called the administering authority, may be one or more states or the Organization itself.

Article 82

There may be designated, in any trusteeship agreement, a strategic area or areas which may include part or all of the trust territory to which the agreement applies, without prejudice to any special agreement or agreements made under Article 43.

Article 83

1. All functions of the United Nations relating to strategic areas, including the approval of the terms of the trusteeship agreements and of their alteration or amendment shall be exercised by the Security Council.
2. The basic objectives set forth in Article 76 shall be applicable to the people of each strategic area.
3. The Security Council shall, subject to the provisions of the trusteeship agreements and without prejudice to security considerations, avail itself of the assistance of the Trusteeship Council to perform those functions of the United Nations under the trusteeship system relating to political, economic, social, and educational matters in the strategic areas.

Article 84

It shall be the duty of the administering authority to ensure that the trust territory shall play its part in the maintenance of international peace and security. To this end the administering authority may make use of volunteer forces, facilities, and assistance from the trust territory in carrying out the obligations towards the Security Council undertaken in this regard by the administering authority, as well as for local defence and the maintenance of law and order within the trust territory.

Article 85

1. The functions of the United Nations with regard to trusteeship agreements for all areas not designated as strategic, including the approval of the terms of the trusteeship agreements and of their alteration or amendment, shall be exercised by the General Assembly.
2. The Trusteeship Council, operating under the authority of the General Assembly shall assist the General Assembly in carrying out these functions.

CHAPTER XIII: THE TRUSTEESHIP COUNCIL

COMPOSITION

Article 86

1. The Trusteeship Council shall consist of the following Members of the United Nations:
   a. those Members administering trust territories;
   b. such of those Members mentioned by name in Article 23 as are not administering trust territories; and
   c. as many other Members elected for three-year terms by the General Assembly as may be necessary to ensure that the total number of members of the Trusteeship Council is equally divided between those Members of the United Nations which administer trust territories and those which do not.
2. Each member of the Trusteeship Council shall designate one specially qualified person to represent it therein.

FUNCTIONS AND POWERS

Article 87

The General Assembly and, under its authority, the Trusteeship Council, in carrying out their functions, may:

a. consider reports submitted by the administering authority;
b. accept petitions and examine them in consultation with the administering authority;
c. provide for periodic visits to the respective trust territories at times agreed upon with the administering authority; and
d. take these and other actions in conformity with the terms of the trusteeship agreements.

Article 88

The Trusteeship Council shall formulate a questionnaire on the political, economic, social, and educational advancement of the inhabitants of each trust territory, and the administering authority for each trust territory within the competence of the General Assembly shall make an annual report to the General Assembly upon the basis of such questionnaire.

VOTING

Article 89

1. Each member of the Trusteeship Council shall have one vote.
2. Decisions of the Trusteeship Council shall be made by a majority of the members present and voting.

PROCEDURE

Article 90

1. The Trusteeship Council shall adopt its own rules of procedure, including the method of selecting its President.
2. The Trusteeship Council shall meet as required in accordance with its rules, which shall include provision for the convening of meetings on the request of a majority of its members.

Article 91

The Trusteeship Council shall, when appropriate, avail itself of the assistance of the Economic and Social Council and of the specialized agencies in regard to matters with which they are respectively concerned.

CHAPTER XIV: THE INTERNATIONAL COURT OF JUSTICE

Article 92

The International Court of Justice shall be the principal judicial organ of the United Nations. It shall function in accordance with the annexed Statute, which is based upon the Statute of the Permanent Court of International Justice and forms an integral part of the present Charter.

Article 93

1. All Members of the United Nations are ipso facto parties to the Statute of the International Court of Justice.
2. A state which is not a Member of the United Nations may become a party to the Statute of the International Court of Justice on conditions to be determined in each case by the General Assembly upon the recommendation of the Security Council.

Article 94

1. Each Member of the United Nations undertakes to comply with the decision of the International Court of Justice in any case to which it is a party.

2. If any party to a case fails to perform the obligations incumbent upon it under a judgment rendered by the Court, the other party may have recourse to the Security Council, which may, if it deems necessary, make recommendations or decide upon measures to be taken to give effect to the judgment.

Article 95

Nothing in the present Charter shall prevent Members of the United Nations from entrusting the solution of their differences to other tribunals by virtue of agreements already in existence or which may be concluded in the future.

Article 96

1. The General Assembly or the Security Council may request the International Court of Justice to give an advisory opinion on any legal question.
2. Other organs of the United Nations and specialized agencies, which may at any time be so authorized by the General Assembly, may also request advisory opinions of the Court on legal questions arising within the scope of their activities.

CHAPTER XV: THE SECRETARIAT

Article 97

The Secretariat shall comprise a Secretary-General and such staff as the Organization may require. The Secretary-General shall be appointed by the General Assembly upon the recommendation of the Security Council. He shall be the chief administrative officer of the Organization.

Article 98

The Secretary-General shall act in that capacity in all meetings of the General Assembly, of the Security Council, of the Economic and Social Council, and of the Trusteeship Council, and shall perform such other functions as are entrusted to him by these organs. The Secretary-General shall make an annual report to the General Assembly on the work of the Organization.

Article 99

The Secretary-General may bring to the attention of the Security Council any matter which in his opinion may threaten the maintenance of international peace and security.

Article 100

1. In the performance of their duties the Secretary-General and the staff shall not seek or receive instructions from any government or from any other authority external to the Organization. They shall refrain from any action which might reflect on their position as international officials responsible only to the Organization.
2. Each Member of the United Nations undertakes to respect the exclusively international character of the responsibilities of the Secretary-General and the staff and not to seek to influence them in the discharge of their responsibilities.

Article 101

1. The staff shall be appointed by the Secretary-General under regulations established by the General Assembly.
2. Appropriate staffs shall be permanently assigned to the Economic and Social Council, the Trusteeship Council, and, as required, to other organs of the United Nations. These staffs shall form a part of the Secretariat.
3. The paramount consideration in the employment of the staff and in the determination of the conditions of service shall be the necessity of securing the highest standards of efficiency, competence, and integrity. Due regard shall be paid to the importance of recruiting the staff on as wide a geographical basis as possible.

CHAPTER XVI: MISCELLANEOUS PROVISIONS

Article 102

1. Every treaty and every international agreement entered into by any Member of the United Nations after the present Charter comes into force shall as soon as possible be registered with the Secretariat and published by it.
2. No party to any such treaty or international agreement which has not been registered in accordance with the provisions of paragraph 1 of this Article may invoke that treaty or agreement before any organ of the United Nations.

Article 103

In the event of a conflict between the obligations of the Members of the United Nations under the present Charter and their obligations under any other international agreement, their obligations under the present Charter shall prevail.

Article 104

The Organization shall enjoy in the territory of each of its Members such legal capacity as may be necessary for the exercise of its functions and the fulfillment of its purposes.

Article 105

1. The Organization shall enjoy in the territory of each of its Members such privileges and immunities as are necessary for the fulfillment of its purposes.
2. Representatives of the Members of the United Nations and officials of the Organization shall similarly enjoy such privileges and immunities as are necessary for the independent exercise of their functions in connexion with the Organization.
3. The General Assembly may make recommendations with a view to determining the details of the application of paragraphs 1 and 2 of this Article or may propose conventions to the Members of the United Nations for this purpose.

CHAPTER XVII: TRANSITIONAL SECURITY ARRANGEMENTS

Article 106

Pending the coming into force of such special agreements referred to in Article 43 as in the opinion of the Security Council enable it to begin the exercise of its responsibilities under Article 42, the parties to the Four-Nation Declaration, signed at Moscow, 30 October 1943, and France, shall, in accordance with the provisions of paragraph 5 of that Declaration, consult with one another and as occasion requires with other Members of the United Nations with a view to such joint action on behalf of the Organization as may be necessary for the purpose of maintaining international peace and security.

Article 107

Nothing in the present Charter shall invalidate or preclude action, in relation to any state which during the Second World War has been an enemy of any signatory to the present Charter, taken or authorized as a result of that war by the Governments having responsibility for such action.

CHAPTER XVIII: AMENDMENTS

Article 108

Amendments to the present Charter shall come into force for all Members of the United Nations when they have been adopted by a vote of two thirds of the members of the General Assembly and ratified in accordance with their respective constitutional processes by two thirds of the Members of the United Nations, including all the permanent members of the Security Council.

Article 109

1. A General Conference of the Members of the United Nations for the purpose of reviewing the present Charter may be held at a date and place to be fixed by a two-thirds vote of the members of the General Assembly and by a vote of any nine members of the Security Council. Each Member of the United Nations shall have one vote in the conference.
2. Any alteration of the present Charter recommended by a two-thirds vote of the conference shall take effect when ratified in accordance with their respective constitutional processes by two thirds of the Members of the United Nations including all the permanent members of the Security Council.
3. If such a conference has not been held before the tenth annual session of the General Assembly following the coming into force of the present Charter, the proposal to call such a conference shall be placed on the agenda of that session of the General Assembly, and the conference shall be held if so decided by a majority vote of the members of the General Assembly and by a vote of any seven members of the Security Council.

CHAPTER XIX: RATIFICATION AND SIGNATURE

Article 110

1. The present Charter shall be ratified by the signatory states in accordance with their respective constitutional processes.
2. The ratifications shall be deposited with the Government of the United States of America, which shall notify all the signatory states of each deposit as well as the Secretary-General of the Organization when he has been appointed.
3. The present Charter shall come into force upon the deposit of ratifications by the Republic of China, France, the Union of Soviet Socialist

Republics, the United Kingdom of Great Britain and Northern Ireland, and the United States of America, and by a majority of the other signatory states. A protocol of the ratifications deposited shall thereupon be drawn up by the Government of the United States of America which shall communicate copies thereof to all the signatory states.

4. The states signatory to the present Charter which ratify it after it has come into force will become original Members of the United Nations on the date of the deposit of their respective ratifications.

Article 111

The present Charter, of which the Chinese, French, Russian, English, and Spanish texts are equally authentic, shall remain deposited in the archives of the Government of the United States of America. Duly certified copies thereof shall be transmitted by that Government to the Governments of the other signatory states.

IN FAITH WHEREOF the representatives of the Governments of the United Nations have signed the present Charter.

DONE at the city of San Francisco the twenty-sixth day of June, one thousand nine hundred and forty-five.

Bibliography

Abrams, Morris B. "The UN and Human Rights." *Foreign Affairs* 47, no. 2 (1969): 363–74.

Ake, Claude. "The New World Order: A View from Africa." In *Whose Order?* edited by Hans Henrick Holm and Georg Sorensen. Boulder, Colo.: Westview Press, 1995.

American Anthropological Association Executive Board. "Statement on Human Rights." Part 1. *American Anthropologist* 49, no. 4 (1947): 539–43.

Annan, Kofi. "Two Concepts of Sovereignty." *The Economist* 352 (September 18, 1999): 49–50.

———. *Secretary General's Speech to the 54th Session of the General Assembly*, September 20, 1999.

Arrigo, Linda Gail. "A View of the United Nations Conference on Human Rights, Vienna, June 1993: From Among the Throng at the Non-Governmental Organization Forum." *Bulletin of Concerned Asian Scholars* 25, no. 3 (1993): 62–72.

Axworthy, Lloyd. "Human Security and Global Governance: Putting People First." *Global Governance* 7, no. 1 (January–March 2001):19–24.

Bliss, Michael. *Right Honorable Men: The Descent of Canadian Politics from Macdonald to Mulroney*. Toronto: Harper Collins, 1994.

Boutros-Ghali, Boutros. *An Agenda for Peace 1995*, 2nd ed. New York: UN Department of Public Information, 1997.

Chesterman, Simon. *East Timor in Transition: From Conflict Prevention to State-Building*. New York: International Peace Academy, 2001.

Clapham, Andrew. "Where Is the EU's Human Rights Common Foreign Policy, and How Is It Manifested in Multilateral Fora?" In *The EU and Human Rights*, edited by Philip Alston. Oxford: Oxford University Press, 1999.

Clark, Roger S. "Human Rights Strategies of the 1960s Within the United Nations: A Tribute to the late Kamleshwar Das." *Human Rights Quarterly* 21, no. 2 (May 1999): 308–41.

Cohen, Andrew. *While Canada Slept: How We Lost Our Place in the World*. Toronto: McClelland and Stewart, 2004.

Cooper, Andrew F., ed. *Niche Diplomacy: Middle Powers After the Cold War*. London: Macmillan, 1997.

Cooper, Andrew F., John English, and Ramesh Thakur. *Enhancing Global Governance: Towards a New Diplomacy*. Tokyo: United Nations University Press, 2002.

Cooper, Andrew F., Richard A. Higgott, and Kim Richard Nossal, eds. *Relocating Middle Powers: Australia and Canada in a Changing World Order*. Vancouver: UBC Press, 1993.

Cox, Robert. *Production, Power and World Order: Social Forces in the Making of History*. New York: Columbia University Press, 1978.

————, ed. *The New Realism: Perspectives on Multilateralism and World Order*. London: Macmillan for UNU Press, 2000.

Crocker, Chester A., Fen Osler Hampson, and Pamela Aall, eds. *Turbulent Peace: The Challenges of Managing International Conflict*. Washington, D.C.: United States Institute for Peace, 2001.

Dell, Sidney. "Contributions of the United Nations to Economic Thinking and Action." *Journal of Development Planning* 17 (1987): 113–23.

Duchêne, François. "The European Community and the Uncertainties of Interdependence." In *A Nation Writ Large: Foreign Policy Problems Before the European Community* edited by M. Kohnstamm and W. Hager. London: Macmillan, 1973.

Emmerij, Louis, Richard Jolly, and Thomas G. Weiss. *Ahead of the Curve? UN Ideas and Global Challenges*. Bloomington: Indiana University Press, 2001.

European Union. *A Secure Europe in a Better World*. Brussels: Secretariat of the Council of the European Union, 2003.

————. *The Enlarging European Union at the United Nations: Making Multilateralism Matter*. Luxembourg: Office for Official Publications of the European Communities, 2004.

Fasulo, Linda. *An Insider's Guide to the United Nations*. New Haven: Yale University Press, 2004.

Foot, Rosemary S., Neil MacFarlane, and Michael Mastanduno, eds. *US Hegemony and International Organizations*. Oxford: Oxford University Press, 2003.

Gaer, Felice. "Reality Check: Human Rights NGOs Confront Governments at the UN." In *NGOs, the UN and Global Governance*, edited by Thomas G. Weiss and Leon Gordenker, 51–66. Boulder, Colo.: Lynne Rienner, 1996.

Gardner, Richard N. *Sterling-Dollar Diplomacy in Current Perspective: The Origins and Prospects of Our International Economic Order*. New York: Columbia University Press, 1980.

Glendon, Mary Ann. *A World Made New: Eleanor Roosevelt and the Universal Declaration of Human Rights*. New York: Random House, 2001.

Gourevitch, Philip. *We Wish to Inform You That Tomorrow We Will Be Killed with Our Families: Stories from Rwanda*. New York: Farrar, Straus, and Giroux, 1998.

Gray, John. *Enlightenment's Wake: Politics and Culture at the Close of the Modern Age*. London and New York: Routledge, 1995.

Greider, William. *One World, Ready or Not: The Manic Logic of Global Capitalism*. New York: Simon & Schuster, 1997.

Griffths, Martin, Iain Levine, and Mark Weller. "Sovereignty and Suffering." In *The Politics of Humanitarian Intervention*, edited by John Harriss. London and New York: Pinter, 1995.

Heinbecker, Paul. "Washington's Exceptionalism and the United Nations." *Global Governance* 10, no. 3 (July–September 2004): 273–79.

Inter-American Conference on Problems of War and Peace, Mexico City, February 21–March 8, 1945. Report Submitted to the Governing Board of the Pan-American Union by the Director General. Congress and Conference series, no. 47. Washington, D.C.: Pan American Union, 1945.

Jordan, Robert S. "Why an NIEO? The View from the Third World." In *The Emerging International Economic Order: Dynamic Processes, Constraints and Opportunities*, edited by Harold K. Jacobson and Dusam Aidjanski. Beverly Hills, CA: Sage, 1982.

Jørgensen, Knud Erik, and Katie Verlin Laatikainen. "The EU @ the UN: Multilateral-ism in a New Key?" Second Pan-European Conference on EU Politics, Bologna, June 24–26, 2004.

Kagan, Robert. "Power and Weakness." *Policy Review* 13 (2002): 3–29.

Kaplan, Robert D. *The Ends of the Earth: From Togo to Turkmenistan, From Iran to Cambodia—a Journey to the Frontiers of Anarchy.* New York: Vintage Books, 1997.

———. *Warrior Politics: Why Leadership Demands a Pagan Ethos.* New York: Vintage, 2002.

Kausikan, Bilahari. "An Asian Approach to Human Rights." *Proceedings of the American Society for International Law 89.* ASIL Proceedings 70 (1995): 146–52.

Keohane, Robert O. *After Hegemony: Cooperation and Discord in the World Political Economy.* Princeton, NJ: Princeton University Press, 1984.

———. *Power and Governance in a Partially Globalized World.* London: Routledge, 2002.

Korey, William. *NGOs and the Universal Declaration of Human Rights: A Curious Grapevine.* New York: St. Martin's Press, 1998.

———. "Human Rights NGOs: The Power of Persuasion." *Ethics and International Affairs* 13 (1999): 51–74.

Krasner, Stephen D., ed. *International Regimes.* Ithaca, N.Y.: Cornell University Press, 1983.

Kumar, Radha. "Sovereignty and Intervention: Opinions in South Asia." *Pugwash Occasional Papers* 2, no. 1 (January 2001): 52–64.

Kupchan, Charles A. "The End of the West." *Atlantic Monthly* 290, no. 4 (2002): 42–45.

———. "The Rise of Europe, America's Changing Internationalism, and the End of U.S. Primacy." *Political Science Quarterly* 118, no. 2 (2003): 205–32.

Laatikainen, Katie Verlin. "Norden's Eclipse: The Impact of the European Union's Common Foreign and Security Policy on Nordic Cooperation in the United Nations." *Cooperation and Conflict* 38, no. 4 (December 2003): 409–41.

———. "Assessing the EU as an Actor at the UN." *CFSP Forum* 2, no. 1 (January 2004): 4–10.

Laatikainen, Katie Verlin, and Karen E. Smith, eds. *The European Union at the United Nations: Intersecting Multilateralisms.* Basingstoke: Palgrave, 2006.

Lasswell, Harold Dwight. *Politics: Who Gets What, When, How.* New York: P. Smith, 1936.

Luck, Edward C. "Steps Toward UN Reform." New York: United Nations Association of the United States, March 19, 1993.

Lyons, Gene. "International Organizations and National Interests." *International Social Science Journal* 144, no. 2 (1995): 261–77.

Maley, William. "The UN, NGOs and the Landmines Initiative: An Australian Perspective." In *Enhancing Global Governance: Toward a New Diplomacy*, edited by Andrew F. Cooper, John English, and Ramesh Thakur. Tokyo: United Nations University Press, 2002.

Manners, Ian. "Normative Power Europe: A Contradiction in Terms?" *Journal of Common Market Studies* 40, no. 2 (2002): 235–58.

Manners, Ian, and Richard G. Whitman. "The 'Difference Engine': Constructing and Representing the International Identity of the European Union." *Journal of European Public Policy* 10, no. 3 (June 2003): 380–405.

Mittelman, James. *Globalization: Critical Reflections.* Boulder, Colo.: Lynne Rienner, 1996.

———. *The Globalization Syndrome.* Princeton: Princeton University Press, 2000.

———. *Whither Globalization? The Vortex of Knowledge and Ideology.* London: Routledge, 2004.

Morsink, Johannes. *The Universal Declaration of Human Rights: Origins, Drafting, and Intent.* Philadelphia: University of Pennsylvania Press, 1999.

Moskowitz, Moses. *International Concern with Human Rights.* Leiden: Sijthoff Publishers, 1974.

Moynihan, Daniel P. *A Dangerous Place.* Boston: Little, Brown, 1978.

Murphy, Craig. *International Organization and Industrial Change.* Oxford: Oxford University Press, 1994.

"Mutual Aid Agreement Between the United States and the Union of Soviet Socialist Republics: June 11, 1942." *Department of State Bulletin, June 13, 1942.* Washington, D.C.: U.S. Government Printing Office, 1942.

"Non-Benign Neglect: America and the Developing World in the Era of Globalization." National Press Club, Washington, D.C., October 14, 1998.

Onuf, Nicholas. *World of Our Making: Rules and Rule in Social Theory and International Relations.* Columbia: University of South Carolina Press, 1989.

Proceedings and Documents of the United Nations Monetary and Financial Conference. Bretton Woods, New Hampshire, July 1–22, 1944, Vol. 2. Department of State Publication 2866. International Organization and Conference Series I, 3. Washington D.C.: U.S. Government Printing Office, 1948.

Puchala, Donald J. "The Secretary-General and His Special Representatives." In *The Challenging Role of the UN Secretary-General: Making "The Most Impossible Job in the World" Possible,* edited by Benjamin Rivilin and Leon Gordenker, 81–97. Westport, Conn.: Praeger, 1993.

———. "The Vienna Conference on Human Rights: Bridge to the Future or Bridge over Troubled Waters." Unpublished Case Study used for Central European University Summer Institute, 2002.

———. *Theory and History in International Relations.* New York: Routledge, 2003.

Puchala, Donald J., and Roger A. Coate. *The State of the United Nations, 1988.* Reports and Papers, no. 2. Academic Council on the United Nations System, 1988.

———. *The Challenge of Relevance: The United Nations in a Changing World Environment.* Reports and Papers, Academic Council on the United Nations System, 1989.

Rapoport, Anatol. *Fights, Games and Debates.* Ann Arbor: University of Michigan Press, 1960.

Ravenhill, John. "Cycles of Middle Power Activism: Constraint and Choice in Australian and Canadian Foreign Policies." *Australian Journal of International Affairs* 52, no. 3 (1998): 309–27.

Ruggie, John G. "Territoriality at the Millennium's End." In *Constructing the World Polity: Essays on International Institutionalization,* edited by John Gerard Ruggie, 173–198. New York: Routledge, 1998.

Schori, Pierre. "Painful Partnership: The United States, the European Union and Global Governance." *Global Governance* 11, no. 3 (July–September 2005): 273–80.

Schwartz, Herman. *States Versus Markets: History, Geography, and the Development of the International Political Economy.* New York: St. Martin's Press, 1994.

Sen, Amartya. *Development as Freedom.* New York: Anchor Books, 1999.

Singer, P. W. *Children at War.* Washington, D.C.: The Brookings Institution, 2004.

Smaghi, Lorenzo Bini. "A Single EU Seat in the IMF." *Journal of Common Market Studies* 42, no. 2 (2004): 29–48.

Spero, Joan Edelman. *The Politics of International Economic Relations.* New York: St. Martin's, 1985.

Stiftung Wissenschaft und Politik. *The Brahimi Report: Overcoming the North-South Divide.* Report of the 6th International Workshop, Berlin, June 29–30, 2001.

Strange, Susan. *Casino Capitalis.* Oxford: Blackwell Publishers, 1986.

———. "The 'Fall' of the United States: Peace, Stability, and Legitimacy." In *The Fall of Great Powers: Peace, Stability, and Legitimacy,* edited by Geir Lundestad, 197–211. Oxford: Oxford University Press, 1994.

———. *Mad Money.* Manchester: Manchester University Press, 1998.

Tessitore, John, and Susan Woolfson, eds. *A Global Agenda: Issues Before the 55th General Assembly of the United Nation.* New York: Rowman & Littlefield, 2000.

United Nations. *Report to the Secretary-General of the United Nations* [The Thornburgh Report]. New York: The United Nations, 1993.

———. *We the Peoples: The Role of the United Nations in the 21st Century* [*Millennium Report*]. A/54/2000, September 2000.

———. *The Responsibility to Protect: Report of the International Commission on Intervention and State Sovereignty.* Ottawa: International Development Research Center, 2001.

———. *We the Peoples: Civil Society, the United Nations and Global Governance* [The Cardoso Report]. A/58/817, June 7, 2004.

———. *A More Secure World: Our Shared Responsibility.* Report of the Secretary-General's High-level Panel on Threats, Challenges and Change. A/59/565, December 2, 2004.

———. *Investing in Development: A Practical Plan to Achieve the Millennium Development Goals.* [Report of the Millennium Project to the Secretary-General], January 17, 2005.

———. *In Larger Freedom: Towards Development, Security and Human Rights for All Report of the Secretary-General.* A/59/2005, March 21, 2005.

———. *2005 World Summit Outcome.* A/60/L/1, September 15, 2005.

United Nations Development Programme. *Human Development Report 1993.* New York: Oxford University Press, 1993.

———. *Human Development Report 1994.* New York: Oxford University Press, 1994.

———. *Human Development Report 1998.* New York: Oxford University Press, 1998.

———. *UNDP Today: Reform in Action.* New York: United Nations, 1999.

Weiss, Thomas G. "The Politics of Humanitarian Ideas." *Security Dialogue* 31, no. 1 (March 2000): 11–23.

Weiss, Thomas G., David P. Forsythe, and Roger A. Coate. *The United Nations and Changing World Politics,* 3rd ed. Boulder, Colo.: Westview Press, 2001.

———. *The United Nations and Changing World Politics,* 4th ed. Boulder, Colo.: Westview Press, 2004.

Wendt, Alexander. "Anarchy Is What States Make of It: The Social Construction of State Politics." *International Organization* 46 (1992): 33–70.

World Bank. *World Development Report 1997: The State in a Changing World.* New York: Oxford University Press, 1997.

———. *World Development Report 2006: Equity and Poverty.* Washington, D.C., 2005.

Young, Oran R. "The Politics of International Regime Formation: Managing Natural Resources and the Environment." *International Organization* 43, no. 3 (1989): 349–75.

———. "Political Leadership and Regime Formation: On the Development of Institutions in International Society." *International Organization* 45 (1991): 281–308.

———. *Governance in World Affairs.* Ithaca, N.Y.: Cornell University Press, 1999.

Zakaria, Fareed. "Culture Is Destiny: A Conversation with Lee Kwan Yew." *Foreign Affairs* 73, no. 2 (March/April 1994): 109–26.

Index